Design Culture

Design Culture

Objects and Approaches

EDITED BY
GUY JULIER,
ANDERS V. MUNCH,
MADS NYGAARD FOLKMANN,
HANS-CHRISTIAN JENSEN
AND NIELS PETER SKOU

BLOOMSBURY VISUAL ARTS
LONDON · NEW YORK · OXFORD · NEW DELHI · SYDNEY

BLOOMSBURY VISUAL ARTS
Bloomsbury Publishing Plc
50 Bedford Square, London, WC1B 3DP, UK
1385 Broadway, New York, NY 10018, USA
29 Earlsfort Terrace, Dublin 2, Ireland

BLOOMSBURY, BLOOMSBURY VISUAL ARTS and the Diana logo are
trademarks of Bloomsbury Publishing Plc

First published in Great Britain 2019
This paperback edition first published 2021

© Guy Julier, Anders V. Munch, Mads Nygaard Folkmann, Niels Peter Skou and
Hans-Christian Jensen and Contributors, 2021

Cover image by Anders V. Munch

All rights reserved. No part of this publication may be reproduced or transmitted
in any form or by any means, electronic or mechanical, including photocopying,
recording, or any information storage or retrieval system, without prior
permission in writing from the publishers.

Bloomsbury Publishing Plc does not have any control over, or responsibility for, any
third-party websites referred to or in this book. All internet addresses given in this
book were correct at the time of going to press. The author and publisher regret any
inconvenience caused if addresses have changed or sites have ceased to exist,
but can accept no responsibility for any such changes.

A catalogue record for this book is available from the British Library.

A catalog record for this book is available from the Library of Congress.

ISBN: HB: 978-1-4742-8984-9
PB: 978-1-3501-9654-4
ePDF: 978-1-4742-8982-5
ePub: 978-1-4742-8983-2

Typeset by Deanta Global Publishing Services, Chennai, India
Printed and bound in Great Britain

To find out more about our authors and books visit www.bloomsbury.com
and sign up for our newsletters.

CONTENTS

List of image credits vii
List of contributors viii

Introducing Design Culture
Guy Julier and Anders V. Munch 1

PART ONE Developing design culture
  Mads Nygaard Folkmann 11

1 Design culturing: Making design history matter *Kjetil Fallan* 15
2 Taste and attunement: Design culture as world making *Ben Highmore* 28
3 Embedding design in the organizational culture: Challenges and perspectives *Alessandro Deserti and Francesca Rizzo* 39
4 Use in design culture *Toke Riis Ebbesen* 52

PART TWO Addressing market and society
  Niels Peter Skou 67

5 A brand for everyone *Sara Kristoffersson* 71
6 Buying into the future: A case study of a Danish brand of fashionable children's clothing *Trine Brun Petersen* 83
7 The Glowing Black of fritz-kola: Aestheticization in design culture *Mads Nygaard Folkmann* 96

PART THREE Positioning design professions
Hans-Christian Jensen 111

8 Design Culture in the sex toy industry: A new phenomenon *Judith Glover* 115

9 Working from home: Fashioning the professional designer in Britain *Leah Armstrong* 131

10 On the professional and everyday design of graphic artefacts *Sarah Owens* 145

11 The fixing I: Repair as prefigurative politics *Gabriele Oropallo* 157

PART FOUR Locating design culture
Anders V. Munch 171

12 Something old, something new, something borrowed: Relocating Kähler's brand heritage *Niels Peter Skou* 175

13 Performing Turkish design in products, collections and exhibitions: Expanding the archive, seeking depth *Harun Kaygan* 189

14 A theoretical straddle: Locating design cultures between national structures and transnational networks *Joana Ozorio de Almeida Meroz and Katarina Serulus* 203

15 The challenges and opportunities of introducing Design Culture in Jordan *Danah Abdulla* 214

Epilogue: Towards design culture as practice
Guy Julier and Anders V. Munch 227

Index 231

LIST OF IMAGE CREDITS

1.1	Kristin Vedel / Research and Development Unit, Department of Design, University of Nairobi, June 1971 18
1.2	Elbil / Norsk Jernbanemuseum 20
2.1	With kind permission of Habitat Retail Limited 34
3.1	Alessandro Deserti and Francesca Rizzo 42
3.2	Alessandro Deserti and Francesca Rizzo 43
4.1	Toke Riis Ebbesen 59
4.2	Silvio Lorusso & Sebastian Schmieg, 2012 61
5.1	Sara Kristoffersson 78
6.1	Trine Brun Petersen 85
6.2	Trine Brun Petersen 86
6.3	Trine Brun Petersen 89
7.1	Fritz-kola 98
7.2	Fritz-kola 99
7.3	Fritz-kola / photographer: Camilla Lorentzen 103
7.4	Fritz-kola 103
7.5	Fritz-kola 104
8.1	Judith Glover 122
8.2	Judith Glover 124
9.1	Colin Tait / source: FHK Henrion Archive, University of Brighton Design Archives 136
9.2	Gee and Watson / Design Council Archive, University of Brighton Design Archives 139
11.1	Gabriele Oropallo 164
11.2	iFixit 166
12.1	Niels Peter Skou 181
12.2	Niels Peter Skou 182
12.3 & 12.4	Kähler Design 184
13.1	Ela Cindoruk 193
13.2	Kunter Şekercioğlu 194
13.3	Koray Gelmez 197
14.1	Private Archive Des Cressonnières, Belgium 207
14.2	Studio Formafantasma 209
15.1	Studio Turbo 224

LIST OF CONTRIBUTORS

Danah Abdulla, University of the Arts London, UK
Leah Armstrong, University of Applied Arts Vienna, Austria
Alessandro Deserti, Politecnico di Milano, Italy
Toke Riis Ebbesen, University of Southern Denmark, Denmark
Kjetil Fallan, University of Oslo, Norway
Mads Nygaard Folkmann, University of Southern Denmark, Denmark
Judith Glover, RMIT University, Melbourne, Australia
Ben Highmore, University of Sussex, UK
Hans-Christian Jensen, University of Southern Denmark, Denmark
Guy Julier, Aalto University, Finland
Harun Kaygan, University of Southern Denmark, Denmark
Sara Kristoffersson, Konstfack, Sweden
Anders V. Munch, University of Southern Denmark, Denmark
Gabriele Oropallo, London Metropolitan University, UK
Sarah Owens, Zurich University of the Arts, Switzerland
Joana Ozorio de Almeida Meroz, Vrije Universiteit Amsterdam, Netherlands
Trine Brun Petersen, University of Southern Denmark, Denmark
Francesca Rizzo, Politecnico di Milano, Italy
Katarina Serulus, KU Leuven, Belgium
Niels Peter Skou, University of Southern Denmark, Denmark

Introducing Design Culture

Guy Julier and Anders V. Munch

The term 'design culture' has emerged into regular academic and professional usage since around 2000. This has opened out in multiple ways, reflecting not just the varying locations where it is used and co-opted but also the different functions it carries. Placing itself across the Arts, Humanities and Social Sciences, it foregrounds the study of design in contemporary societies, paying attention to the networks and relationships between the domains of design practice, production and everyday life. This book is focused on opening it out for inspection through case studies and theoretical explorations.

Sharing some approaches and, indeed, much of its geniality with related fields of discourse and scholarly study, we nonetheless claim some distinctive territory for Design Culture studies as an academic focus of study. Design History has developed since the 1970s, broadening its historical and geographical scope, while maturing its own historical methods and key arenas of interest. Contrastingly, Design Culture[1] focuses intensively on design's contemporary manifestations, seeking historically grounded understandings that are, nonetheless, relevant to emergent fields of scholarly enquiry and design practices.

Concurrently, Design Studies has grown from an initial concern with design processes to include its philosophies, theories and histories. Design Culture maintains a sharper emphasis on the deep understanding of design objects and their interrelationships with the multiple actors engaged in their shaping, functioning and reproduction. As such, Design Culture takes in – and contributes to – research and discourses in business and management studies, human geography, anthropology, media and communications studies and cultural studies, to name but a few of its cognate disciplines. It may be taken to be more outward looking and permeable in its disciplinary borders.

Design Culture goes beyond the classic dispute between Design Studies as understood in the United States and Design History as having emerged in the United Kingdom (Margolin 1992). This dispute has revolved around whether scholarship in Design Studies or Design History should serve design practice (as classically understood) or whether they should forge an independence as stand-alone discipline (Huppatz and Lees-Maffei 2013; Fallan 2013). Contrastingly, while this book serves as an investigation of scholarly possibilities within Design Culture studies, we do not necessarily take it to represent a bounded, singular and consistent discipline. And this is consonant with the field of design itself in contemporary society. It reaches into many parts of society and culture, and there are, now, many more actors, professions and scientific disciplines that are part of its constitution, rendering normative methods and epistemologies redundant. For example, the rise of so-called user-experience (UX) design since around 2010, that engages ethnography, Human–Computer Interaction (HCI), human factors and ergonomics, data analytics, digital coding and many other intersecting specialisms, underlines the ever shifting boundaries and porosity of what design might involve. Thus, in its scholarly practices, Design Culture shares, for instance, its very broad scope with Cultural Studies of design (Highmore 2009) and Material Culture studies. But it is also informed by shifting professions, institutions and debates of design – the 'designer culture', if you like (Sparke 1986).

When Kjetil Fallan (2010) argues that Design History will get further impact on a broad field of historical and cultural sciences by striving towards a 'history of design culture' or a 'cultural history of design', it is in close dialogue with Design Culture. The main scope of Design Culture is the more recent developments and constitutions forming our contemporary design culture rising since the 1980s and 1990s showing new densities, convergences, mediations and disciplinary constellations both inside and beyond the professional cultures of the designers. Historical antecedents or re-uses, however, may also come into view to open out conceptions of design culture. As an example, the recent so-called New Nordic Design seems to be a re-performance of the values of Scandinavian Design of the 1950s, but, at the same time, it is also driven by new kinds of firms and 'design-editors' that produce and promote their outputs globally and depend on contemporary approaches to branding and new media platforms (Skou and Munch 2016).

It is not a coincidence that Design Culture studies has grown at the same time that conceptions of what design is and could have developed dramatically. We have moved beyond solely regarding design as concerned with singularities, be these spatial, material or visual or the serial reproduction of objects. Design, these days, also includes the orchestration of networks of multiple things, people and actions. This may, for instance, be found in brand strategies where an identity is deployed across several interlinked platforms. Systems that bring products and services together, such as cycle sharing schemes or smartphones, require complex interweaving of material and immaterial artefacts. Or, for example, it is manifested in city programmes where architecture, design and cultural planning are configured as part of urban boosterism (Julier 2005).

In such articulations, design cultures become the objects of study, rather than the individual objects per se that populate them. We place the term in the plural here in recognition of the multifarious scales through which these exist. Thus, for example, they may operate through national or professional systems and identities, or may exist as implicit or explicit defining sensibilities among firms or groups. Each case may have its distinctive features and dynamics but these are not necessarily independent of each other. They exist and act in relation to each other.

At the same time, design cultures not only involve distributed and multilevel thinking and action in and about design, but also new dispositions and sensibilities on the part of their publics. In this, and in agreement with Marres and Lezuan (2011), we see publics as multi-scalar entities that are constituted through 'socio-material settings of engagement' rather than 'discursive, linguistic or procedural terms'. Everyday life is 'object-dependent' (Marres and Lezuan 2011: 490). By extension, the social practices that are held within particular publics are entangled with their material constituent parts. Design cultures come into being through the agency of their objects and people. In seeing them as ongoing constitutions and re-constitutions, they are both beings and becomings. And this is where we see the shift from design to design culture. This takes us from the consideration of singularized objects of design to multiple assemblages and also requires a shift of conception. This also takes us from linear flows of meaning to complex, multi-linear ecologies that involve ongoing interactions between design and its human and other participants.

Design cultures offer themselves as unstable, dynamic and variegated homologies. In this, they are objects for study. They invite a particular form of disciplinary enquiry that, at the same time, reflects their plurality in the ways by which this is done. Finally, the proximity of the researcher to their everyday qualities combined with a necessity for their macro-contextual understanding produces, we suggest, a particular form of practice. Design culture may be both an object and a discipline.

Let us, for the time being, take the first two propositions and explore what they have to offer.

Design culture as an object

If a design culture is to be viewed as an object in itself, then it invites particular methods of enquiry. Its constituent parts may be analysed in a direct, transactional sense. Visual or material 'reading' may take place. But as a whole, a design culture requires a more extended and, perhaps, embedded mode of investigation. It is something to be inhabited, to move within, following the connections and flows through it so that its existence isn't just understood as the sum of its individual nodes but, in addition, the movements and translations that take place between them. The researcher thus becomes the curious traveller, engaged in multi-linear micro-journeys, with or without maps.

As we have already noted, these ecologies exist in different scales and through distinct networks, from the home to the neighbourhood to the city to the nation and beyond. Indeed, they may not even be spatially bounded as we think of their diasporic, interlocking or hybrid instantiations. And within them, different constellations of people, interests and objects take place. Distinctive trajectories and dynamics are enacted within them.

This is partly an issue of representation that is still being argued out. Many design museums question whether the exhibition of singularized objects does justice to contemporary conceptions of design in society (Farrelly and Weddell 2016). A 2016 exhibition on 'mediagenic' chairs showed the massiveness of media representations, brand space stagings and social media appropriations of just a few, popular chairs – and raised the question, why should such huge material not be covered by the acquisitions of design museums to document contemporary design culture (Satell 2016)? Popular design publications continue to provide photos of reified objects, images and spaces, floating in space. At the same time, a new language of design photography attempts to 'naturalize' the design environment through showing it in use, held in moments of everyday life (Bouchez 2013). In both these cases, the challenge of representation is moving towards an anthropological account.

But if we release ourselves out of the museum halls or from the pages of the design magazine – if we turn ourselves back into the wild outside these rarefied environments – what is this network of design culture? What are its limits? How do its routes of enquiry differ, say, from media culture, architecture culture, the art scene or, even, political activism? There are three broad differences, as follows:

First, the *things*, the people, the institutions and so on (taken together we mean the actors) that would be the points of contact within a design culture field that would differ as would the practices among these. We're not talking about advertisements, buildings or works of art here that might be part of the constitution of media culture, the world of architecture or the art scene. So the routes between the constituent parts of design culture would differ too. For example, Jensen et al. (2017: 144–5) identify riding on a subway as involving 'trains, platforms, compartment design, gateways, ticket systems, CCTV systems, station architecture etc. ... [and] fellow passengers, train stewards, newspaper agents, coffee shop attendants, maintenance people and subway police'. Overlaps with other cultural assemblages do exist (news media or food retail for instance, in this case), but this example illustrates the heterogeneity and extensity of a system that may be regarded as forming of a set of (not necessarily consistent or stable) intentions, practices and experiences.

Second, and at the same time, design culture interlocks with these other cultures, providing form and content to them in ways that these others do not necessarily do for each other. In other words, design culture involves a measure of dependency and contingency on other fields of cultural practice while also having its own field of practice. For example, as a profession architecture largely constitutes itself through distinct and normative understandings and knowledge-fields. Contrastingly, as a professional field, design defines itself relationally to other knowledge domains (Wang and Ilhan 2009). Without a singular internal professional definition, designers largely identify their work as a service to other interests (users, consumers, firms, governments etc.).

Third, design more obviously (though not necessarily explicitly) attempts to reach into multiple domains of everyday practice through its varied materializations. The other 'cultures' listed above are more or less optional. We can skip art exhibitions, avoid television and digital media, ignore advertisements and act contrarily to the schemes of architecture and planning. But design relentlessly intervenes into the quotidian world so that it becomes our world and we become in it.

This process of becoming relates to the complexity of the contexts within which design situates itself. Design's multiple publics, objects and processes require it to be in a constant 'unfinished' state (Knorr Cetina 2001). Such is this complexity that design's relations are in constant flux. Therefore, if design defines itself in relation to its contexts that are – in the contemporary economic and social circumstances – always on the move, so design is too. In turn, design contributes to this dynamism and is shaped by it (Brassett 2015).

Attempts to understand design cultures are therefore attempts to understand not only their internal logics and illogicalities, but their relationship to other 'cultures'. But they are also accounts of how these relations are performed in dynamic ways. It makes for an unstable discipline as we discuss below.

Design culture as discipline

Following Thompson (2016: 322–3), we identify a discipline as having three key features. First, there is a unity in a discipline's 'problematics, categories and techniques of investigation'. In this there is a singular and uniform object of study, in this case, a (or multiple) design culture(s). Second, there is an agreed degree of rigour that is in force and is applied to its methodologies and procedures. Third, the discipline is autonomous in that it maintains an intellectual and procedural territory that is not subject to encroachment from other disciplines. In this, it carries its own disciplinary institutions such as identified departments, conferences and publishing infrastructure.

Given the unfolding, contingent and dynamic nature of design culture, it is perhaps difficult to imagine it as a unitary academic discipline at the same time. Design Culture, at least to date, shares the three prerequisites that are described above, but only partially. Degree courses in the Design Culture exist in several European universities. They largely function to educate their students in an understanding of the complexities and meanings of design in contemporary society. However, none of these courses existed before the year 2000. Some of their pedigree, particularly among the academics who staff them, is mostly in a development from the delivery of core 'history and theory' components to practice-oriented design courses. Others come through Cultural Studies, Art History or other branches of the Humanities or Social Sciences.

Thus, in many respects, its background is historically constituted and formed through its relations to other disciplines (e.g. design studies, design history, media and communications). And it is often positioned in a balance between traditional academia and new innovative sciences. To establish Design Culture studies or research at a design school, a museum, a polytechnic or university, a business school or in the humanities is a very different disciplinary act, poised between various, and sometimes competing, intentions and aspirations of the academy. As such, we suggest that it might just have the capacity to side-step intense bureaucratization where, for example, canonical texts are established in order to provide a tick-box level of legitimation for study in order to meet targets, provide performance indicators and show that the job is being done (as in, 'I've read this or that so I now know how to *do* and evaluate my work within this academic discipline') (Smith 2005).

The hybridity of Design Culture was underlined by the 2014 conference Design Culture: Object, Discipline and Practice that took place at the University of Southern Denmark in Kolding, Denmark. This book stems from that encounter. It was mostly populated by specialists from other fields such as design studies, design history, anthropology or media and communications who, nonetheless, gathered around a core academic support of and concern for Design Culture studies. Equally, the peer-reviewed journal that currently comes closest to Design Culture studies would be *Design and Culture* that, however, also exists as the official journal of the American-based Design Studies Forum and includes, for instance, articles about design history and design philosophy.

What kind of disciplinarity does this suggest, then? It seems that Design Culture embraces three kinds.

Following Barry and Born (2013), we may take *multidisciplinarity* approach to involve bringing several distinct disciplines together to focus on a particular object from the point of view of their particular specialism. In our case, we may see design culture filtered through the lenses of human geography, media and communications, sociology, economics, management, philosophy, design history and so on. If these viewpoints are aggregated and synthesized then there is an *interdisciplinarity* going on. The strength of the specific disciplinary contributions to the object of analysis that they lend is maintained; at the same time their relationships are reassembled and reconfigured. Design Culture studies, however, becomes disruptive of the integrity of separate disciplines when practiced in *trans-* or *cross-disciplinary* mode. In this, new ways of understanding, knowing and feeling may be enacted. And in this, new purposes for a discipline may be discovered.

These three kinds of disciplinarity echo the notion of design culture as an object, as a discipline and, as we later expand in our Epilogue to this book, as a practice. A design culture as a singular, yet complex, object with its specific materialities and socialities that can be studied from various viewpoints suggests a multidisciplinary approach. A design culture as something that has contingency and relationality with other cultural assemblages suggests the synthesizing processes of interdisciplinarity. As something that involves transcendence and disruption of everyday worlds, so a cross-disciplinarity in Design Culture studies engages new ontologies and epistemologies.

In short, then, Design Culture studies is a complex hybrid of voices, approaches and interests. As a mongrel of academia, it can also be undisciplined. And as such, it becomes propositional rather than reactive, climbing out of its service-mode to other disciplines (in particular, traditional design practice, institutions and business) to posit its own, particular form of practice.

Contributions of this book

This book might not present all aspects of the continuously evolving design cultures. It may not represent all mentioned disciplines contributing to Design Culture either. But it presents a wide range of different approaches to the manifold challenges and possibilities of design cultures between private domesticity and public spaces, between users, professions and economic stakeholders, between markets, medias and museums.

The chapters of the first part, 'Developing Design Culture', explain the relevance and importance of investigating design to understand our contemporary culture. They point to general developments that design is part of in society: sustainability, digitalization and changes in the environments of everyday life, organizations and understandings and experiences of use. They also discuss the development of Design Culture as a disciplinary field in relation to Design History, Cultural Studies, Material Culture and the Management Sciences. In so doing, this part refines and positions Design Culture studies.

The chapters of the second part, 'Addressing Market and Society', present different understandings of design culture as cases, where design approaches market and society in different ways. Designers, and to some extent firms that are highly profiled in design culture, occasionally express reformist approaches to the relations of market forces to product culture as part of a cultural critique. This means that both marketing and professional discourses have introduced many intricate ways of addressing relations of design, market and its impacts on society, showing configurations of political agendas, professional ideologies, consumer segments and subcultures, all of which characterize design culture.

The chapters of the third part, 'Positioning of Design Professions', look at how designers act according to the challenges of the professional and commercial fields of design. As designers don't count as a profession in a classic, well-defined sense and there is a heavy competition from other professional actors with different educations as well as non-designers, designers have constantly to position themselves and their educational background in the liberal market of design services. A tracking of this continued positioning in an institutional and professional field is an important contribution to the mapping of design culture.

The chapters of the fourth part, 'Locating Design Culture', position design culture in different geographical contexts and relations – local, national, regional and global. As such it provides an additional opportunity to push Design Culture studies beyond traditional parameters and outwards toward a mesh of transnational relations beyond the heavily branded design nations as well as beyond the Western, modernist design canon. The cases come from Denmark, Turkey, Belgium, the Netherlands and Jordan, but go beyond the frame of the nation-state in different ways, as transnational constellations and national conditions alter. The last chapter exemplifies design culture in the context of the Arab region by looking into design education and practice in Jordan. It suggests that the introduction of Design Culture studies and research would make designers more aware of their local and regional contexts and conditions – and in this way work against the Westernization and blind borrowing from Western design that characterizes both institutions and business.

This look into future possibilities is taken up in our Epilogue, where we reflect on the question of, how Design Culture could be said, not only to find its way as a discipline, but also into different kinds of practice in business and society. We see the development of design culture as object, discipline *and* practice as a vital source of understanding, critique and action in addressing the many challenges of contemporary life. This may take place in both local and global ways and in all its complexities and simplicities.

Note

1 In this introduction we use 'Design Culture' (upper case) to signify the academic discipline and 'design culture' (lower case) to signify it as a phenomenon. As editors, we have left this issue of capitalization to be employed for other authors in this book as they see appropriate.

References

Barry, A. and Born, G. (eds), (2013), *Interdisciplinarity: Reconfigurations of the Social and Natural Sciences*, London: Routledge.

Bouchez, H. (2013), '"*I don't care what it is for, I want it*": The flow of meaning of *high design* in Flanders from 1980–1910, through the dynamics between producer, media and consumer', PhD, Katholieke Universiteit Leuven.
Brassett, J. (2015), 'Poised and Complex. Deleuze, Design and Innovation', in B. Marenko and J. Brassett (eds), *Deleuze and Design*, 31–57, Edinburgh: Edinburgh University Press.
Fallan, K. (2013), 'De-tooling Design History: To What Purpose and for Whom Do We Write?', *Design and Culture*, 5(1): 13–9.
Fallan, K. (2010), *Design History: Understanding Theory and Method*, Oxford: Berg.
Farrelly, L. and Weddell, J. (eds), (2016), *Design Objects and the Museum*, London: Bloomsbury Publishing.
Highmore, B. (ed.), (2009), *The Design Culture Reader*, London: Routledge.
Huppatz, D. J. and Lees-Maffei, G. (2013), 'Why Design History? A Multi-national Perspective on the State and Purpose of the Field', *Arts and Humanities in Higher Education*, 12(2–3): 310–30.
Jensen, O., Bendix Lanng, D. and Wind, S. (2017), 'Artefacts, Affordances and the Design of Mobilities', in J. Spinney, S. Reimer and P. Pinch (eds), *Mobilising Design*, London: Routledge, 143–54.
Julier, G. (2005), 'Urban Designscapes and the Production of Aesthetic Consent', *Urban studies*, 42(5–6): 869–87.
Knorr Cetina, K. (2001), 'Objectual Practice', in T.R. Schatzki, K. Knorr Cetina and E. Von Savigny (eds), *The Practice Turn in Contemporary Theory*, London: Routledge, 184–96.
Margolin, V. (1992), 'Design History or Design Studies: Subject Matter and Methods', *Design Studies*, 13(2): 104–16.
Marres, N. and Lezaun, J., (2011), 'Materials and Devices of the Public: An Introduction', *Economy and Society*, 40(4): 489–509.
Satell, R. (2016), *Instant Icon*, Copenhagen & Kolding: Strandberg & Trapholt Museum of Art and Design
Skou, N. P. and Munch, A. V. (2016), 'New Nordic and Scandinavian Retro: Reassessment of Values and Aesthetics in Contemporary Nordic Design', *Journal of Aesthetics & Culture*, 8: 1–12.
Smith, M. (2005), 'Visual Studies, or the Ossification of Thought', *Journal of Visual Culture*, 4(2): 237–56.
Sparke, P. (1986), *An Introduction to Design and Culture in the 20th Century*, London: Allen and Unwin.
Thompson, G. F. (2016), 'Interdisciplinary Complexities', *Journal of Cultural Economy*, 9(3): 322–9.
Wang, D. and Ilhan, A. O. (2009), 'Holding Creativity Together: A Sociological Theory of the Design Professions', *Design Issues*, 25(1): 5–21.

PART ONE

Developing design culture

Mads Nygaard Folkmann

The title of this section carries a twofold question of how to develop design culture. We may develop our understanding of *what* to look at as the object of investigation and we may develop methods of *how* to look at this object. Of course, we may as researchers and students of design not forget to also ask *why* design is important to study: What is the motivation to privilege design as an entry to investigate and understand our cultures, historically as well as in a contemporary perspective?

The contributions in this section discuss possible developments in the field of design culture, both as an object to be analysed and scrutinized, and as a multifaceted, interdisciplinary discipline still in its becoming. In their different approaches to investigating the design as a cultural phenomenon, the contributions do not necessarily build up Design Culture as a homogeneous discipline with an established methodology of investigation and a common theoretical ground, but they explore different analytical and theoretical settings for understanding the importance of design.

The starting point for Kjetil Fallan's chapter, 'Design culturing: Making design history matter', is that even if design is ever more central to our societies and cultures, design seems to gain only little academic interest in the social sciences and the humanities. Fallan discusses the disciplinary demarcations of Design Studies, Design Culture and Design History and argues for the latter as a focal methodological entry for investigating also the developments in contemporary society. Consequently, Fallan argues against the objections against Design History for delving into historical studies without relevance to contemporary concerns. On the contrary, Fallan demonstrates his methodological point by pointing to three key recent developments in design – 'designification', 'sustainification' and 'digitalization' – which pose challenges for how design can be studied, but all can be studied with the prism of Design History in its interest in 'design as deeply entangled in social and cultural networks and processes, portraying a much more complex design culture'. Ultimately, Fallan's point is that history writing is also concerned with the present, and that the methodological tools we employ in our analytical enterprises also 'actively configures design culture'.

In the chapter 'Taste and attunement: Design culture as world making', Ben Highmore continues the discussion of design culture as a methodological approach. He does not, however, take his starting point in a discussion of disciplinary demarcations (which also may be a question of institutional conditions in design schools and universities). Instead he experimentally explores what it means to position design at the centre of our interest, and how an interest in design culture enables 'us to see the world as particular sets of qualities, feelings and meanings as well as a purposefully fashioned material environment'. In Highmore's view, the term 'design culture' orients the investigation of design towards a larger consideration of the 'world-forming activity of design'. As a prism, design culture may direct the attention towards constitutive factors in design studios, manufacture and consumption, but also look at modern society at large with all its tools, technology and shaping of the physical as well as mental environment. In this sense, Highmore advocates for regarding design as a 'cultural form' and employs this as a platform for analysing the emergence of the duvet in the United Kingdom as a cultural form. Through the duvet case, it is demonstrated how the duvet is a physical object as well as engaging in a cultural configuration, including the history of bedding and media and marketing discourses.

In the chapter 'Embedding design in the organizational culture: Challenges and perspectives', Alessandro Deserti and Francesca Rizzo make a case of applied design culture methodology. They question and explore how design culture approaches can be productive in understanding how companies and organizations operate according to their cultural setting. Taking a starting point in a discussion of the concept of Design Thinking (which, indeed, has been a strong conceptual currency in the last fifteen years), Deserti and Rizzo argue that this notion 'tends to be fixed as an abstract design model applicable independently from the context and the object of design', whereas the concept of design culture introduces a situated, dynamic and context-dependent approach which 'emphasizes the peculiar "way of doing things" of an organisation or system'. Through the cases of Apple and Samsung, which have similarities in the field of consumer electronics, but have quite different company cultures, Deserti and Rizzo demonstrate that the specific cultures of understanding and conceptualizing design are reflected in the organizational culture of the companies. In their analysis, design is not only a strong determinant in giving shape to new products, but may also, through the concept of design culture, be a driver of development and innovation in the organization.

In the final chapter, 'Use in design culture,' Toke Riis Ebbesen examines the status of the concept of use within the disciplinary framework of Design Culture and other recent approaches oriented towards an understanding of design being embedded in and a product of cultural, social, economic and political contexts. Ebbesen argues that 'the concept of use in design is, if not overseen, then at least under-prioritized, both in practice-related design fields and within the fields of history, theory and criticism of design'. Employing semiotic concepts for a better understanding of the character and role of use in design, Ebbesen proposes 'a model of use in context' which points out how users can make inferences about material properties, potential use schemes and typical discursive valuations and relationships on the basis of concrete products and their formal and material properties. Ultimately, the chapter not only argues for a 'revival of the concept of use in the study of design as culture' but also seeks to demonstrate how the conceptual framework of Design Culture can (re-)connect to a concept of use.

CHAPTER ONE

Design culturing: Making design history matter

Kjetil Fallan

Introduction

Ours is a culture of design (Highmore 2008; Fallan 2013a). Design is the interface between us and the world. Everywhere. Always. But why, as Stuart Kendall asks, is this so poorly reflected in current research in the humanities, 'when design, in all of its myriad forms, is manifestly both the most significant force shaping our lives today and so widely misunderstood?' (Kendall 2011: vii). In the following I will make a case for how design history – arguably the most established form of humanistic design studies – can best contribute to our understanding of design culture – understood both as an object of study and as a field of inquiry – and thereby regain the relevance to contemporary concerns some of the discipline's critics claim it has lost (Fry 2009: 122; Tonkinwise 2014; Julier and Narotzky 1998). One possible strategy for doing this is turning the attention of design history to key developments in contemporary society rather than the less obviously relevant phenomena of the distant past. This is not to subscribe to a crude instrumentalist approach demanding of scholars they maximize the social relevance of their work, but rather to argue that design historians can and should *also* address topics of more immediate concern to contemporary challenges.

Although design culture can certainly be a useful shorthand for describing the subject matter of a design history more attuned to the socio-cultural embeddedness of design than its biographies and iconologies (Fallan 2010: 149–50), the term is probably even more interesting as a dynamic, a course of action – something that we *do*, *produce* or *configure*, rather than something we observe (Kendall 2014: 364). One way of explicating this would be to coin the neologism 'design culturing' as a paraphrase of Tony Fry's concept 'design futuring' (Fry 2009). Just like, for Fry, the future of design is not something that is just 'out there' waiting to be discovered, but has to be facilitated, so can the culture of design be conceived as *configured* rather than preconditioned. Importantly, this *con*-figuration is a relational, networked process inhabited by people and things alike (Atzmon and Boradkar 2014: 145; Boradkar 2010: 4–5).

A processual approach to design culture has the advantage of highlighting the open-ended, constantly shifting nature of its subject matter – a familiar challenge in all types of contemporary history. It also requires scholars to acknowledge our status as actors in the world we engage with rather than as disinterested observers, and thus forces us to reflect on our subjectivity (Fallan and Lees-Maffei 2015). Another consequence of this line of reasoning is that those who study design culture are as complicit in its configuration as is design, designers, mediators and consumers. Therefore, we should choose our objects of study with care – after all, we only ever get the design culture we deserve. Let me briefly outline, then, a few key themes in contemporary design culture – as object – that warrant closer attention from design historians and that hold the potential to increase the extrinsic, or exogamous, relevance of design history.

Designification

First, we might make the modest move from stating that ours is a culture of design to describing the situation in more processual terms as the *designification* of society. Design practice, design awareness, design terminology and even 'design thinking' seem to permeate society to an ever-increasing degree, creeping into every nook and cranny of our existence. Of course, as many scholars have noted, design culture is nothing new – it can be claimed to be as old as homo faber (Huppatz 2010; MacGregor 2010; Margolin 2015). Jean Baudrillard (1981: 185–6) points to the Bauhaus as 'the genesis of the universal extension of design' (Holt 2016: 56). But there is an argument to be made that its sheer pervasiveness has escalated significantly in the course of just the last decades, even. We now have not only 'designer' furniture and 'designer' clothes, but also 'designer' diapers and 'designer' dildos. Pretentious hairdressers become 'hair designers'; and even God is nowadays referred to as a 'designer' – at least by creationists. The use of design lingo and designer signatures in marketing is no longer restricted to high-end furnishing companies, but equally eagerly embraced by mass-market actors like IKEA and Target.

It is this development – this profusion and de-elitification of design – that apparently offended Hal Foster's aesthetic sensibilities and prompted him to decry the current situation 'when the aesthetic and utilitarian are not only conflated but all but subsumed in the commercial, and everything – not only architectural projects and art exhibitions but everything from jeans to genes – seems to be regarded as so much *design*' (Foster 2002: 17). Being an art critic rather than a design historian, Foster, of course, is late in the game, beaten to it by some thirty years by Wolfgang Haug (Haug 1971).

These criticisms of the *designification* of society, though, are in reality criticisms of the *commodification* of society, and as such can be thought of as a more design-centred version of Frankfurt school critique of the *Kulturindustrie* and the aestheticization of society (Featherstone 1991). Or, perhaps more specifically, they are criticisms of the commercial and market-driven nature of design – at least of the kind of design under attack. In this logic, of course, 'the aesthetic' does not refer to a more general notion of sensory qualities or experiences, but rather to a narrower sense of 'visual appeal'. Similarly, products are reduced to signs, carriers of symbolic meaning, ignoring their functional properties, social purposes and emotional values (Stockmarr 2014: 54; 67). Nevertheless, this type of criticism is not without merit on some counts, especially when it targets the excessive attention to seductive and fetishistic features in so much of contemporary design whose 'added value' adds little or no value to humanity or society (Russo 2013; Carmagnola 2013).

But the *designification* of society does not necessarily have to be construed as synonymous to the aestheticization of society. It may also describe the immersion and expansion of design competence into new domains. Whereas it is true, of course, that design is often used to turn cheap utensils into more expensive lifestyle accessories (Jensen 2012), one might argue that it is also increasingly being put to use in less hedonistic contexts. Although perhaps not a radical change, it is worth noting that designers are now working in a broader range of industries beyond the narrow segment of 'lifestyle' consumer products. And because the latter category has dominated historical studies of design culture, the current state of design practice should prompt us to recalibrate our selection criteria and analytic lenses. There is, in short, a world of goods out there that continue to fly under the radar of design historians (Fallan 2015).

Other developments in contemporary practice that design history will have to engage with include the move into areas producing less tangible outputs such as web design, interaction design and service design. Despite, in relation to the first example, important initiatives like the Way Back Machine Internet Archive and Design Museum Denmark's Webmuseum.dk based on Ida Engholm's pioneering history of web design (Engholm 2003), writing histories of such forms of design practice will be challenging to a breed of scholars accustomed to scrutinizing material artefacts.

More radically, perhaps, design practice has – in parallel to its growing contribution to the hyperinflation of consumption – also, at times, been dancing to a different and less overtly commercial tune. One iteration of this, the radical design movement, has been the subject of considerable interest from design historians for some time (see for example Rossi 2013). Another category, which thus far has received less attention, is what might be called 'design aid', or design for development. A contemporary example of this type of practice is the activities coordinated by the Design without Borders programme organized by the Foundation for Design and Architecture in Norway, which uses design work and design competence to improve conditions in developing countries through concrete design projects ranging from landmine clearing equipment to urinals for use in slum areas (Ramberg and Verdu-Isachsen 2012).

FIGURE 1.1 *Page from* Media of transportation by use of human forces on or by the body. Report on a joint project of 2nd Year Product Design students and the Design Research and Development Unit, *produced by Kristian Vedel's colleagues and students in the Department of Design, Faculty of Architecture, Design and Development, University of Nairobi, June 1971. Courtesy of Ane Vedel.*

Despite its limited visibility in design history, design aid has a fairly long track record, stretching back into the 1950s at least. If we stick to Scandinavian examples, Danida (the Danish Ministry of Foreign Affairs' development cooperation) sent the designer Kristian Vedel (Figure 1.1) to Kenya in 1968 where he spent three years establishing the industrial design programme at the University of Nairobi (Dybdahl 2006: 58). Later, in the early 1980s, the Norwegian Agency for Development Cooperation (Norad) commissioned designer Bjørn A. Larsen to develop school furniture intended for production in Tanzania (Fallan 2011: 36). In the 1960s and 1970s these Nordic governmental organizations also sent architectural aid along the same lines – a history which was explored at the Nordic pavilion at the 2014 Venice Biennale Architettura with the exhibition *Forms of Freedom: African Independence and Nordic Models*. So, as design aid gains greater public and official traction, it certainly is ripe for design historical investigation (see for example Clarke 2016; Lie 2016). Importantly, one of the most significant criticisms of Design without Borders has come from a design historian (Banu 2009), demonstrating the fertility and societal relevance of this material.

No matter which version of the *designification* of society we home in on – the beautification of consumer products; the expansion of design competence into new fields; or 'design for the real world' (Papanek 1971) – it should be clear that there is no dearth of design cultures of contemporary relevance for design history to explore. As Mads Nygaard Folkmann reminds us, whether we are considering its most audacious or its most austere manifestations, design is 'creating a dominant and omnipresent culture of the aesthetic as the filter through which we experience the world' (Folkmann 2013: 60).

Sustainification

Tony Fry's depiction of design history's understanding of design as 'historically decontextualized' and 'a particularist concern' (Fry 2009: 122), the significance of which 'is trivial' (Fry 2015: 8), seems rather exaggerated and unwarranted in light of the field's development over the last decades, but he does have a point that it has hitherto not contributed much by way of connecting design's pasts to its role in creating sustainable futures (Fry 2015: 9). Design history would do well to accept his challenge.

Today, sustainability is an essential parameter in all design practice, education, research and mediation. However, the history of design's relationship to sustainability, ecology and the environment is still an embryonic field (Fallan and Jørgensen 2017). This is not for lack of interest – quite the contrary: Recent scholarship has pointed out the need to pursue this topic, but has thus far made only cursory attempts. These include charting the historical importance of Victor Papanek, which has received some attention, but remains fragmentary (Clarke 2010; Fiender and Geisler

2010; Lie 2016). Systematic efforts at documenting and analysing the development of sustainable design have yet to emerge. Although concerned more with architecture that with design, Panayiota Pyla has noted that 'now that sustainability has the added burden of no longer being at the margins, but at the center of design concerns, the realm of design has the responsibility to vigilantly consider how this "magic word of consensus" came about' (Pyla 2012: 276).

Twenty years ago, Pauline Madge (Madge 1993) provided a pioneering and very valuable historiographical review that sought to link work relating to sustainability issues in design activism and environmental history to design history and thereby provide a basis from which to develop a design history of sustainability. It is high time her call is heeded, as historical understanding of and critical reflection on the rise of sustainability as the primordial trope in design discourse is essential to building a solid knowledge base and to underpin present and future decision making. Fully in line with this, Clive Dilnot recently pointed to design history 'as a site of the possible redemption of the future-now-lost' in confronting the looming ecological crisis: '*To redeem the hopes contained in the [designed] past is to recover the deeper contents contained in the assumption of design's virtue*' (italics and brackets in original)

FIGURE 1.2 *The design history of electric vehicles remains to be written. This project for an electrically powered van developed by the Norwegian coachbuilding company Strømmens Værksted around 1970 was motivated specifically by environmental concerns. It featured an aluminium frame and a fiberglass-reinforced polyester body designed by Terje Meyer and Bjørn A. Larsen. Courtesy of Norsk jernbanemuseum.*

(Dilnot 2014: 63). Scrutinizing past policies on sustainability will provide a unique vantage point for asking tough questions of current and future policies – a strategy which has been proposed as perhaps the best way of making historical research relevant to contemporary and future concerns (Cox 2013).

The links between 'design culturing', as understood here, and Tony Fry's concept of 'design futuring' are also quite clear, because in order to facilitate desired future developments of the design field, a comprehensive understanding of the cultural and social significance of design is absolutely crucial. As Fry writes, 'the common goals of creating sustain-ability will only stand a chance of realization if pursued in socio-culturally plural ways' (Fry 2009: 91). Given the immense societal significance of sustainability and the crucial role played by design in its past, present and future, historical studies of sustainability and unsustainability in design will have great relevance to contemporary design discourse broadly defined, from pedagogy and policy to consumption and criticism (Figure1.2).

Digitalization

Arguably, the digitalization of design and manufacturing processes (through Computer Aided Design, Computer Aided Manufacturing, Computer Numerical Control, Rapid Prototyping, etc.) has been the greatest paradigm shift in the design profession and the manufacturing industry since the industrial revolution – in fact, the recent flurry known as the 'maker movement' often refers to the development of affordable 3-D printing as 'the third industrial revolution' (Knott 2013: 61) and endows it 'with powerful utopian capacities' (Stein 2017: 4). Now as mundane and obvious part of any design student's toolkit as a pencil, in historical terms CAD technology is a recent invention. Nevertheless, the profusion of such technologies begs the design historians' questions: What are their key developmental trajectories? How have they changed design practice? How have they changed designed objects? How have they changed industrial organization and manufacturing practices? What roles have they played in the globalization of design and production, where products may be 'designed ... in California' but 'assembled in China'? Such questions are only slowly being explored, but their urgency heralds an emerging literature on the topic (e.g. Steenson 2017). Digital design processes are followed by digital design objects, that is, physical products incorporating and relying on digital technologies. Such objects are fundamentally different from 'analogue' products in that their augmented functionalities bear no direct relation to their material properties in a conventional sense. This is what Gert Selle (2014: 42) has labelled 'Halb-Dinge' in recognition of their hybrid character. Paul Atkinson (2010; 2013) has explored computers as design culture, and the recent surge on digital objects and the rise of the Internet of things will no doubt beget more studies akin to Barry Katz' (2015) history of Silicon Valley design.

A corollary to the digitalization of design practice and objects is the digitalization of design mediation and design consumption. It seems uncontroversial by now to claim that the World Wide Web has brought about changes to the mediation and consumption of design as profound as those induced by CAD and related technologies in design and production. But what have these changes consisted of, and what are their consequences? Mediation of design through websites – which are, of course, themselves design objects in their own right with a design history of their own (Engholm 2003) – be it manufacturers' promotional sites, online stores, online magazines, blogs, or other forms, differ quite substantially from conventional forms of mediation – most notably in that the sheer materiality of the mediated design remains imaginary, invoked purely by visual and textual proxies. This type of digital culture has become a favoured topic in media studies, but design is rarely given much consideration. How does this 'triumph of the virtual', as it were, affect us as readers/viewers, consumers and users? How is meaning and value constructed in this 'dematerialized' design culture? In considering design's move 'from object to image' Dario Russo has pointed out that 'paradoxically, if the aesthetic is becoming more "factual", because it condenses in the object of use, design is becoming virtual, taking shape towards a calculated dissemination of the image' (Russo 2013: 12). A related issue arises from the fact that more and more designed objects are (seemingly) immaterial: How does the ever more prevalent consumption and use of digital interfaces, services and products differ from the consumption and use of conventional, material objects? And what are the relations between the immaterial and the material (say, between software and hardware – the domain of Human–Computer Interaction, a design discipline of rapidly increasing significance (Tonkinwise 2014: 27–8))? Crucially, though, histories of digital design are not immaterial histories (Atkinson 2010; 2013; Gabrys 2011; Katz 2015). Design historians have perhaps more than anyone else proved apt at interrogating the materiality of things; a sensitivity that needs to be retained also when the subject matter is seemingly immaterial: 'Contrary to pervasive narratives of the digital, computational transactions are not invisible, nor weightless. They are socially and materially constructed. As a theory and contract of such transactions, software – its history, its design, its irreducibly material dimension – must be approached as a crucial subject of discussion and debate in design' (Cardoso Llach 2015: 54).

A third strand of digital design culturing could turn the focus on digitalization from subject to method. By exploring the emerging field of the digital humanities, we can investigate new research methods based on digital technology and their potential application to design history. Digital humanities are becoming a new exciting modality of research taking advantage of the computer and the internet in archiving and examining large amounts of data, providing and producing various tools that can be used for accessing and examining digital archives. Even for conventional archives, digitalization has great potential. 'We have the means to build stepping stones between archives to represent connections across institutional divides', writes Catherine Moriarty (2016: 56) of the University of Brighton Design Archives, arguing that digitalization provides 'the capacity to use the codified descriptions of archives as an environment in which to identify and establish points of connection'. It is not just about the organization of, and access to, the material, though – as Moriarty (2016: 57) points out, mobilizing the digital data in design archives can also 'start to answer ... how visualization techniques might animate design's history afresh'.

Digital humanities seem an especially promising modality for studies that deal with the examination of non-textual material, and design is therefore integral to the endeavour (Burdick et al., 2012). The digitalization of design culture – both as object and as practice – is a rich and thus far virtually unexplored terrain for design history, and certainly one that holds the potential of reconnecting design history with design practice.

Disciplination

In a recent 'state-of-the-art' survey of the merits of design studies as a scholarly field Cameron Tonkinwise engaged in some serious design history bashing – a sport that non-design historians seem to take pleasure in from time to time. A particularly notorious example is Daniel Miller's characterization of the field, 'as conventionally studied', as 'clearly intended to be a form of pseudo art history, in which the task is to locate great individuals ... and portray them as the creators of modern mass culture' (Miller 1987: 142). Now, whereas Miller can be – partially, at least – absolved of his dim view of design history based on the date of his criticism, Tonkinwise should have informed himself better of the development of design history over the last decades before dismissing design history as 'Research of a design(er)'s histories' (Tonkinwise 2014: 10). Such a 'Great Designer and his Great Design' approach has been firmly relegated to the coffee table book segment, and has little or nothing to do with the field's research front. Recent academic design history, on the other hand, tends to consider design as deeply entangled in social and cultural networks and processes, portraying a much more complex design culture. If design studies neglects design history, it is to the detriment of the former. In the words of Clive Dilnot: 'It is precisely the almost complete lack of historical perspective in design research that renders what it produces all but null-and-void as genuine understanding' (Dilnot 2014: 59).

Tonkinwise also claims that 'In few other professions is the history of the profession useful' (Tonkinwise 2014: 12). First, as mentioned, design history is not synonymous with the history of the profession, as it recently has been more interested in the mediation and consumption of design than in its production (Lees-Maffei 2009). Second, a recent case study has poignantly demonstrated just how useful design students find design history in their work (Pollen 2015). Moreover, though, it seems odd to assume that students of art, engineering and economics – to name but a few relevant fields – are consistently being taught the history of art, the history of technology and business history, respectively, if the knowledge of the history of their professions that these branches of historical scholarship (also) provide has no value.

I have pointed to these parallels elsewhere, while arguing that a more significant problem is that design history is all too often considered subservient to design practice education rather than a branch of historical scholarship in its own right (Fallan 2013b). Although Tonkinwise asks the same question of design studies – why it isn't located in a humanities or social science context rather than in design schools (Tonkinwise 2014: 10) – he seems unwilling to acknowledge the value of such a 'de-tooled' design history. Harking back to the 'design studies versus design history' debate of the mid-1990s, we could here be at the core of what distinguishes – or perhaps *should* distinguish – design studies from design culture in the disciplinary sense: The former seems to be faithfully wedded to design practice and design education, whereas the latter can maintain a far more casual relationship to that sphere, while at the same time nurturing its liaisons with relevant branches of the humanities and social sciences, and thus cultivate a less instrumentalist and therefore more culturally significant discourse on design.

We are currently in a situation where there is considerable interest in design culture also outside the realm of design practice and design education. I have previously argued that thinking of design history as 'the history of design culture or as the cultural history of design' might be a way of forging stronger relations between design history and other disciplines within the humanities and social sciences engaged in the study of culture (Fallan 2010: 150). Today, recognizing the opportunity to mitigate what Guy Julier and Viviana Narotzky (1998) described as 'the redundancy of design history' to design practice and research, I would add that by engaging in *design culturing* more explicitly, along the lines suggested in this chapter, design history might improve its relevance to, and contribution to, contemporary design discourse as well.

History writing is concerned as much with the present as with the past. Writing about design culture is not some detached, objective endeavour – it is an enterprise that actively configures design culture. Conceiving of our remit as *design culturing*, then, might be a way of deliberately making design history matter.

References

Atkinson, P. (2010), *Computer*, London: Reaktion.
Atkinson, P. (2013), *Delete: A Design History of Computer Vapourware*, London: Bloomsbury Academic.
Atzmon, L. and Boradkar, P. (2014), 'Introduction: A Design Encounter with Thing Theory', *Design and Culture*, 6(2): 141–52.
Banu, L. (2009), 'Defining the Design Deficit in Bangladesh', *Journal of Design History*, 22(4): 309–23.
Baudrillard, J. (1981) [1972], *For a Critique of the Political Economy of the Sign*, St. Louis, Mont.: Telos Press.
Boradkar, P. (2010), *Designing Things: A Critical Introduction to the Culture of Objects*, Oxford: Berg Publishers.
Burdick, A., Drucker, J., Lunenfeld, P., Presner, T. and Schnapp, J. (2012), *Digital_Humanities*, Cambridge, MA MIT Press.
Carduso Llach, D. (2015), 'Software Comes to Matter: Towards a Material History of Computational Design', *Design Issues*, 31(3): 41–54
Carmagnola, F. (2013), 'Design ed estetica oggi', in *Il design e la sua storia: Primo Convegno dell'Associazione Italiana degli Storici del design*, Milan: Lupetti, 45–60.
Clarke, A. (2010), 'The Anthropological Object in Design: From Victor Papanek to Superstudio', in A. Clarke (ed.), *Design Anthropology: Object Culture in the 21st Century*, Vienna: Springer Verlag, 74–87.
Clarke, A. (2016), 'Design for Development, ICSID and UNIDO: The Anthropological Turn in 1970s Design', *Journal of Design History*, 29(1): 43–57.
Cox, P. (2013), 'The Future Uses of History', *History Workshop Journal*, 75(1): 125–45.
Dilnot, C. (2014), 'Is there an Ethical Role for the History of Design? Redeeming through History the Possibility of a Humane World', in Helena Barbosa and Anna Calvera (eds), *Traditions, Transitions, Trajectories: Major or Minor Influences? Proceedings of ICDHS 2014 the 9th International Committee for Design History and Design Studies, 8, 9, 10, 11 July, Aveiro, Portugal*, Aveiro: UA Editora/University of Aveiro, 57–80.
Dybdahl, L. (2006), *Dansk design 1945–1975*, Copenhagen: Borgen.
Engholm, I. (2003), *WWW's designhistorie: website udviklingen i et genre- og stilteoretisk perspektiv* [PhD thesis], Copenhagen: IT University of Copenhagen.
Fallan, K. (2010), *Design History: Understanding Theory and Method*, Oxford: Berg Publishers.
Fallan, K. (2011), 'The "Designer"—The 11th Plague': Design Discourse from Consumer Activism to Environmentalism in 1960s Norway', *Design Issues*, 27(4): 30–42.
Fallan, K. (2013a), 'Culture by Design: Co-Constructing Material and Meaning', in K. Aukrust (ed.), *Assigning Cultural Values*, Frankfurt am Main: Peter Lang, 135–63.
Fallan, K. (2013b), 'De-tooling Design History: To What Purpose and for Whom Do We Write?', *Design and Culture*, 5(1): 13–19.
Fallan, K. (2015), 'Nordic Noir: Deadly Design from the Peacemongering Periphery', *Design and Culture*, 7(3): 377–402.

Fallan, K. and Lees-Maffei, G. (2015), 'It's Personal: Subjectivity in Design History', *Design and Culture*, 7(1): 5–27.

Fallan, K. and Jørgensen, F. A. (2017), 'Environmental Histories of Design: Towards a New Research Agenda', *Journal of Design History* 30(2): 103–21.

Featherstone, M. (1991), *Consumer Culture and Postmodernism*, London: Sage.

Fiender, M. and Geisler, T. (2010), 'Design Criticism and Critical Design in the Writings of Victor Papanek (1923–1998)', *Journal of Design History*, 23(1): 99–106.

Folkmann, M. N. (2013), *The Aesthetics of Imagination in Design*, Cambridge, MA: MIT Press.

Foster, H. (2002), *Design and Crime (And Other Diatribes)*, London: Verso.

Fry, T. (2009), *Design Futuring: Sustainability, Ethics and New Practice*, Oxford: Berg Publishers.

Fry, T. (2015), 'Whither Design/Whether History', in T. Fry, C. Dilnot and S. Stewart, *Design and the Question of History*, London: Bloomsbury, 1–130.

Gabrys, J. (2011), *Digital Rubbish: A Natural History of Electronics*, Ann Arbor: The University of Michigan Press.

Haug, W. F. (1971), *Kritik der Warenästhetik*, Frankfurt: Suhrkamp.

Highmore, B. 2008, 'General Introduction: A Sideboard Manifesto: Design Culture in an Artificial World', in B. Highmore (ed.), *The Design Culture Reader*, London: Routledge, 1–11.

Holt. M. (2016), 'Baudrillard and the Bauhaus: The Political Economy of Design', *Design Issues*, 32(3): 55–66.

Huppatz, D. J. (2010), 'The Cave: Writing Design History', *Journal of Writing in Creative Practice*, 3(2): 135–48.

Jensen, H. C. (2012), 'Jacob Jensen and the Lifa Kitchen: Branding the "Lifestyle" Kitchen with Designer Personality and Mythology', in K. Fallan (ed.), *Scandinavian Design: Alternative Histories*, London: Berg Publishers, 152–67.

Julier, G. and Narotzky, V.. (1998), 'The Redundancy of Design History'. Paper presented at the Practically Speaking conference at the University of Wolverhampton, 14–15 December 1998.

Katz, B. M. (2015), *Make it New: The History of Silicon Valley Design*, Cambridge, MA: MIT Press.

Kendall, S. (2011), *The Ends of Art and Design*, Chadron, NE: Infra-Thin Press.

Kendall, S. (2014), 'Positioning Design Studies: An Institutional Challenge', *Design and Culture*, 6(3): 345–68.

Knott, S. (2013), 'Design in the Age of Prosumption: The Craft of Design after the Object', *Design and Culture*, 5(1): 45–68.

Lees-Maffei, G. (2009), 'The Production-Consumption-Mediation Paradigm', *Journal of Design History*, 22(4): 351–76.

Lie, I. K. (2016), '"Make Us More Useful to Society!": The Scandinavian Design Students' Organization (SDO) and Socially Responsible Design, 1967–1973', *Design and Culture*, 8(3): 327–61.

MacGregor, N. (2010), *A History of the World in 100 Objects*, London: Allen Lane.

Madge, P. (1993), 'Design, Ecology, Technology: A Historiographical Review', *Journal of Design History*, 6(3): 149–66.

Margolin, V. (2015), *World History of Design* [Volume 1], London: Bloomsbury Academic.

Miller, D. (1987), *Material Culture and Mass Consumption*, Oxford: Blackwell.
Moriarty, C. (2016), 'Monographs, Archives, and Networks: Representing Designer Relationships', *Design Issues*, 32(4): 52–63.
Papanek, V. (1971), *Design for the Real World Human Ecology and Social Change*, New York: Pantheon Books.
Pollen, A. (2015), 'My Position in the Design World: Locating Subjectivity in the Design Curriculum', *Design and Culture*, 7(1): 85–105.
Pyla, P. (2012), 'Sustainability's Prehistories: Beyond Smooth Talk—Oxymorons, Ambivalences, and Other Current Realities of Sustainability', *Design and Culture*, 4(3): 273–8.
Ramberg, T. and Verdu-Isachsen, L. (eds), (2012), *Design without Borders: Creating Change*, Oslo: Foundation for Design and Architecture in Norway.
Rossi, C. (2013), 'Crafting a Design Counterculture: The Pastoral and the Primitive in Italian Radical Design, 1972–1976', in G. Lees-Maffei and K. Fallan (eds), *Made in Italy: Rethinking a Century of Italian Design*, London: Bloomsbury Academic, 145–60.
Russo, D. (2013), *Il lato oscuro del design*, Milan: Lupetti.
Selle, G. (2014), 'Ding, Halb-Ding, Nicht-Ding, In-Ding, Über-Ding', in J. H. Gleiter (ed.), *Symptom Design: Vom Zeigen und Sich-Zeigen der Dinge*, Bielefeld: Transcript Verlag, 39–67.
Steenson, M. W. (2017), *Architectural Intelligence: How Designers and Architects Created the Digital Landscape*, Cambridge, MA MIT Press.
Stein, J. A. (2017), 'The Political Imaginaries of 3D Printing: Prompting Mainstream Awareness of Design and Making', *Design and Culture*, 9(1): 3–27.
Stockmarr, P. (2014), *Det æstetiske i design: En diskussion af æstetikbegrepets historiske rolle og aktuelle status i designlitteraturen med henblik på en identifikation af mulige afsæt for en fornyet designfaglig æstetikdiskussion* [PhD thesis], Copenhagen: The Royal Danish Academy of Fine Arts, Schools of Architecture, Design and Conservation.
Tonkinwise, C. (2014), 'Design Studies: What Is It Good For?', *Design and Culture*, 6(1): 5–43.

CHAPTER TWO

Taste and attunement: Design culture as world making

Ben Highmore

Introduction

This chapter is a speculative attempt to position 'design culture' at the centre of our descriptions and understandings of the world. In it I argue that 'design culture' allows us to see the world as particular sets of qualities, feelings and meanings as well as a purposefully fashioned material environment. But rather than claiming that design *is* at the centre of the world (a claim that, to my mind, would be no less spurious than any other claim for the centrality of one particular phenomenon) I want to more modestly explore what it would mean to *position* design at the centre. In other words, my interest is in the generative affordance of inquiries that treat design as somehow foundational to how the world seems to us (the qualia of our being in the world). In some ways this centrality is already assumed by the actual term 'design culture', which orients the ambition of investigation about design towards considering the world-forming activity of design. 'Culture', as a qualification for the word 'design', offers significantly different capacities than the word 'history' or 'social', for instance. At its most limited 'design culture' might suggest a form of attention aimed at investigating the practices and values enacted, say, by a particular design studio, in the same way that anthropologists might want to look at practices and values of a group of Trobriand Islanders. At its most extensive, though, 'design culture' might well try to attend to any and every aspect of society where tools, technology, clothing and the fashioning of an environment are central.

Within our contemporary scholarly institutions this extensive understanding of 'design culture' might simply look unhelpful. Isn't it just too broad? And, perhaps more importantly, doesn't it start encroaching on disciplinary arenas that are already engaged in the close study of homo faber: archaeology, anthropology, material culture, science studies and so on? In a scholarly world where disciplinary success might depend on recruiting students to identifiable courses, organizing well-attended conferences, and producing highly regarded journals, such an indiscriminate attention to both 'design' and 'culture' might be seriously over-reaching. And yet doesn't such over-reaching accord with certain characteristics that might be at the very heart of how the world is experienced and how the world 'seems' to us? It might make sense within disciplinary fields to want to divide up the world, and our experience of it, into discrete entities, but this isn't often how the world is concretely experienced. Words like 'private' and 'public', 'work' and 'leisure', can often only vaguely gesture towards a complex world of gyms, smartphones, internet access, commuting, shopping, and domestic labour. It is this messy assemblage that the term 'culture' gestures towards.

In this chapter, I'm going to explore the world-making capabilities of material culture, and to claim this as a central component to studying design culture. My case study is the emergence and consolidation of the duvet as the dominant form of bedding in the UK. But before that I need to establish what it means to approach design as a cultural phenomenon.

Culture and design culture

In the 1950s, the cultural theorist and novelist Raymond Williams, drew on the resources of literary criticism and anthropology to fashion an attention to culture as 'a whole way of life' (Williams 1958: 4). It is worth pausing a while to consider what 'whole' could mean in this context: it could, for instance, mean something like unified or coherent. Indeed, since the time of Williams' statement, 'culture' in this anthropological sense, has often been used to designate a unified and relatively discrete and stable arena of meanings and activities: for instance, it is not unusual to hear people talk about 'rave' culture or the culture of stamp collecting, so as to draw out a set of established and normative protocols and values. But for Williams such an understanding of culture would seriously undermine the ambition of the term. 'Whole', in the sense that Williams used the word, is similar to the concept of 'totality' for existential Marxism: it is a heuristic invitation to consider *everything* relationally, without assuming that there is an underlying foundation holding it all together (see Poster 1975). A 'whole way of life' is a question and a challenge, rather than pointing to a readily and easily knowable entity. Indeed, throughout his career Williams constantly insisted on the dynamism and fragmentation of culture, drawing our attention to the way that a range of practices, feelings and thoughts were constantly jockeying for position, and that while some were on their way out, some were taking poll position and some were only just emerging.

To invoke 'design culture' in the light of Williams' insistence that culture is a 'whole way of life' might mean that we must start with our most ordinary experiences of living in a world that has been, and is being, designed in both extensive and intensive ways. Like many people today who are living in the relatively wealthy global North, and with a professional income to boot, I can afford up-to-date communicative hardware. I can sit watching TV, on a comfortable couch, while 'drifting' around the internet and social media on a tablet computer, in a room that has central heating and electric lighting. If I observe this scene I can see that I am sitting on a purple sofa that is constantly shedding feathers, that the TV is showing the Olympic Games live from Brazil and that I am looking up recipes on my tablet device as it is my turn to cook tonight. I'm looking for culinary inspiration. I am aware that the production of the website that I am looking at has involved lots of people at various levels (from graphic designers to algorithmic coders) so that my browsing for recipes is relatively 'user-friendly'. I recognize that it is also delivering me to various advertisers and siphoning off information about me to sell to others. Some of the people involved in supplying this online experience will go by the name of 'designers' other will not, but it is hard to imagine that anyone in this great chain of production isn't also involved in shaping my particular experience. What would I gain from claiming that the tablet computer is 'designed', but not the recipe that I'm looking at? Or that my television is a designed object but not the intricately staged spectacle that I am only half watching? Or the plug and socket that supplies the television with energy but not the national grid system that orchestrates a supply of energy from a variety of sources? If we can think of 'design' as the purposeful shaping of environments (both virtual and physical), and that this shaping alters practices, affects our feelings and orchestrates sensorial perception, then to my mind it makes no sense to designate what will and will not count as design culture in advance of analysis.

When Raymond Williams turned his attention to the study of television in the mid-1970s, he treated it as both a technology and a 'cultural form' (a phrase that he had adopted from Ruth Benedict's *Patterns of Culture*, published in 1934). 'Cultural forms' for Benedict were social arrangements that might differ from one society to another (marriage and kinship patterns would constitute a cultural form, for instance). For Williams to treat something like television as a cultural form meant trying to ascertain the particular phenomenal form of TV as a general condition. This meant spending less time analysing specific programmes and more time looking at what he called the 'flow' of television; the rhythmic dispersal of advertising that interrupted dramatic forms (such as narrative films), the endless 'coming soon' that established 'anticipation' as a key feeling within this cultural form, the repetition of news and weather which produced broadcast television as a specifically temporal form and so on (Williams 1990). It would be hard to point to any one agent in particular for 'designing' the cultural form of television in this way, yet it is also clear that as an orchestration it has particular characteristics that make it different from newspapers, or going to the cinema or theatre.

The concept of 'cultural form' is particularly useful for looking at design culture and for looking at my specific case study. The duvet (or 'continental quilt', as it was once called) is hardly a 'designed' object in the way that a new tablet computer is. It is a vernacular form that has emerged over centuries into the various forms that it takes today. Today, of course, there are a host of design agencies that are involved in the production, distribution and promotion of duvets: from the design of duvet covers to the marketing of new duvet 'technologies' (usually associated with their capacity for thermal insulation; the 'tog' rating). My concern is to see the duvet in Britain as part of a 'whole way of life', to treat it as part of design culture, *in general*. And this will mean looking at the way it interconnects with other cultural elements and to see it as an agent in fashioning the tastes and attunements of a society.

Bedding as cultural form

People who are interested in design as innovation, as visual culture, as formal complexity, might well find that the duvet (or doona in some parts of the world) is relatively resistant to their attentions. As a discrete object of scrutiny there isn't much to describe, nor is there much variety within duvets such that different versions can usefully be compared beyond their insulating capacities. The duvet is a large bag filled with thermal insulating material (sometimes synthetic, but often down or feathers or wool). To stop the insulating material from bunching up in one area of the bag, the bag is quilted into a grid of pockets such that the insulating material is evenly spread across the duvet. The bag is enclosed within another bag (in the same way that a pillow is enclosed within a pillow case) which can be removed and washed.

To see it as a cultural form, though, would require seeing it as embedded (if you will excuse the pun) within a history of bedding and within a set practices and feelings associated with bedding. It is also to see it within histories that are at once both national and international, material and virtual. My case study is only concerned with the take-up of the duvet as the dominant form of bedding within Britain, but this intricately connects with changes that are taking place across Europe and the global North, as well as changes around national and international outlooks and attitudes within Britain. Today the situation is that the vast majority of bedding in Britain consists of a mattress with a sheet covering and a pillow that the sleeper sleeps on, with a duvet placed on top of this, covering the sleeper's body.

An informal poll conducted by the British newspaper *The Daily Telegraph* (a deeply conservative newspaper) in 2013 revealed that roughly 84 per cent of the respondents favoured sleeping under a duvet, while 16 per cent slept under blankets (Wallop 2013). In 1960 a very generous estimate might suggest that 5 per cent of Britons slept under a duvet.

Before the duvet came to Britain, bedding consisted of a bottom sheet, a top sheet, and then, depending on the time of year and whether a house had central heating or not (central heating only became a dominant domestic technology in the 1980s), there would be a series of blankets, followed by an eiderdown and counterpane or bedspread on top of that (an eiderdown would be dispensed with in the summer). The duvet could quite easily be seen as a 'soft technology', a design solution that managed to bundle a set of properties that had been distributed across four or five items (top sheet, various blankets and covers and an optional 'comforter' or eiderdown) into one composite item (duvet and duvet cover). The move from blankets to duvet is, from this angle at least, an act of efficiency and simplicity. A rational choice.

For the 'early adopters' of duvet technologies in Britain, efficiency was only part of what was being offered by the duvet. In the 1960s to acquire a duvet in Britain meant either the exorbitant cost of buying it from the elite London retailers Harrods (who had stocked them since the 1950s and prided themselves on being able to source any commodity on earth), or it meant sending off to a number of specialist suppliers. In 1967, as part of a series of publications by the Design Centre (which was the public face of the Council of Industrial Design), Dorothy Meade published *Bedrooms: Practical Bedrooms for Today*. She proselytizes on behalf of the new technology of duvets: 'Why not scrap all those separate top layers – sheet, blankets, eiderdown – and use one top cover only? With a fitted sheet below, one quick flip and the bed is made' (Meade 1967: 30). But she recognizes that the population at large is absolutely committed to blankets and eiderdowns and the practices that go with them and quotes a duvet supplier as saying that 'if you tell an ordinary Briton that his bedclothes are not going to be tucked in at the sides he will start shivering before you have finished speaking' (Meade 1967: 30). Meade's book is positioned in the pre-dawn of the duvet becoming the main component of popular bedding in Britain. But the book is clearly situated in other transitional moments too, and one of the main priorities of the book is the possibility that bedrooms might adapt to 'daytime uses':

> A room of one's own ... is a necessity at some time for all but the gregarious few: somewhere to think, or read, or work, or sulk, or weep, or do nothing at all – alone; somewhere to entertain private friends and keep private possessions. The room where one sleeps is as good a place as any, if it is warm and welcoming and suitably equipped.
>
> (Meade 1967: 4)

The emergence of the British duvet coincides with the possibility of a room that might be warm and welcoming (which in a cold climate, means some form of heating). And central heating, being an immobile investment, requires patterns of home ownership rather than renting (in the 1960s considerably less than half of households were owner occupied).

If we follow this moment across what are now called 'shelter magazines' we can get a sense of some of the other configurations in which the duvet is situated. If we look in issues of magazines like *Good Housekeeping* and *Homes and Gardens* that came out in 1967, we can see several themes and issues being prioritized both in the features and in the advertising. Central heating is a consistent theme (*Good Housekeeping* makes this a specific feature of its October 1967 issue) as are mortgages. Where there is reference to bedding, the emphasis is on blankets, which are often given full page colour adverts. Duvets (as Continental Quilts or other cognate terms) are only featured in the 'small ads': the short black-and-white adverts which are relatively inexpensive and which can include up to sixteen on a page. Here adverts for continental quilts keep company with adverts for 'Nordic' home saunas and for 'family planning' (i.e. contraceptives) that you can order by post.

Duvets become mainstream 'high-street' items within Britain when the retailer Habitat starts stocking and promoting them in the early 1970s. And this is where the cultural form of the British duvet emerges in its most emphatic way as an item that is involved in what can be thought of as a reconfiguration of values, feelings and practices. In the 1973 catalogue, for instance, the duvet publicity shows a young sleepy couple nestling under a duvet.

The 1977–8 catalogue shows a man making the bed (Figure 2.1); another image shows a couple spooning beneath a duvet. From a contemporary perspective these images look innocuous enough, but at the time the picture of the supine, and possibly post-coital couple enraged many people and Habitat were inundated with complaints. Similarly, by showing a man making the bed, while a couple is getting up in the morning, the image signifies a gendered distribution of tasks that is a considerable departure from dominant ideas of the roles of the sexes at the time. Habitat encouraged the association between the duvet and a more liberated attitude towards sex to the point of adjusting the counter-culture, anti-Vietnam slogan 'make love not war', to its promotional strategy in 1980: 'make love not beds with the help of a duvet' (Habitat catalogue 1980/1: 75). Looking back at this moment, Habitat's creative director Terence Conran remembers: 'I had been in Sweden in the 1950s and was given a duvet to sleep under. I probably had a girl with me and I thought this was all part of the mood of the time – liberated sex and easy living. It was wonderful that when you came to make your bed, it was just a couple of shakes' (Parkinson 2015).

To see the emergence of the duvet in Britain as a cultural form that is part of a 'whole way of life' requires seeing a range of configurations and

FIGURE 2.1 *Habitat Catalogue 1977–8, page 80, with kind permission of Habitat Retail Limited.*

reconfigurations taking place within Britain. Some of these bear directly on the condition of possibility for the duvet becoming a popular form of bedding, some of these reconfigurations are actually performed with the help of the duvet, and other configurations while seemingly tangential to the duvet aren't fully imaginable without it. We could begin to list some of the elements that we would need to put in place to see the duvet as being in among other socially active ingredients: contraceptive pills (which started becoming widely available in the UK in 1961); a new availability for mortgages as well as the increase in modern (i.e. centrally heated) social housing; affluence across the classes in the 1960s that alters some of the cultures of class society; challenges to gender norms through second-wave feminism in the 1970s; changing attitudes towards children and teenagers (the emergence of the teenage bedroom as a cultural form); and so on. The UK-duvet is neither explained by these items, nor is it an explanation of these features: it is both determined and determining. It is part and parcel of a general 'redistribution of the sensible' (Rancière 2004) that is ideological and material, emotional and practical.

Yet an object like the duvet, which replaces other objects and practices, has to also be characterized by what it isn't, what it doesn't achieve and by the losses that it effects. Blankets, eiderdowns and bedspreads were heavy. And they weren't just physically heavy; they were culturally heavy too. And this heaviness was often the weight of family history and familial relations. To adopt the duvet in the 1970s was to break with the traditions of a parent culture and with some of the sociality that went with that. For instance, wedding presents were often a way of materially connecting a newly married couple to the past, as a previous generation passed on decorative quilts, embroidered eiderdowns or bequeathed quality blankets and counterpanes. Such practices stretch back to a time when bedding would have been among the most expensive items in the home and had often been part of a marriage dowry (Flanders 2014; Worsley 2011). To choose duvet bedding instead of layers of blankets, eiderdown and counterpane would have constituted a moment of domestic rupture: in the 1960s and 1970s it would have been to turn your back on the tradition of the previous generation and their involvement in fashioning the look and feel of your bedroom. No doubt it was a moment of liberation, a moment of shrugging off the mantle of a previous generation. But it also emptied bedding of the densely connected webs of familial continuity and support. For a previous generation to peek into a bedroom and see a duvet covered bed, might be to see a room newly thinned.

Taste and attunement

The ambition and the danger of design culture, as I perceive it, is that it very quickly starts sprawling beyond the confines of discrete objects. It is profligate in its purview, promiscuous in its object choices. But if this is the danger it is also the ambition. In this regard it shares more than a passing affinity with the sociology of taste that has, since the work of Pierre Bourdieu, sought to treat culture, not as discrete objects that require interpretation, but as bundles of preferences that go together to produce taste-subjects who are socially positioned via these choices (Bourdieu 1989). And these taste bundles can, at times, qualify and adjust other forms of social and economic power (and powerlessness). Taste, for certain sociologists, is how some social groups exert their superiority, while for others it is what lets them get positioned as inferior.

But while design culture might share this tendency in connecting and bundling objects together, it also offers a real challenge to the sociology of taste. It is clear, for instance, that in the sociology of taste the material world of objects is primarily symbolic in value: indeed, it is often *only* through their symbolism that culture can perform the work of social stratification. As an article of faith the sociology of taste has often had to depart from any attempt to attend to the actual and innate qualities of culture (material or virtual) seeing 'value' as only related to forms of socially ascribed and relative worth in the negotiation of social stratification. Design culture, as I see it, is much keener to attend to the sensorial capacities of culture, and takes its investigative sensibilities from the sociological traditions that are descended from Georg Simmel, where attention to fashion, trade exhibitions and urban forms is something that requires detailed attention to the sensorial forms, and the material sensibilities such phenomena produce (see Frisby and Featherstone 1997 for a representative sample). To pursue this form of sociology, as distinct from the dominant protocols of the sociology of taste, is not to ignore questions of class. A cultural sociology descended from Simmel starts, however, from a different place and suggests that rather than class culture bestowing value on design culture, design culture may be something that produces class and, potentially at least, changes social classifications that would include class but would also include other social taxonomies.

To relate this to my example of the UK-duvet, we could say that today it is clear that having a duvet isn't particularly symbolic (though using blankets and an eiderdown might well have a symbolic aspect, for instance, in a very expensive and traditional hotel). Perhaps at one point the UK-duvet would have been symbolic. Perhaps in 1967 if you had followed the advice of Dorothy Meade and become an early adopter of the UK-duvet it might have allowed you to achieve social distinction among your neighbours. My point, and the point of the kinds of analysis that a design culture approach can foster, is that design culture is always 'technoaesthetic' (Boscagli 2014: 4) *before* it is symbolic. The term 'technoaesthetic' insists that we should always recognize the sensorial form of any new materials, and the technological aspect of new designs. The duvet's capacities of warmth-with-lightness were a material fact that distinguished it from blanket bedding. It's abilities to turn a practice that had been a scene for intense disciplinary activity (the command 'make your bed' was transformed with a duvet) and a gendered division of labour into something altogether 'lighter' was reliant on its material capacities. The UK-duvet didn't symbolize a more modern set of attitudes (towards sex, say, or domestic chores) it was the material affordance for the practice of a certain form of what it was to be modern in late twentieth-century Britain. And for this the UK-duvet emerged as part of an assemblage of 'technoaesthetic' objects that might include Japanese paper lampshades, Ryvita crispbreads, pizza and pasta. All such items could be seen to bundle together material practices of convenience, economic capacities of inexpensiveness, social informality and symbolic and non-symbolic dimensions of a particular form of 'domestic' cosmopolitanism. They were also, importantly, technoaesthetic objects that could signify and embody the modern without signifying and embodying 'North America' as their ultimate referent. Many of these items also had peasant roots which were then re-articulated as a mark of authenticity (in a similar way that 'artisanal' is used today).

If we take the 1960s as the decade that marks the emergence of the UK-duvet and the 1970s and 1980s as the period of its consolidation as it enters the mainstream, then this history coincides with a number of other histories. For instance, we could connect this history to the history of furnishing and household goods retailing: the 1960s saw the birth of the shop Habitat which became so dominant in the 1970s and 1980s to be superseded by IKEA in the 1990s and after. We could connect this to changes in food consumption (Habitat opened the same year that Pizza Express opened), changes in manners, changes in attitudes towards children and teenagers and so on. We can also see this as a period when there are profound changes in national identity (particularly in relation to race and racism), gender and sexuality, and class. Crucially it is a period that sees the birth of a 'new middle class' of white-collared workers: of people working in service industries and technical industries, of social workers and lecturers, of shop managers and industrial engineers, who embrace the modern over the staid. The duvet wasn't a symbol of the new middle class. The new middle class was the outcome of a range of changes in manufacturing and the economy; it was shaped by changing social attitudes which included social 'informalization'. But such a sentence is just an abstraction if it can't also identify the concrete circumstances and the technoaesthetic cultural forms that can embody and perform these abstractions. The UK-duvet is one such object: it is an agent in class formation; it is part of that class's compositional circumstance, and the very fact that a duvet is mainstream (as are Japanese lampshades and pizzas) is a symptom of the changing cultural landscape of class in the UK.

Conclusion

The emergence and dominance of the UK-duvet acted on a population: it provided a material sensorial lesson in the lightness and looseness of a new form of the modern. It attuned a population to different manners and protocols: to convenience, to the unregimented and spontaneous (Wouters 2007). It also detuned them from the values and relationships that were embedded in previous objects and practices. The UK-duvet wasn't a recipient of taste; it was a prime mover in its production. And it was also part of a bundle of unfulfilled desires and unrealized promises: of an incomplete sexual liberation; of a new 'democratic' and 'equal' culture that disguised more ingrained and structural inequalities. It would have been absurd to think of duvets and Japanese lampshades overcoming inequality: but it would be hard to think of the flourishing of the inequalities of neoliberalism without neoliberalism itself being camouflaged by the (false) social promises embedded in such a technoaesthetic assemblages of objects.

The potential of 'design culture' for understanding our world is not premised on the centrality of design in the world. Design culture's critical productivity is not premised on its ability to understand and explain 'design'. Its critical cargo is of value inasmuch as it can help us understand our world. To do this we need to recognize the way that design is an active agent in producing this world, of 'worlding' this world: of shaping its meanings, its practices and its qualia. How the world seems to us, how it feels to us, is materially embedded in the technoaesthetic assemblages which are design culture's natural objects.

References

Benedict, R. (1934), *Patterns of Culture*, Boston: Houghton Mifflin Company.
Boscagli, M. (2014), *Stuff Theory: Everyday Objects, Radical Materialism*, New York and London: Bloomsbury.
Bourdieu, P. (1989), *Distinction: A Social Critique of the Judgement of Taste*, translated by R. Nice, London and New York: Routledge.
Flanders, J. (2014), *The Making of Home*, London: Atlantic Books.
Frisby, D. and Featherstone, M., eds. (1997), *Simmel on Culture*, London: Sage.
Meade, D. (1967), *Bedrooms: Practical Bedrooms for Today* (A Design Centre Publication), London: Macdonald and Co.
Parkinson, J. (2015), 'Almost 300 Years without a Duvet', *BBC News Magazine*, 25 December 2015, http://www.bbc.co.uk/news/magazine-34848546 – accessed on 23 November 2016.
Poster, M. (1975), *Existential Marxism in Postwar France: Sartre to Althusser*, Princeton: Princeton University Press.
Rancière, J. (2004), *The Politics of Aesthetics: The Distribution of the Sensible*, translated by G Rockhill, London and New York: Continuum.
Wallop, H. (2013), 'Duvets or Blankets? Bedding Debate Splits the Nation', *The Telegraph* 24 January 2013, http://www.telegraph.co.uk/lifestyle/9823911/Duvets-or-blankets-Bedding-debate-splits-the-nation.html – accessed on 23 November 2016.
Williams, R. (1958), 'Culture is Ordinary', in *Resources of Hope: Culture, Democracy, Socialism*, London: Verso, 1987, 3–18.
Williams, R. (1990), *Television: Technology and Cultural Form*, London: Routledge.
Worsley, L. (2011), *If Walls Could Talk: An Intimate History of the Home*, London: Faber and Faber.
Wouters, C. (2007), *Informalization: Manners and Emotions since 1890*, London: Sage.

CHAPTER THREE

Embedding design in the organizational culture: Challenges and perspectives

Alessandro Deserti and Francesca Rizzo

Design Thinking has been indicated by many scholars (Brown 2008; Dorst and Cross 2001; Liedtka and Mintzberg 2006) as a powerful new approach to enhance innovation within and across organizations by combining the creative and the analytical mind (Martin 2009); creating products and services that are both profitable and humanly satisfying (Boland and Collopy 2004). At the same time, its collaborative and human-driven approach helps many organizations to overcome barriers to innovation (Martin 2009; Norman and Verganti 2014). While some authors suggest that designers can stimulate change in organizations due to their positive attitude towards change itself (Michlewski 2008), very little attention has been dedicated to the complexity of organizational change processes associated with a design-led innovation approach.

However, while experiments of adoption of design processes and tools are flourishing all over the world, the question of how the new knowledge that they generate can be integrated within organizations emerges as a key question. Experimentation produces knowledge connected to both new arrangements and new processes, thus leading to a twofold problem: how the results and the knowledge can be integrated back into the organizations.

This chapter faces the issue of the diffusion of design as a culture that triggers and provokes changes in the organizational cultures it interacts with. Fundamental questions addressed by the chapter are: How do organizations develop design culture? Is it possible to set up processes meant to cultivate design culture in organizations?

To answer these questions the authors move from the perspective that the introduction and the development of design competences within an organization are not neutral but always trigger a reaction in the established organizational culture and eventually induce a change (Deserti and Rizzo 2014).

The chapter starts from the premise that a profound difference exists between the concept of design thinking (as a generic innovation management model) and design culture (as a set of situated practices, instruments, competences and values). It then investigates some of the main characteristics of design as a culture (Julier 2014, 2006; Kimbell 2011, 2012) and discusses them in the light of two case studies on how the introduction and management of design within an organization is tied to the larger organizational culture within which design is embedded and vice versa.

Confronting design thinking with design culture

Design Thinking (Buchanan 1992; Cross 2006) and design culture (Julier 2014) can be both described as concepts, but while the first tends to be fixed as an abstract design model applicable independently from the context and the object of design, the latter is situated and dynamic. The concept of design culture is based on the idea that design is not only an attitude, but also, and first of all, a system of knowledge, competences and skills that operates in a specific context to sustain the development of new products and services (Julier 2014; Deserti and Rizzo 2014). To achieve an improvement of the innovation performances, this system must be acquired, integrated and combined with the already-established processes of organizations (Bertola and Teixeira 2003).

In other words, the notion of design culture is context-dependent, and emphasizes the peculiar 'way of doing things' of an organization or system. By consequence, we cannot individualize a generic design culture, but many different cultures, depending on a variety of factors that characterize a particular organization.

In the recent *DMI Review* issue dedicated to 'Design Thinking and Doing' many contributions (e.g. McCullagh 2013; Collins 2013) agree that Design Thinking was oversold as a panacea for all manner of business ills, but that it played a fundamental role in introducing design into business, and that it can be rethought and reconfigured to cope with some of its pitfalls.

Lucy Kimbell (2011, 2012) clearly pointed out how all the current interpretations of Design Thinking (Design Thinking as a cognitive style, as a general theory of design and as a resource for organizations) rely on the supposed dualism between thinking and doing, ignore the diversity and the situatedness of design practices and rest on theories that consider the designer the main agent of design practices. Kimbell introduces the concepts of design-as-practice and designs-in-practice as useful to investigate and understand the nature of design, concluding that their application leads to rethink Design thinking as 'a set of contingent, embodied routines that reconfigure the sociomaterial world' (Kimbell 2012: 141).

The description of the notion of embeddedness of design culture refers to the idea that a piece of something will become an 'integral part of a surrounding whole by, at the same time, keeping its own logic and rules and, hence, intensively interacting with surroundings' (Vetterli 2016: 14). Assuming the above-mentioned definition allows us to formulate a critique to the notion of Design Thinking as an abstract process, whose usage seems much closer to the practice of experiments in a controlled environment, which can always succeed if adequately repeated.

The notions of embeddedness and situatedness bring with them different questions: How is design understood by different organizations? How is design used in different organizations? What is embedded and at what organizational level(s)?

In our perspective, one of the most significant risks in introducing Design Thinking into companies as a set of tools for (disruptive) innovation, is that its de-contextualized nature typically leads to the generation of many solutions that do not take into account contingencies, and that rarely cross the threshold of real development, manufacturing and commercialization. The gap between the phases of generation of new ideas and those of development is, in our experience of applied research, one of the most critical aspects of the design activity. The generation of new ideas is in fact pretty simple whenever we reduce the number of constraints and we operate outside the real contingencies: we might produce a great number of innovative ideas, but we miss the point that the design processes are not only the result of the work of designers, and that they can be effective only through the necessary mediation and negotiation for dealing with different situations and stakeholders and the constraints they bring about (Figure 3.1).

This point was well defined by Vandenbosh and Gallagher (2004): while contemporary managerial practice is fraught with the idea of out-of-the-box thinking, what should be learnt from design is not a further push towards creativity but the capacity of staying 'inside the box' considering all the constraints.

The lack of contextualization and situatedness, combined with the split of the ideation and the development processes and the idea of a top-down practice that principally affects the management rather than the whole enterprise, is in our opinion the main fault of Design Thinking as it was introduced into the managerial world.

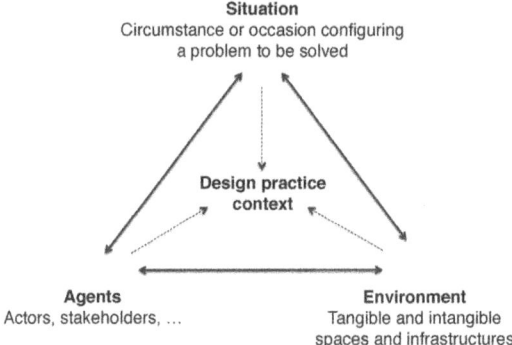

FIGURE 3.1 *The Situatedness of Design Culture.*

Connecting design culture with organizations' culture

In our opinion, to be effective within organizations, design must become part of their culture: enterprises and other organizations should develop their own design culture by integrating design through continual processes of learning, negotiation and alignment. This calls for a different perspective, where design culture can be described as a system of knowledge, competences and skills in use within a situated context to develop new solutions and pursue innovation (Deserti and Rizzo 2014).

Here the problem is not only how to create knowledge, but also how to make it flow through all the levels of the organization. A clear connection between design processes and learning (Beckman and Barry 2007) seems necessary to create the conditions to better exploit the innovation endeavours. Once again, this perspective shifts our interest from the sheer positive results – that is new successful products or services – to capacity-building and to the connection between design and the organizational culture.

The discourse on the relation between design and culture is usually based on the idea that we should link design to the cultural context where it occurs/operates to better understand or guide it. The cultural context is then interpreted as a recipient for the design of products or services, which will be better conceived (if we look at the process from a professional perspective) or interpreted (if we look at the process from a historical perspective) by linking them with the cultural context. Therefore, culture is referred to the end-user at an individual or at a social level: products can be interpreted as the result of their context of destination in its multifaceted dimensions, which include the cultural dimension.

Some scholars introduced the concept of 'culture-oriented product design' (Moalosi, Popovic and Hickling-Hudson 2010), assuming the idea that designers should not just focus on needs but also on the culture of the end-user. The concept explains that culture can be seen as a catalyst for designing innovative products if and when designers are able to incorporate a specific culture into the design of products thereby giving space to the interpretation of local characters in contrast with the globalization of solutions. This line of thinking can be associated with the vast literature on the reasons and modes of making design interact with the context of destination, primarily but not only represented by the end-user, leading to solutions that properly solve a specific set of problems and fit a specific context (Bannon 1991; Jordan and Green 1999; Frascara 2006).

While we do not want to neglect the importance of the cultural context of destination, we would like to note a gap: a product can be interpreted not just as the result of its context of destination but also, and in some cases primarily, as the result of its original context (Figure 3.2). If this is true, as we will try show in the case studies, a new product or service must also be seen as the result of the culture of the organization that produces and delivers it. If we look at the context of destination as the main force that influences the design process, then we are primarily driven to consider the culture of the end-user, but if we look at the original context as the main force that influences the design process, then we are primarily driven to consider the culture of the organization.

In our view, new products and services result from the complex interaction between these two levels: the user-centricity of contemporary design is in constant tension with the fact that organizations do what they are able to, and what they believe is right to do. Quite often this is not perfectly correspondent to the needs and wants of users or consumers, but introducing a more user-centred perspective is not always simple and fast, as it calls for the transformation of the culture of the organization.

In the following, we will introduce two cases, Apple and Samsung, showing that a specific design culture is clearly reflected in the characteristics

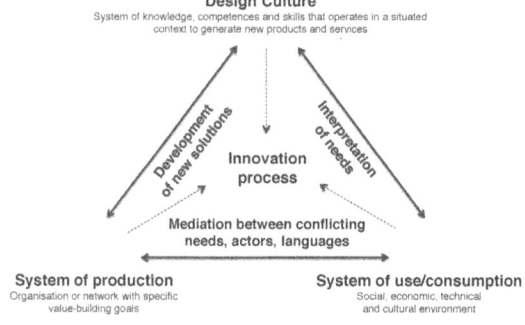

FIGURE 3.2 *Innovation as a Process Shaped by the Interaction of Diverse Systems and Competences.*

of the processes and of the same offering of companies, and that this culture is part of the overall organizational culture.

The cases will highlight how the original context is a strong determinant in giving shape to new products (or whole offerings, entrepreneurial ventures and organizations in general), and how the specific design culture of the organization rather than the generic notion of Design Thinking is the driver of its development, and of innovation in a broader sense.

The Apple case

As one of the most famous global brands Apple needs no introduction. More than its tangible products, which were already widely described in managerial and design literature, here we would like to examine the company's attitude towards adopting closed software solutions that run only on Apple products. By doing this, we want to demonstrate how a low degree of openness of information resources (the core feature of the new generation of smart products) is a result of the company's culture, and that the design of products and services, or else the design culture of the organization, is profoundly affected by its overall culture. To reach this goal, we will take the smartphone sector as an example, assuming that the same 'way of doing' is adopted by Apple in the different sectors in which the company operates.

The smartphone sector is populated by different software platforms, and even if an important manufacturer like Samsung invests in its own proprietary platform, the three main competitors, Symbian, Apple and Google, comprise almost the entire market.

While we might notice a convergence in the design of the hardware of the different smartphone brands, and even in the design of the interaction experience (one of the central issues in the recurrent legal war between Apple and Samsung), choices regarding the openness of the software make a significant difference. The three main platforms are actually characterized by divergent philosophies on open and closed systems.

To make it simple, while a closed system is bound to specific hardware, an open system can work with hardware from different manufacturers. In a more accurate definition, the degree of openness of a mobile platform can be evaluated in terms of *access to* and *control of* the elements of the platform, mainly the mobile operating system as the core element of the platform (Schlagwein, Schoder and Fischbach 2010). The access to information resources can be open, exclusive to the platform leader, or limited to a specific group of partners, while control can be internal (fully controlled by the platform leader), external (controlled by an external company) or shared (the case of open source, normally controlled through licenses). In terms of hardware specifications and system core, Symbian and Google developed open and shared systems, while Apple developed an exclusive and internal system. The only area where Apple partially opens its platform is in the realm of application development by releasing software development kits that provide a programming environment and tools for development that are fully controlled by Apple. This is, in fact, a forced choice because the development of applications is a necessity both for Apple's business and for the satisfaction of its customers' needs.

> More recent research, especially on today's complex ICT industries, has argued that a platform is not solely a technology but also the outcome of a set of business behaviours and relationships between actors in an ecosystem. This ecosystem for modern high-tech platforms is characterised as having high levels of interdependence between actors. ... As a result, even those firms with clear market dominance in one area ... are dependent on the innovation of complementary firms to maintain their leadership position. Hardware firms and software firms rely on each other to push technology forward. Even Apple and its relatively closed iOS depend upon thousands of application developers to continue to create desirable apps for end-users. (Kenney and Pon 2011: 2)

Even if Mac iOS is originally built on top of open-source software, Apple's general philosophy is to adopt closed systems that can only run on Apple's hardware with strong control over all of the information resources. We see this choice as linked to the culture of the company, as it was widely presented through the many public declarations of its founder, Steve Jobs. The obsession with tight control over the characteristics of the products, together with the choice to operate within a strict regime of secrecy in the development of the new products, are linked to a traditional conception of competition that is opposed to the spreading idea of open innovation. The many declarations against companies following Apple's lead are part of this conception: Steve Jobs always presented Apple as the innovation leader, developing new bright ideas that became the prey of their competitors. While the identity of the Apple brand was built around the idea of freedom from the very beginning (just think about its famous 1984 commercial), the company's culture is in reality quite closed, and linked to the company's attempt to protect information in the constant fear of being imitated by rivals. Schein's idea (1985) that exterior signs can be misleading in evaluating the corporate culture is fully applicable to Apple: a company that conveys the idea of freedom but is actually closed. The whole philosophy behind the development of the new products is bound to the company's culture. While open source and open innovation are widely discussed (Chesbrough, Vanhaverbeke and West 2006), Apple demonstrates its competitive attitude through the protection of information that results in 'closed' products that mirror the company's culture.

The company's attitude is confirmed by recent facts: Apple got to the point to set up an upgrade to the iPhone 6 software that blocks any functionality of the handset when it detects the intervention of unauthorized technicians (the so-called error 53'). Apple first explained this clearly unfair feature as a security measure in favour of consumers, and withdraw it only after widespread negative publicity, when thousands of iPhone 6 users started protesting and when it was served with a class action lawsuit in the United States and attention from a competition watchdog in Australia.

The sacredness of design at Apple is also somehow part of the same overall corporate culture. Jonathan Ive, Apple's chief designer, and his quite small team appear and are often described as the caste of guardians of the secrets of the new products (Parker 2015), an attitude which is opposite to Samsung's, where a large number of designers without any famous chief shows a much more working-class style.

The Samsung case

Just like Apple, Samsung doesn't need any introduction. Unlike in the case of Apple, a brand considered a flag of contemporary design, Samsung's relation with design is quite ambiguously described in recent literature – this is probably right because Samsung does not correspond to the standard set by Apple and other design champions.

We may discuss if Apple is a true innovator, or if its core capacity is that of assembling, recombining and attributing meaning to already existing innovations, but Apple for sure would be generally considered an innovation leader. On the other hand, Samsung's approach to innovation is usually narrated including its transition from ODM to OBM: from manufacturing inexpensive, imitative electronics for other companies, to establishing and developing its own brand worldwide (Yoo and Kim 2015).

In our view, Apple and Samsung's different approaches to design actually reflect their different histories, but we'll try to also highlight that they depend on different cultural settings, and on different product portfolio strategies.

Samsung's OEM mentality is still conditioning the relationships between the different functional areas. Despite the great investment of the company and the commitment of the top management, design has to fight its way to take part in decision making. In the very words of Kyungmook Kim, principal designer at Samsung Electronics' Corporate Design Center: 'Despite strong support from top management, the company's designers continue to face constant challenges stemming from its efficiency-focused management practices, which are deep-rooted. Shifting to an innovation-focused culture without losing an engineering edge is not a simple matter. It involves managing a number of very real tensions' (Yoo and Kim 2015: 72).

Samsung's product portfolio strategy is also playing a great role in making its approach to design quite different from Apple's. First, Samsung's portfolio is much wider, as it comprises microwave ovens, refrigerators, air conditioners, washing machines, cameras and camcorders, televisions, laptops, printers, tablets and mobile phones. Second, it is also much deeper, both in functional variations and in price points. Even if Samsung is being pushed out of the low-end market segment by the Chinese competitors (Go 2015), its portfolio strategy is still that of extensively covering the market, and to offer a great variety of products with slightly different features, in the attempt to satisfy the larger number of customers. While Apple tries to cover the high-end market with a very limited number of iconic products, Samsung tries to compete with a few flagship models, and to use the halo effect that they produce to sustain its competitiveness in the mid/low-end market segments, primarily based on economies of scale.

> Samsung's revenue model relies on the high volume and low margins of countless SKUs that are more or less variations on the same product, whether it's a smartphone or a vacuum cleaner. Samsung doesn't sell just one point-and-shoot camera. They have a dozen at various price points carefully calculated by the cost of their raw components and features, each more or less asking its customer, 'Am I the right camera for you? No? Then try my little brother'. (Wilson 2015)

Samsung perfectly corresponds to what Ciborra (1996) used to describe as a 'dynamically stable organization', an organization where well-established processes sustain the fast turnover of the product portfolio.

Case studies comparison

While Apple's brand promise is a holistic experience granted by carefully designed products and services, Samsung's brand promise is still bound to product features and performance. To compete in the high-end mobile phones market, in 2010 Samsung had to launch the Galaxy sub-brand as its original brand name was associated with cheap flip phones. Despite Samsung's capacity to challenge Apple on its same ground and to turn Galaxy into a cool brand (Kovach 2015), the same invention of the 'phablet' is – in our view – more related with the obsession with hardware and performances than with the design of the user experience.

According to Wilson (2015), Apple's product portfolio strategy – based on a handful of carefully designed products – is not exclusive to Apple, as many Silicon Valley brands like Jawbone, Tesla, Fitbit, Nest and Amazon successfully applied it. In his view, such a strategy is tightly connected to a specific (Western) way of attributing a sort of heroic role to design, which does not fit with the Korean (and likely with the whole Asian) mentality. This is why Apple chief designer is a superstar, while Samsung's is almost unknown. This is also why consulting for Asian companies is so difficult to Western design offices: companies like Samsung heavily invested in hiring Western design consultants, with quite unsatisfactory outcomes for both parts (Wilson 2015). The turning point for Samsung was in fact to invest in creating in-house design capacities, or else to interiorize design as core knowledge. This was originally done through hiring faculty members of the ArtCenter College of Design in Los Angeles to set up an extensive training programme from the company's internal designers. This way Samsung started embedding design in the organization, a quite complex process full of difficulties and tensions, but with much more satisfactory results than outsourcing. According to Yoo and Kim (2015), the decision to internalize design knowledge was fundamental in challenging and slowly changing the whole company's culture, and to make designers capable of setting up an emphatic relation with the rest of the organization.

Another interesting insight we draw from Yoo and Kim's account of the internalization of design culture at Samsung is the variety of tasks attributed to designers. Although Samsung is a clearly product-focused enterprise, the progressive shift from exploration to exploitation (March, 1991) defines many temporal horizons for the designs: some are meant to explore quite distant futures, and some are meant to enter the market quite soon, which calls for different attitudes of the designers, and for different – even if interconnected – work streams in which they will take part.

Conclusion

The cases clearly show that design can (and should) be interpreted as part of the culture of an organization, or of the culture of a specific place in a specific period.

In this perspective, the introduction of design in an organization can be seen as a process of cultural transformation: design processes have a pervasive nature, as they typically stand at the intersection of some of the most relevant functional areas of a company, and need to be related to all of them.

The existing frameworks describing the introduction of design in organizations actually depict a process made of different stages (e.g. The Danish Design Ladder; Gardien and Gilsing's Design Maturity Level Grid; Porcini's five phases of design integration) primarily bound to a specific interpretation of the role of design which seems in contradiction with the evidences from our case studies (Danish Design Centre, 2001; Gardien and Gilsing, 2013; de Vries, 2015).

First, they often appear too much predictive: particularly in large organizations, diverse kinds of tasks require particular design competences and skills that the existing frameworks would locate at different steps of the ladder while in reality they peacefully coexist in the same organization at the same time.

Second, they are all based on the analysis of processes that occurred in large Western commercial corporations. In our view, further investigation would be needed to capture the differences that may emerge if we change any of the above-mentioned features: non-Western corporations, small-medium enterprises and non-commercial organizations. This opens interesting perspectives for future studies.

Embedding design culture implies coping with the overall cultural setting where the organization itself is embedded (Deserti and Rizzo 2011), a quite complex task that may end up being even more complex and difficult when designers operate outside of the organization.

Becoming aware that design is a much more complex and stratified concept than what is commonly perceived, and that there is no easy formula to integrate it as a source of value, is the main challenge that organizations must overcome to include it as a stable and relevant part of their culture. While at the same time it would become a relevant part of the designers' training curricula.

References

Bannon, L. J. (1991), 'From Human Factors to Human Actors', in J. Greenbaum and M. Kyng (eds), *Design at Work: Cooperative Design of Computer Systems*, Hillsdale: Lawrence Erlbaum Associates, 25–44.

Beckman, S. L., and Barry, M. (2007), 'Innovation as a Learning Process: Embedding Design Thinking', *California Management Review*, 50(1): 25–56.

Bertola, P. and Teixeira, C. (2003), 'Design as a Knowledge Agent: How Design as a Knowledge Process Is Embedded into Organizations to Foster Innovation', *Design Studies*, 24(2): 181–94.

Boland, R. J. and Collopy, F. J. (2004), *Managing as Designing*, Stanford: Stanford University Press.

Brown, T. (2008), 'Design Thinking', *Harvard Business Review*, 6: 84–92.

Buchanan, R. (1992), 'Wicked Problems in Design Thinking', *Design Issues*, 8(2): 5–21.

Chesbrough, H., Vanhaverbeke, W. and West, J. (2006), *Open Innovation: Researching a New Paradigm*, Oxford: Oxford University Press.

Ciborra, C. U. (1996), 'The Platform Organization: Recombining Strategies, Structures, and Surprises', *Organization Science*, 7(2): 103–18.

Collins, H. (2013), 'Can Design Thinking Still Add Value?', *DMI Review*, 24(2): 35–9.

Cross, N. (2006), *Designerly Ways of Knowing*, Berlin: Springer.

Danish Design Centre (2001), *The Danish Design Ladder*. Retrieved from http://ddc.dk/wp-content/uploads/2015/05/Design-Ladder_en.pdf

de Vries, J. (2015), 'PepsiCo's Chief Design Officer on Creating an Organization Where Design Can Thrive', *Harvard Business Review*, 93(9): 1–9.

Deserti, A. and Rizzo, F. (2011), 'Co-designing with Companies', *Proceedings of IASDR11*. 31 October–4 November, Delft, The Netherlands: 1–10.

Deserti, A. and Rizzo, F. (2014), 'Design and the Cultures of Enterprises', *Design Issues*, 30(1): 36–56.

Dorst, K. and Cross, N. (2001), 'Creativity in the Design Process: Co-Evolution of Problem–Solution', *Design Studies*, 22(5): 425–37.

Frascara, J. (2006), *Design for Effective Communications: Creating Contexts for Clarity and Meaning*, New York: Allworth Press.

Gardien, P. and Gilsing, F. (2013), 'Walking the Walk: Putting Design at the Heart of Business', *DMI Review*, 24(2): 54–66.

Go, S. J. (2015), *Strategic Analysis of Samsung's Smartphone Product Portfolio: Countering the Challenge from Chinese Competitors* (master's thesis), Cambridge, MA: MIT Sloan School of Management.

Jordan, P. W. and Green, W. S. (1999), *Human Factors in Product Design: Current Practice and Future Trends*, London: Taylor & Francis.

Julier, G (2006), 'From Visual Culture to Design Culture', *Design Issues*, 22(1): 64–76.

Julier, G. (2014), *The Culture of Design*. London: SAGE Publications.

Kenney, M. and Pon, B. (2011), Structuring the Smartphone Industry: Is the Mobile Internet Os Platform the Key? *Social Science Research Network*. Retrieved from http://ssrn.com/abstract=1851686.

Kimbell, L. (2011), 'Re-thinking Design Thinking. Part I', *Design and Culture*, 3(3): 295–306.

Kimbell, L. (2012), Re-thinking Design Thinking. Part II', *Design and Culture*, 4(2): 129–48.

Kovach, S. (26 February 2015), 'How Samsung Won and then Lost the Smartphone War' *Business Insider UK*. Retrieved from http://uk.businessinsider.com/samsung-rise-and-fall-2015-2?r=US&IR=T

Liedtka, J., and Mintzberg, H. (2006), 'Time for Design', *Design Management Review*, 17(2): 10–18.

March, J. G. (1991), 'The Opposable Mind: How Successful Leaders Win Through Integrative Thinking', *Organization Science*, 2(1): 71–87.

Martin, R. L. (2009), *The Opposable Mind: Winning through Integrative Thinking*, Boston: Harvard Business Press.

Martin, R. (2009), *The Design of Business*, Boston, MA: Harvard Business School Press.

McCullagh, K. (2013), 'Stepping up: Beyond Design Thinking', *DMI Review*, 24(2): 32–4.

Michlewski, K. (2008), 'Uncovering Design Attitude: Inside the Culture of Designers', *Organization Studies*, 29(3): 373–92.

Moalosi, R., Popovic, V. and Hickling-Hudson, A. (2010), 'Culture-Orientated Product Design', *International Journal of Technology and Design Education*, 20(2): 175–90.

Norman, D. A., and Verganti, R. (2014), 'Incremental and Radical Innovation: Design Research Versus Technology and Meaning Change', *Design Issues*, 30(1): 78–96.

Parker, I. (23 February 2015), 'The Shape of Things to Come. How an industrial designer became Apple's greatest product', *The New Yorker*. Retrieved from http://www.newyorker.com/magazine/2015/02/23/shape-things-come

Schein, E. H. (1985). *Organizational Culture and Leadership*, San Francisco: Jossey-Bass Publishers.

Schlagwein, D., Schoder, D. and Fischbach, K. (2010), 'Openness of Information Resources. A Framework-Based Comparison of Mobile Platforms', *Ecis 2010. 18*th *European Conference on Information Systems*.

Vandenbosh, B. and Gallagher, K. (2004), 'The Role of Constraints', in R. J. Bolland and F. Collopy, *Managing as Designing*, Standford, CA: Stanford University Press.

Vetterli, C. (2016), *Embedded Design Thinking*, PhD Dissertation, Dissertation no. 4501, Bamberg: St Gallen University Gallen.

Wilson, M. (2015), 'Why Samsung Design Stinks. Co.Design'. Retrieved from http://www.fastcodesign.com/3042408/why-samsung-design-stinks

Yoo, Y. and Kim, K. (2015), 'How Samsung Became a Design Powerhouse', *Harvard Business Review*, 93(9): 72–8.

CHAPTER FOUR

Use in design culture

Toke Riis Ebbesen

Introduction

Within the broader design culture, conceptually oriented design comprises a tangled field of digital practices, such as augmented reality and virtual reality concepts, but also service design, social design, emotional design and other disciplines where more intangible phenomena such as innovation, social change, services and management, not the creation of physically perceivable artefacts, are claimed to be the central aims of design practice (Kimbell 2011). Sometimes, design is described as a practice of creating 'interfaces for intangible processes' (Secomandi and Snelders 2011), in which the crux of design is to create tangible means that merely *facilitate* non-product outcomes, like a service or an organisational change. Furthermore, other conceptually inclined design movements, such as critical and speculative design, seem even less concerned with creating products of use. Instead, they aim to question ideologies of design and stimulate thoughts, reflections and critical discourse (Raby 2008), aiming to cause social change through people, rather than through designed products, which would be the more modest proposition, as suggested by Manzini (2014). Proponents of what, for brevity, shall be referred to as *critical design*, have even argued against the very concept of usefulness of design products, to instead 'imagine, argue and design the useless' (Rosenbak 2015: 5.15), or to design the 'post-optimal' or even 'user-unfriendly' (Dunne 1999: 32).

While all these movements towards the non-use and conceptuality of design may represent interesting challenges to taken-for-granted ideas about the culture of design, they share a common conflation of a basic distinction between use and discourse, in essence obviating the creation of useful artefacts as the primary aim of design, in favour of conceptual work. In short, the concept of use in design is, if not overseen, then at least underprioritized, both in practice-related design fields and within the fields of history, theory and criticism of design. This contrasts with the extensive proliferation of consumer reports, product tests and customer reviews of products on the Internet. These seem to indicate that consumers are very interested in the practical use potential of products, not their discursive values. Cameron Tonkinwise has argued that 'design has another realm that differentiates it from all other forms of culture – use' (Tonkinwise 2014: 15).

By employing the use of books, print and digital, vernacular and art oriented, as recurring examples, this chapter then argues for a revival of the concept of use in the study of design as culture. Following the introduction of a perspective on materiality, use and discourse based in pragmatic semiotics, the chapter suggests perspectives for integrating the acts of use, in which people are involved in the physical handling of designed products, with broader issues of design culture.

A contested concept in design

The concept of use seems to have gained a tarnished reputation in current design discourse. Originally, conceptions of the similar concept, 'function', were intimately connected with the development of design modernism. Early pioneers of the modernist design movements, such as Sullivan, boiled their design approaches down to slogans such as 'form follows function'. Rather than a descriptive assessment of existing artefacts, this served through the twentieth century as normative prescription within architecture, product design and related disciplines: Ornament, style and other features were to be avoided in favour of more 'honest' design that better revealed the basic function of artefacts. The pioneers of design modernism, such as Jan Tschichold, set the standard for modern print typography by renouncing earlier form in favour of more sober, 'objective' forms (cited after Tschichold, Hendel, Kinross and McLean 2006), regularly connecting more or less utopian visions of social revolution with normative and limited conceptions of what constituted such objective functions (Greenhalgh 1990: 18). Twentieth-century design communicators, such as Bruno Munari, argued for a close connection of function with aesthetics, in term of 'formal coherence' of form and function, writing that a designer was the 'artist of today', who 'helps the object … to make itself by its own proper means', responding to 'the human needs of his time, and helps people solve certain problems without stylistic preconceptions and false notions of artistic dignity derived from the schisms of the arts' (Munari 2008: 31–2). This line of thinking continued as a dominating narrative, both within design practice and design theory, which not only described but also evaluated design morally by referring to terms such as function, utility or relevance. Even prominent critics of design modernism's inherent alliances with the dominating capitalist production system in terms of social and environmental sustainability, such as Victor Papanek, at least until the 1970s, still argued in terms of optimizing the way things work, invoking austere images of design utility with a strong moral and social profile (see for example Papanek and Hennessey 1977).

This normative functionalism in design has been criticized on many levels, for instance, for focusing too narrowly on function as something that designers hold the power to determine through imbuing form with intention (Vermaas and Houkes 2006: 31). Other sources of criticism argue that the modernist notion of function was never only about function, in the sense of strict technical or structural function, exactly because of its underlying ideological and moralizing intentions (see Malpass 2017: 71). Nevertheless, as has been well documented, modernist functionalist design did not achieve many of its original social and moral goals. It soon developed into what was later seen as an austere and dehumanizing post-Second World War environment (Greenhalgh 1990). Since the happy days of high modernism, claims of function or utility as the normative basis for design have been diluted, contested or outright rejected, at least at the level of theoretical discourse, to be supplemented by movements such as postmodernism, emotional design or speculative design.

In the disciplines reflecting design, the *use* of design artefacts seems to play a similar small role in the theoretical discourse. 'New' design history, began with the foundation of the Design History Society in 1979 with an explicit rejection of earlier functionalist approaches to design, in favour of wider cultural and social dimensions in the description of design (Walker 1989). Widely cited works in the field that could be broadly characterized as design culture studies conceptualize design processes and products as intertwined in production, consumption and mediation, and as discourses and practices, located in broader cultures of design or social and economic conditions (du Gay et al. 2013; Julier 2014; Lees-Maffei 2009; Lees-Maffei 2017). However, the defining book in the field, Guy Julier's *The Culture of Design* champions a conception of design culture, which briefly subsume use under the concept of consumption, as 'prosaic activities' which 'express, knowingly or unknowingly, a wider set of cultural and ideological systems' (Julier 2014: 69). While Julier's book promotes use as part of consumption, it is mostly concerned with artefacts as mediators for external and immaterial traits. Characteristically, features like demography, social relations, taste and psychological response are listed under 'Consumption' in the book's model overview of the domains of the culture of design (Julier 2014: 15). Thus, the book is mainly occupied with how design gains meaning in wider cultural systems of meaning in which people are consuming products (see also McCracken 1989), not with the aforementioned 'prosaic activities' of use, which involve physical handling and interaction with the material artefacts. As will be argued, these activities in which people are involved with artefacts are not only expressive of value systems external to the designed artefact, they are also central for understanding much design.

To be fair, both design culture and its siblings in the broader fields of design history, theory and criticism have been influenced by a broader material turn within the humanities, which considers the agency of objects in the constitution of the cultural practice of design, production and consumption, bannered by texts such as Attfield's *Wild Things* (2000). These have interacted with a range of disciplines, like anthropology (Miller 1987), cultural studies (Hebdige 1983, 1989; Hall 1997), archaeology (Tilley 2016), sociology (Dant 1999) and recently also with actor-network-theory (Yaneva 2009) and script analysis (Fallan 2008). Nonetheless, Tim Ingold argues that studies within this field seem to be concerned with material artefacts insofar as they mirror aspects of immaterial values and cultural discourse, not their use and assemblage as material configurations (Ingold 2007). While the normativity of design modernism still demands critical questioning, the description of use, which relates directly to the physical handling of the artefact, not to its discursive valuation, remains important. Hence, there is an argument for taking a closer look at what constitutes such prosaic use of material artefact configurations in relation to cultures of design.

The following is therefore a closer examination and revival of the concept of use in designed artefacts, without the normative assumption of design modernism that usefulness is better or preferred and with a focus on use as the physical handling of material artefacts. The aim is not to abandon earlier approaches to understanding the culture of design. Instead, the argument proposed here is in favour of a balanced approach where cultural phenomena, discourse in communication and media relate to how most designed artefacts are *also* useful.

An inferential perspective

The pursuit of the questions outlined in this chapter is indebted to the interpretative methodology of design analysis proposed by Giampaolo Proni (Proni 2002, 2010), inspired by a C.S Peirce's pragmaticist semiotics, and on other inferential perspectives on design (Suchman 1987) and material culture (Schiffer 2002). This approach is particularly valuable because it understands cultural significance in relation not only to communicative and linguistic meaning-negotiation, but also to the embodied, physical and interactional contexts of design, understood from the perspective of users handling artefacts. A basic tenet of the approach is that users make inferences about the meaning of physically perceivable features of artefacts to interact with them in their situational context (Suchman 1987: 53). These inferences range from 1) *perceptions* of the material properties of the artefact itself, to 2) inferences connecting the perceived properties of artefacts causally to past *production* or future *use* and to the situational context of the artefact, to 3) more or less developed *discursive associations*, relating the perceived material features to non-causal, conventional and metaphorical meanings of culture, often far removed from the local context of use (Guldberg 2012: 93).

All inferences develop from pragmatic interactions with artefacts, people and other externs (Schiffer 2002: 33) in the life-world of users. Thus, although inferences about artefacts can be of a personal or of a more conventional, socially developed character, they tend to be shaped by continuous interactions with the thing at hand, what Peirce called the 'Outward Clash' of the real (quoted after Houser and Kloesel 1992: 233). Hence, there will normally be a difference between three-dimensional artefacts, which users purposefully interact with on a multisensory, bodily level, or 'do something' with, and other, more ephemeral signs, such as spoken words or visual signs. As Proni subtly writes, 'Until we can drink beer ads, it would be better to consider them as something different from beer,' (2002: 41). Accordingly, artefacts are normally used for some practical purpose. Hence, users interact and make inferences about artefacts on the assumption that they represent such a use programme. It can be contended whether such purposefulness represents a use plan, that is, structured sequence of *considered* actions (Vermaas and Houkes 2006: 29), or whether the purpose is less conscious and more related to the habits of practice. A pragmatic suggestion would be that the more practical experience users have with an artefact, the less this use will be consciously planned. Hence, over time, perceptual inferences become embedded in the bodily actions of the user and in the configurations of related para-artefacts, necessary to perform the use sequence (Vermaas and Houkes 2006: 41), and find expression in secondary associations. Thus, use can be modelled as a feedback process of action and perception in which, according to Proni, 'a subject acts to attain a goal (cognitive or practical) in interaction with an artifact which offers the support and sets the limits of its constitution' (Proni 2002: 48).

Central to the argument here proposed, designed artefacts are then not *only* a cultural or discursive phenomenon. However, while the meaning of the design is contextual and defined by users in interplay with the cultural and social forces in which they make inferences, something, for example an artefact, is created as an inter-subjectively perceivable configuration of material properties during the design process. Hence, the role of designers is to create configurations of materials through design processes (Ingold 2007). Although designers may try to anticipate user inferences before they design, they first and foremost create tangible artefacts, which can be touched, felt and otherwise interacted with by users. By extension, even media artefacts, like books or social media posts, are not only interesting as mediators of their contained texts, but also in terms of their perceivable sensorial material properties, which indicate possibilities of use. Many such 'flat', media may at a superficial reflection seem to be non-artefacts. Nonetheless, the pages of a book is not just a medium, but a special type of artefact that can be used to communicate, because it is built to communicate, in a standardized way, integrating various textual, visual or auditory modalities.

In contrast to artefacts whose use is for most users non-communicative, for example an office chair, the use of media artefacts like books always depends on multisensory para-artefacts located in the situational context of users, often unrelated to them, but still necessary for their use (Steward 2015). Likewise, a post on a social media platform, such as Facebook, is dependent on a smartphone or computer to be 'liked' or otherwise interacted with. As any remediation is affected by the materiality of the media that re-mediates it (Bolter and Grusin 1996; Wiberg 2014), use and discourse will never produce exactly similar inferences. However, people still interact and make inferences about the artefacts of their everyday life on the assumption that they represent a practical means of use.

An outline of the useful

The codex form of the book, the stack of printed text sheets, bound in a cover, is one of the most well-established material and cultural forms. On the other hand, the book and its use are undergoing radical changes and re-inventions, following radical reconfigurations of production, distribution and consumption patterns due to digitization and globalization of book business (Murray and Squires 2013). In addition, there is a proliferation of 'post-artifact' books (Mod 2011) and sculptural 'bibliobjecs', or 'bookworks' (Steward 2011) with much more conceptual aims than the simple act of reading. This makes books, print and digital, particularly interesting as examples that both extend and challenge conceptions of useful artefacts in general, and thus creates a space for discussing the contribution of the concept of use within a design cultural perspective.

Use was earlier defined as a process in which some user acts to achieve a purpose in interaction with an artefact. However, purposes vary; sometimes they may be related to basic needs, other times to mere entertainment, or something completely different. As Guy Julier and others have mentioned, the possession and display on a shelf of an anomalous object like the Juicy Salif may communicate an impression of a certain level of aesthetic and social sophistication of its owner, not use value (Julier 2014: 88ff).

In the case of books, common parlance has that they are 'read' by 'readers'. Nevertheless, a book not only carries the text of a novel to be read, it is also designed with a set of material properties that supports certain use patterns. These, which Proni calls *use schemes*, and which Houkes and Vermaas call *use plans* (2006), are the possible and likely sequences of interactions or handlings of the artefact (Proni 2002: 49). Use schemes follow a syntax of use. This syntax may be linear or more tree-like, with several possible outcomes, sub-sequences and with several conditionals and feedback-loops built in (Martinec and Van Leeuwen 2009).

Some insights into such use schemes can be gained from the *interaction codes* which users draw from in inferring the use schemes of an artefact. The basic implicit book interaction code for English language books could be stated like this: 'I am a book, read me by opening the cover and read the following pages one by one, from left to right, top to bottom.' Thus, a book may be read from beginning to end, by turning page by page. This is the case with most reading of novels in print and audiobooks. But, as in the instance of textbooks, technical literature and many other genres, a book may also be used in numerous other orders. Sometimes interaction codes are explicit, for example as found in built-in help functions of digital e-book reading devices, such as the Kindle, or as in teachers' guides for elementary school textbooks, that is, in communication about the artefact. Sometimes interaction codes are implicit and culturally transmitted among users. They then exist mostly as habitualized patterns in the performative practices of user communities. The implicit 'read me' code for using a book is strong, and to a large degree never explained in detail to children learning to read. Hence, while most students have appropriated individual interaction codes for reading in general, they can most often benefit from being taught one or more of the efficient explicit interaction codes available, to develop better reading strategies in their academic study (Mokhtari and Reichard 2002).

Although they may be designed for a certain purpose, artefacts never enforce a certain use. They lend themselves to certain more probable use schemes than others, as they physically allow or 'afford' users to engage in some perceptual inferences and actions (Gibson 1979) and on the other hand constrain or even forbid others (Knappett 2005: 111–16; Proni 2010: 194). Other uses of an artefact are more loosely connected with physical limitations, and more determined by discursive associations. These may change over time and in relation to social contexts and relations of power. Some editions of holy books are only for use at special occasions, limited by written and unwritten prescriptions. In analysis, it is therefore necessary to make a distinction between the model user and the socially coded user of an artefact. The model user is only limited by the physical constraints of an artefact, such as when a book is written with tiny lettering, making it difficult to read for near-sighted persons. The socially coded or 'preferred' user is limited by the cultural expectations, which will be manifest in cultural discourse about the artefact. Such a user is delimited by the cultural expectations on who 'ought' to use them, not by the material or technical dimensions of the artefact. A math book, aimed at first grade in primary school, is socially coded for children at a specific and culturally defined level. However, only the skill level in understanding the math problems, contained in the text, limits who can use the book. Furthermore, even this limit is a socially coded difference, a resistance in the content of the text, not a design differentiation, embedded in its materiality. The model user in case is a much wider population: anyone who can physically handle the book.

A model of use in context

To sum, the proposed perspective models how users make inferences about material properties, potential use schemes and typical discursive valuations and relationships. (See the diagram in Figure 4.1). On the basis of perception of the material qualities on an artefact, users infer a) how they can be used and b) how they came into being, that is, their contexts of production – who or what produced them, stylistic inspirations, and so on. Subsequently, these inferences will inevitably be associated with discursive interpretations. Such associations are not unitary. Instead they form a network of many discursive meaning potentials of the artefact which users may associate with the artefact (dotted arrows). These associations develop over time and differ widely from user to user, according to his or her personal experience, social location and position within the domains of design culture. In turn, discursive associations then influence how the use of the artefact is subsequently perceived and used. Users therefore inevitably invoke discursive associations before, during and after the use of artefacts. Importantly, however, when concerned with tangible artefacts, these associations are created, not out of thin air, but in response to and in pragmatic interplay with the material properties and built-in indices of potential use of the artefact (thick curved arrow). This is how artefacts differ from pure communicative signs of meaning, and why mediations of design are something different than designed products themselves.

In the analysis of a designed artefact, one is thus interested in making a model of how a community of users would habitually use it, since inferences are shaped in continuous interactions with the artefacts in hand. These use schemes both shape and are shaped by discourse.

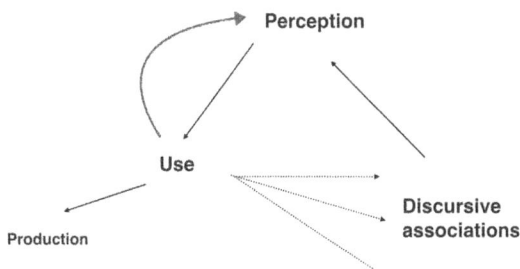

FIGURE 4.1 *A Model of the Design Analytical Methodology Inspired by Proni (2002).*

In the suggested inferential perspective, the task of designers normally is not to imbue artefacts with meaning per se. Designers create configurations of material properties, that is, form, which users and other stakeholders may infer from their material properties, expected use plans and cultural association potentials. What designers of artefacts *can* do is then to assemble material properties (or corresponding sketches, blueprints or models for the production of artefacts) that anticipate probable use schemes, in terms of anticipated affordance and constraints involved in habitual interaction codes, on the basis of their heuristic expert knowledge of how users will successfully interact with the material properties of artefacts (see Lawson 2004: 5). Designers may also anticipate the cultural discourse which users may associate with the artefact. Designers may then supplement the artefact with explicit interaction codes, written in user manuals and other media and para-artefacts that may (with luck and skill) determine its actual usage. Designers both anticipate use schemes and communicate them.

Exceptions and fringe-cases of use

The perspective presented here aims to rejuvenate the concept of use in understanding design culture. While this outline has established a vocabulary for understanding use in context, it can be argued that some artefacts and practices of design blur the limits of the concept of use in relation to design considerably. Hence, it could be argued that such artefacts and practices be taken into consideration in order to fully understand the full contextual picture of design culture.

Returning to the case of books, Garrett Steward argues that some books that attract attention in terms their opaqueness as mediating tools, seem to be interesting in terms of their 'lexical or graphical codes of inscription' rather than their content (Steward 2011: 130). In other words, they are not interesting mainly as books to be used in the sense of physical handling proposed here. These 'bookworks' are removed from their usual context and re-appropriated by artists (2011: 3). By using the original artefact as materials for the construction of a quite different artefact, these artefacts claim to create a new aesthetic experience while at the same time drawing attention to the absence of the materiality of the original artefact consumed in the production of the new artefact.

An example is the work '56 broken Kindle Screens', by Silvio Larusso and Sebastian Schmieg (Schmieg and Larusso 2012). It consists of a paperback edition and various e-books published in Kindle format. Its sole content is image footage of broken Kindle e-book reader screens which the creators found on the Web (see Figure 4.2). According to its creators, this work 'serves as an examination into the reading device's materiality. As the screens break, they become collages composed of different pages, cover illustrations and interface elements' (Schmieg and Larusso 2012). In other words, the destruction and re-contextualization of the more familiar useful artefact produces an aesthetic effect, which arises through the breakdown of the original artefacts' usefulness.

Such breakdowns, modifications, hybridizations and re-contextualizations can be interesting and thought-provoking, as they are clearly not simple malfunctions (Houkes and Vermaas 2010: 101) nor simple conversions of an old to a new purpose. Although they cannot be understood as design practices in the sense of creating artefacts of use suggested here, they can trigger creative new discursive associations in the minds of designers and other stakeholders involved in the cultural dimensions of design. Indeed, such effects are crucial to conceptual design movements, like 'critical design' (Dunne 1999) or 'speculative design' (Dunne and Raby 2013), which seek to 'to raise issues, to ask questions and to challenge assumptions' (Raby 2013).

However, circulating mainly in the spheres of the conceptual art scene or academic settings, such as 'art galleries, conference halls and academic publications' (Blythe, Yauner and Rodgers 2015: 83), such critical design artefacts rarely enter the situational contexts of everyday life (Bardzell and Bardzell 2013). This may be the case, either because they don't have the 'boundaries of commercial products' (Auger 2012), that is, they never enter the market, or because they are never noticed nor accepted and acquired by any significant number of consumers. Hence, the full effect of these remains to be seen in any larger scale, in terms of actual changes of design practices. It can be argued that in practice critical design mainly serves as discursive

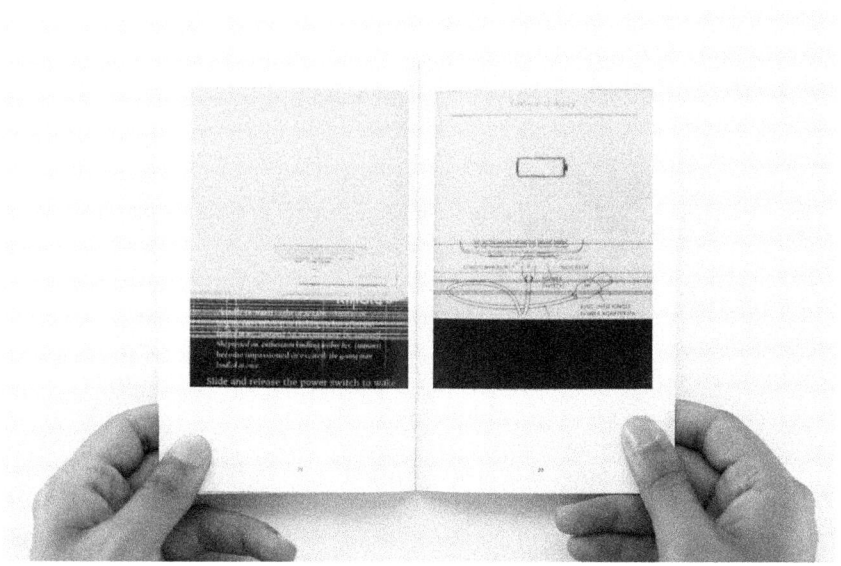

FIGURE 4.2 *56 Broken Kindle Screens* © *Schmieg and Larusso (2012).*

sparks or 'wake-up calls', aimed at other designers. Nonetheless, all these proposed effects are performed on a non-artefactual level; hence, they are not about use in the sense discussed in this chapter.

The heuristics of use in research

What are the ramifications for the conception of a culture of design that take this model of use seriously? Crucially, in contrast to discourse, use sets some practical limits on the study of design artefacts as culture. While discursive associations can be gathered for analysis in communication about and for the artefact – in the multiple mediations of the artefact in documents, in designer sketches, in design magazines and so on, use is not necessarily easy to document. Handling and playing with the possibilities of the artefact is a prudent first step. However, this will rarely reveal more than a basic knowledge of the use potential. Of course, the closer connected the researcher is in time and proximity to the community of use whose inferences are studied, the more credibility his or her interpretation may gain. Sometimes, this can be achieved through participation and observation of rituals, exchanges and everyday-use routines in which users, individually and in communities of practice, handle the artefact. As communities of users tend to cooperate and communicate, as artefacts are modified over time in order to optimize their use within their given cultural setting (Petroski 1992) and since inferences are shaped in continuous interactions with the artefacts in hand, use can be modelled for analysis by studying communities of practice (Wenger 1998) over time. An interesting avenue of research would also be the various rituals of appropriation suggested by McCracken (1989). Moments of use, like the waxing of new-bought cars or the unboxing video phenomenon on YouTube (O'Connell 2013) where perceptions of use are translated into discursive associations or vice versa. At other times, the concept of use may serve as a methodological reminder that the study of design discourses is not the same as the study of actual design use. In the cultural mesh surrounding design, use overlaps, entwines and interleaves with discourse.

In final analysis, even though use is in constant flux, and even though the use scheme of an artefact may be blurred through suboptimal user interfaces, and even though artefacts may malfunction, the use of a designed artefact is always also something else than the discourse about artefacts. In contrast, a conceptually oriented design practice does not create artefacts of use. It distorts, loosens or hinders dominant cultural anticipations, hence implies on a breakdown of dominant implicit interaction codes of use, and a move towards discourse through design, not useful artefacts. Moreover, since no artefacts can speak for themselves, especially when usual conventions of meaning are not available for user decoding, conceptual design relies on help in the form of communication about the artefact. Hence, conceptualizing design artefacts and practices remain dependent on associations with designers with excellent communication skills, or on accompanying communication para-artefacts that help consumers interpret actual use by various discursive means.

Alternatively, design of non-useful artefacts can be conceived more humbly as an integral communicative part of the design process. Alternatively, critical design may serve a more modest role as tools in the early phases of the design process for generating creative insights (Sanders and Stappers 2014: 7), similar to 'design fiction' (Lindley and Coulton 2015). The concept of the useless may, in the simplest sense, support the one of the basic tenets of 'design thinking', that is, broadening the field of ideation, or 'reframing' the problem (Dorst 2010). However, considering design as non-use, it is much more interesting to imagine *not* to produce an artefact at all. This may address the suggestion by Cameron Tonkinwise to steer studies of design, including the culture of design, in the direction of being 'for something' (Tonkinwise 2014: 31). In other words, a focus on non-use could possibly lead to a radical rethinking of the production imperative inherent in an economy of design based on growth (Julier 2017). This could then entail 'a commitment to re-localizing and decarbonizing economies' (Tonkinwise 2014: 31), in order to create genuine design culture of 'sustainment', a future with a future, not just a contingent preferred future (Fry 2017) through design. In other words, to engage in genuine critique, the study of design culture would be legitimized by anchoring the broader contexts in concerns with local contexts of use, as well as in questions of actual use by users of design as an important aspect of interrogating consumption aspects of design culture.

References

Attfield, J. (2000), *Wild Things. The Material Culture of Everyday Life*, London & New York: Berg.
Auger, J. (2012), *Why Robot?: Speculative Design, the Domestication of Technology and the Considered Future* (Doctoral dissertation. Royal College of Art*)*.
Bardzell, J. and Bardzell, S. (2013), What is Critical About Critical Design? In *Proceedings of the SIGCHI conference on human factors in computing systems*, 3297–306. ACM.
Blythe, M., Yauner, F. and Rodgers, P. (2015), 'The Context of Critical Design: Exhibits, Social Media and Auction Houses', *The Design Journal*, 18(1): 83–105.
Bolter, J. D. and Grusin, R. A. (1996), 'Remediation', *Configurations*, 4(3): 311–58.
Dant, T. (1999), *Material Culture in the Social World*, Philadelphia: Open University Press.
Dorst, K. (2010), The Nature of Design Thinking. In *Design thinking research symposium*. DAB Documents.

Dunne, A. (1999), *Hertzian Tales*, London: Royal College of Art.
Dunne, A. and Raby, F. (2013), *Speculative Everything: Design, Fiction, and Social Dreaming*, Cambridge, MA & London: MIT Press.
Fallan, K. (2008), 'De-scribing Design: Appropriating Script Analysis to Design History', *Design Issues*, 24(4): 61–75.
Fry, T. (2017), 'Design for/by "The Global South"', *Design Philosophy Papers*, 15(1): 3–37.
du Gay, P., Hall, S., Janes, L., Madsen, A. K., Mackay, H. and Negus, K. (2013), *Doing Cultural Studies: The Story of the Sony Walkman*, Los Angeles: SAGE.
Gibson, J. J. (1979), *The Ecological Approach to Visual Perception*, Boston & London: Houghton Mifflin.
Greenhalgh, P. (ed.), (1990), *Modernism in Design*, London: Reaktion Books.
Guldberg, J. (2012), 'Design and Iconicity: Design, Materiality and the Meaning of Things', in *Design and Semantics of Form and Movement*, Proceedings of the conference DeSForM 2012: MEANING.MATTER.MAKING: 88–98.
Hall, S. (1997), *Representation: Cultural Representations and Signifying Practices*, London & Thousand Oaks, CA: Sage.
Hebdige, D. (1983), 'Travelling Light: One Route Into Material Culture', *RAIN*, (59), 11–13.
Hebdige, D. (1989), *Hiding in the Light*, London: Comedia.
Houkes, W. and Vermaas, P. E. (2010), *Technical Functions. On the Use and Design of Artefacts* (Vol. 1), Dordrecht: Springer Netherlands.
Houser, N. and Kloesel, C. J. W. (1992), *The Essential Peirce, Volume 1: Selected Philosophical Writings*, (1867–1893), Bloomington: Indiana University Press.
Ingold, T. (2007), 'Materials Against Materiality', *Archaeological Dialogues*, 14(01): 1.
Julier, G. (2014 [2001]), *The Culture of Design* (Third Edition edition), Thousand Oaks, CA: Sage Publications Ltd.
Julier, G. (2017), *Economies of Design*, London: Sage.
Kimbell, L. (2011), 'Rethinking Design Thinking: Part I', *Design and Culture*, 3(3): 285–306.
Knappett, C. (2005), *Thinking through Material Culture: An Interdisciplinary Perspective*, Philadelphia: University of Pennsylvania Press.
Lawson, B. (2004), 'Schemata, Gambits and Precedent: Some Factors in Design Expertise', *Design Studies*, 25(5): 443–57.
Lees-Maffei, G. (2009), 'The Production-Consumption-Mediation Paradigm', *Journal of Design History*, 22(4): 351–76.
Lees-Maffei, G. (2017), Design History: The State of the Art. *Caa.Reviews*.
Lindley, J. and Coulton, P. (2015), 'Back to the Future: 10 Years of Design Fiction', in *Proceedings of the 2015 British HCI Conference*, New York, NY, USA: ACM, 210–11.
Malpass, M. (2017), *Critical Design in Context: History, Theory, and Practices*, London: Bloomsbury.
Manzini, E. (2014), 'Making Things Happen: Social Innovation and Design', *Design Issues*, 30(1): 57–66.
Martinec, R. and Van Leeuwen, T. (2009), *The Language of New Media Design: Theory and Practice*, London; New York: Routledge.
McCracken, G. (1989), *Culture and Consumption*, Bloomington and Indianapolis: Indiana University Press.

Miller, D. (1987), *Material Culture and Mass Consumption*, Blackwell Publishers.

Mokhtari, K. and Reichard, C. A. (2002), 'Assessing Students' Metacognitive Awareness of Reading Strategies', *Journal of Educational Psychology*, 94(2): 249–59.

Munari, B. (2008), *Design as Art (1971)*, translated by P. Creagh, London: Penguin.

Murray, P. R. and Squires, C. (2013), 'The Digital Publishing Communications Circuit', *Book 2.0*, 3(1): 3–23.

O'Connell, Mark (11 July 2013), 'The Cult of Unboxing: How I became Slightly Addicted to these Strange, Homemade Videos, with their Smugness and Exhilaration', *CNN Money*, last accessed 19 September 2017 from http://tech.fortune.cnn.com/2013/07/11/the-cult-of-unboxing/

Papanek, V. and Hennessey, J. (1977), *How Things Don't Work*, New York: s.n.

Petroski, H. (1992), *The Evolution of Useful Things: How Everyday Artifacts—From Forks and Pins to Paperclips and Zippers—Came to be as they are*, New York: Vintage.

Proni, G. (2002), Outlines for a Semiotic Analysis of Objects. *Versus – Quaderni Di Studi Semiotica*, (91/92), 37–59.

Proni, G. (2010), 'The Function of Nonfunctional Objects. Semiotics of Functionalism', in S. belkhamsa and B. Darras (eds), *Objects et communication*, Paris: L'Harmattan, 185–96).

ProQuest Ebook Central Reader. (n.d.). Retrieved 22 July 2017, from http://ebookcentral.proquest.com/lib/sdub/reader.action?docID=811354&ppg=12

Raby, F. (2008), 'Critical Design', in M. Erlhoff and T. Marshall (eds), *Design Dictionary: Perspectives on Design Terminology*, Basel: Birkhäuser Basel, 94–6.

Rosenbak, S. (2015), 'Prototyping a Useless Design Practice: What, Why & How?', *Artifact*, 3(4): section 5–10.

Sanders, E. B.-N. and Stappers, P. J. (2014), 'Probes, Toolkits and Prototypes: Three Approaches to Making in Codesigning', *CoDesign CoDesign*, 10(1): 5–14.

Schiffer, M. B. (2002), *The Material Life of Human Beings: Artifacts, Behavior and Communication*, London: Routledge.

Schmieg, S. and Larusso, S. (2012). 56 Broken Kindle Screens [Website]. Retrieved 19 February 2017, from http://silviolorusso.com/work/56-broken-kindle-screens/

Secomandi, F. and Snelders, D. (2011), 'The Object of Service Design', *Design Issues*, 27(3): 20–34.

Steward, G. (2011), *Bookwork : Medium to Object to Concept to Art*, Chicago & London: University of Chicago Press.

Steward, G. (2015), 'Between Print Matter and Page Matter: The Codex Platform as Medial support', in B. Herzogenrath (ed.), *Media Matter: The Materiality of Media, Matter as Medium*, New York & London: Bloomsbury Publishing USA, 47–68.

Suchman, L. A. (1987), *Plans and Situated Actions: The Problem of Human-Machine Communication*, UK: Cambridge University Press.

Tilley, C. (2016), *Material Culture and Text: The Art of Ambiguity,* London: Routledge.

Tonkinwise, C. (2014), 'Design Studies—What Is It Good For?', *Design and Culture*, 6(1): 5–43.

Tschichold, J., Hendel, R., Kinross, R. and McLean, R. (2006), *The New Typography: A Handbook for Modern Designers*, Berkeley: University of California Press.

Vermaas, P. E. and Houkes, W. (2006), 'Use Plans and Artefact Functions: An Intentionalist Approach to Artefacts and their Use', in A. Costall and O. Dreier (eds), *Doing Things with Things: The Design and Use of Everyday Objects*, Hampshire: Ashgate Publishing, Ltd, 29–48.

Walker, J. (1989), *Design History and the History of Design*, London: Pluto Press.

Wenger, E. (1998), *Communities of Practice: Learning, Meaning, and Identity*, Cambridge, UK: Cambridge University Press.

Wiberg, M. (2014), 'Methodology for Materiality: Interaction Design Research Through a Material Lens', *Personal and Ubiquitous Computing*, 18(3): 625–36.

Yaneva, A. (2009), 'Making the Social Hold: Towards an Actor-Network Theory of Design', *Design and Culture*, 1(3): 273–88.

PART TWO

Addressing market and society

Niels Peter Skou

The title of the second part mirrors the overall aim of the book in addressing design culture both as object and approach. We may thus both ask how designers and companies address market and society through strategies of design and marketing and reflect on the methodological questions which arise in the investigation of these strategies. What happens if we shift the focus from designers and products to their distribution and consumption? Which meanings are produced and which concepts and analytical tools do we need to describe them?

   The concept of design in relation to market and society is intricate since design discourse historically has been less than convinced that the interests of the market and the society were coinciding. From its offset in the Arts and Crafts movements as a reaction to the formation of industrialized capitalism it has been a recurring ideological figure in the European design tradition to take a critical stance towards the state of the market and capitalist product culture as such. This has, however, been combined with the emphasis on the reform of product culture as the key to a reform of society at large. It has thus been a characteristic of design both as ideological discourse and practice not only to develop products for the markets but at the same time to reflect on the societal impact of its activities on a more general level.

The chapters in this part present a series of case studies where at the surface quite disparate company cases are bound together by a shared reflexivity in the way the companies address the market. Sara Kristoffersson and Trine Brun Petersen present two Scandinavian cases, the Swedish Cooperative Union's series of 'basic products' in the 1970s, and Katvig, a Danish brand of children's clothing existing between 2003 and 2013. The historical distance apart both cases can be said to continue the somewhat paradoxical tradition of addressing the market in a way that is supposed to transform the very conditions of the market in order to pursue ethical goals such as in these cases equality, transparency and sustainability. The last case, the German soft drink company fritz-kola investigated by Mads Nygaard Folkmann cannot be said to share the same idealism since it is rather based on a demonstrative hedonism. It shares, however, some characteristics with the Katvig case, which might be said to characterize the current consumer culture. Where the Cooperative Union in the 1970s tried to create 'a brand for everyone', as the title of the chapter states, both Katvig and fritz-kola are characterized by a consciousness of addressing a specific sub-segment of consumers who furthermore are addressed with an increasing sophistication of aesthetic strategies and a marked public presence of the company founders as representatives of the brand.

In *A Brand for Everyone* by Sara Kristoffersson, the historical case of the Swedish Kooperativa Förbundat (KF) and its strategy for creating unbranded basic goods informed by the criticism of consumer society in the wake of the 1970s is investigated as an example of trying to use market strategies to reform consumer culture. In an attempt to eliminate the manipulation of marketing and branding, KF created a unified blue-and-white series of packaging, which paradoxically became a strong brand in itself. This way they made an appeal to a consumption based on rationality and equality rather than emotion and conspicuous consumption. This appeal had links back to Scandinavian modernism and the Swedish tradition of thrift but it can also be rediscovered in present critical design discourses. The study points, however, also to the inherent paradoxes in the design programme, which ultimately became the swan song of the Cooperative Union. It was out of tune with the neo-liberal development of the 1980s where commercial companies like H&M and IKEA came to dominate the market for clothing and furnishing.

The Danish company for children's clothing Katvig, which is at the centre of Trine Brun Petersens *Buying into the Future*, had, even though it was founded in 2003, strong links to the 1970s both aesthetically and ideologically. This way it works as an interesting example of the tensions in trying to revitalize this ideological heritage in the present design culture. The company was part of a series of companies introduced in the early noughties as fashion brands for children but differentiated itself by an increasing focus on promoting sustainable production and consumption patterns. The tension inherent in this case lies in the way the company can be viewed as a representative of a clothing industry increasingly based on globalized production networks and logics of fashion and segmentation while it, at the same time in its communication, made strong appeals to the ideal of a tight-knit, local and transparent design culture. This way the chapter also illustrates how issues of Design Culture and Fashion Studies may fertilize each other even though studies of clothing has been at the periphery of Design Culture studies up till now.

A methodological focus on expanding the conceptual range of Design Culture is also central to Mads Nygaard Folkmann's *The Glowing Black of fritz-kola. Aestheticization in Design Culture* where fritz-kola and its marketing strategies form the backdrop of an argument to reconsider the role of aesthetics in Design Culture and Design History where it historically has been marginalized. It is thus shown how aesthetic elements and mechanisms of sensory appeal and reflective potential are produced in a broad staging of the product through visual identity, advertising, shopping environments and brand spaces and even further reproduced by the consumers in their own staging of the products through social media.

The three studies are thus bound together by a shared focus on the means by which the companies address the consumers and the importance of packaging, visual identity and communication in attaching values and meaning to the products. In these processes design plays a double role: on the one hand a set of activities increasingly directed towards communication and meaning production, and on the other an explicit or implicit category producing differentiation in an otherwise homogenized market – a logic that even a deliberate attempt at de-segmentation as the KF basic goods programme could not escape. Furthermore the chapters show how Design Culture as discipline in its endeavour to study these dynamics may be strengthened by including aspects and insights of other academic traditions like Fashion Studies or aesthetic theory.

CHAPTER FIVE

A brand for everyone

Sara Kristoffersson

In 1971 members of KF – the Swedish Cooperative Union – demanded that the organization should reject the use of marketing ploys like special offers and branded products: 'Let us reform society. No, let us reform the entire world. Down with the tyranny of luxury goods. We are a moral world' (Compilation Consumer Congress 1971). The union's stores should be selling well-made and inexpensive basic products.

One year later KF launched a collection of 'basic' garments as a sensible alternative to what was regarded as a generally treacherous assortment of clothing in the marketplace. Towards the end of the decade the basic garments were joined by basic furniture. The term 'basic' signalled the opposite of luxury and excess and the style of design was defined as timeless and universal: freed from unnecessary fashion details and passing trends. A style to suit everyone.

As though it was a three-step plan a series of 'non-branded' household items were also introduced. Uniform and objectively designed packaging indicated only the contents of the item: toothpaste was packaged as 'Toothpaste' and porridge oats as 'Porridge Oats'. The question here is how one communicates an ideologically coloured message: which ideas, concepts and values are produced and manifested by the products?

Given the political climate of the 1970s the campaign came at the right time and it testifies to the critique of the consumer society current at that time. It should also be viewed in a historic perspective or, more correctly, as an expression of a fairly rigorous ideology with a tendency to embrace a planned economy with collectivist attributes. KF's projects manifested great claims to objectivity with educative and disciplinary aspects, aesthetic as well as moral. It has also roots in a Swedish tradition.

The cooperative movement began in the UK in the nineteenth century but consumer cooperation grew into a particularly strong movement in Sweden and it played an important part in the development of the Swedish welfare state. For decades prior to and after the Second World War, KF in Sweden acted as something of a state within the state with express ambitions of enlightening and educating the citizens about nutrition, consumption and domestic aesthetics.

The goal was in line with a restrictive attitude towards luxury and the consumer society which was stronger in Sweden than elsewhere. The years from the end of the nineteenth century and up until the 1970s were marked by the promotion of personal thrift: a normative idea that people should use their money carefully and should be wary of consumerism. KF became emblematic of what Peder Aléx has described as rational consumption, which was a matter of educating consumers in self-control, thrift and carefully planned purchases. It was a matter of shaping and disciplining the consumers (Aléx 1994).

Furthermore, KF was a major actor in the political landscape with a great influence on design culture in Sweden. The programme of basic goods can be regarded as a last big project with a clear ambition to produce a consumer with values related to the welfare state. (Mattsson 2012: 81). With the programme the cooperative movement tied in with its classical ideology and its tradition as a democratic popular movement. The initiative can thus be viewed as an attempt to maintain the old ideals in the face of new social paradigms.

What was intended to be an investment in the future can retrospectively be regarded as a sort of farewell. The 'timeless' basic goods soon became hopelessly outmoded. The virtue of thrift was totally contrary to the consumer society of the 1980s and the new market conditions. Thus the project also tells us something about the general changes in Swedish society and the transformation of the welfare state.

Designing the Swedish model

KF, the Swedish Cooperative Union, was born into a society in which there was a huge disparity between the rich and the poor. At the turn of the last century Swedes lived in more cramped conditions than almost anywhere else in Europe. There was widespread poverty, poor hygiene and very bad health conditions. The aim of uniting some forty cooperative unions in 1899 was to reduce the cost of food to consumers and to lessen dependence on private tradesmen. The movement grew rapidly. During the first half of the twentieth century the cooperative movement in Sweden grew into an extensive operation with a network of retail shops, department stores and factories. In the background was the enthusiastic support of the members as well as backing from unions and from politicians. KF thus acquired a unique position on the market that was rooted in contemporary society. At the same time Sweden was transformed from a poverty-stricken agrarian country into a welfare state with a very high standard of living. The social-democratic party – which governed Sweden from the 1930s up until the 1970s – introduced numerous reforms that created social and financial security at a unique level.

In Sweden the term 'folkhemmet' or 'people's home' is used interchangeably with 'the Swedish model'. The 'people's home' is a metaphor for a society where no one should feel excluded but it also acts as the hub of a welfare policy in which a home is regarded as a citizen's right. As modern Sweden literally took shape, Swedish functionalism became something of the house of architectural style. Progressive architects received official support from the various layers of government and KF played an important role in this context.

As early as 1924 the cooperative movement started its own architectural office, hereafter referred to as KF Architects. Ten years later it had become the largest architectural practice in Sweden. Its main task was to design KF's numerous shops but it undertook many other briefs. The office designed housing, factories, theatres, civic centres, school premises and restaurants. KF Architects had a profound influence on architecture in Sweden and this influence was not just on account of the number of commissions. From an early stage the office embraced a modernist ideal that was tied up with the cooperative movement throughout Sweden (Brunnström 2004).

KF Architects was the architectural practice that most consistently contributed to the spread and ultimate dominance of modernist architecture in Sweden. At the 1930 Stockholm Exhibition, which launched modernist architecture on a broad front, KF Architects was at the forefront. The principles and style were perfectly suited to the cooperative movement's aims of concern for the future and support of progressive ideas. The ambition was that the architecture and the interior design of buildings used by the cooperative movement should have a clearly collectivist character. Standard solutions in a large number of buildings naturally led to conformity (Brunnström 2004).

KF Architects seem to have embraced a specific house style, a uniformity that would have made Le Corbusier proud. There can be no doubt that Eskil Sundahl, the leading architect, and his colleagues at KF Architects were inspired by a vision of creating a better society with the help of radical architecture. At the core of their activities was an express ambition to work with long series of designs and with new norms for the entire Swedish society. But the modernist aesthetic also played an important role in the movement's identity. The cooperative movement was not responsible for creating the style, but it adopted it as its hallmark; which makes it reasonable to talk about a sort of branded architecture (Brunnström 2004).

The stress on residential accommodation as a means of modernizing the population is a particularly Scandinavian phenomenon. The housing policy of welfare-state Sweden was not just concerned with building more apartments but also on teaching people how to furnish their homes. In Sweden there is a long tradition of a public, highly normative discourse on how people should furnish their homes which is characterized by links between aesthetics and ethics. People are to be educated to recognize the difference between good and bad design, between what is practical and what is not. Besides study circles, courses and advisory pamphlets there were even home inspections (Björkman 2007).

Architects, interior designers, home advisors and social planners took part in the educational programmes and a whole new research industry developed, focused on the home. The target for the experts was 'ill-judged' conventions and in the official rhetoric there is a particular aesthetic that dominates: blond, simple and functional. Ungainly interiors with dark drab furniture were to be exchanged for light and practical items, while flower-patterned wallpapers should be replaced by white walls that symbolized purity and authenticity. The ideal was to embrace what was functional and simple, while items that were overly decorated were regarded as in bad taste (Göransdotter 1999).

KF was one of the driving forces in this context. The movement's aesthetic curriculum dominated the period between 1930 and 1950, promoted also by the Swedish Society of Crafts and Design. It was an aesthetic of rationality and it was often taught in a strikingly direct and arrogant manner. In KF's own course materials from the 1930s two glass tumblers are compared: 'Which of these tumblers is the most tasteful?'. The answer is inevitable: 'The one on the right, because it has a simple shape and strict and simple décor' (Giertz and Strömberg 1999: 128, Translation by the author).

This aesthetic is also in line with KF's views about the consumer society. Right from the beginning of the century the movement preached the importance of moderation and it became a notable representative of the Swedish ideal of thriftiness. The movement was not against consumption as such. Consumption was seen as a path into the future and mass production was regarded as a force for democratic change. The goal was to educate people so that they made rational consumer choices. Instead of being motivated by cravings and passion, consumers were to be taught to be more disciplined and controlled in making purchases (Aléx 1994).

During the decades following the Second World War Swedish incomes rose markedly. This increase in wealth is historically unique. Between 1950 and 1975 purchasing power doubled and people began to develop forms of consumption that, a few decades earlier, they would hardly have been able to dream of. Increased wages, and with them higher levels of consumption, gave people completely new opportunities for realizing their lives with the help of the consumer society. Living in a welfare state was no longer just a matter of social security but also experiencing a material standard with room for private consumption.

The 1960s were marked by an offensive strategy on the part of KF and are generally known as the department-store era. Smaller retail outlets in the countryside shut down and were replaced by stores that were defined first and foremost as sales outlets. Financial calculations took charge. KF Architects lost not only its acuity but actually contributed to a tragic chapter in Sweden's architectural history. The department stores destroyed the traditional town centres in town after town (Brunnström 2004).

During the same decade KF developed a new graphic profile, the most comprehensive and the most expensive that had ever been undertaken in Sweden. The movement's various units, activities and associations throughout the country had previously had their own trademarks and typography. Now their unity was to be clarified with a single, joint logotype. A unified image was considered essential in meeting the competition in the marketplace and the campaign was primarily defined as a financial measure (Hjalmarsson 1967).

The symbol of a blue Möbius band was launched in January 1967 and was used on motor vehicles, façades and banners as well as in advertisements, notepaper and packaging. After a mere two weeks almost half of the Swedish population could recognize the new symbol and by the end of the year just about everyone was familiar with it, according to KF's own calculations. By this time KF had become a business empire in the bosom of Sweden. The transformation from popular movement to major industry gave rise to criticism. The debate focused on dying ideals, on centralization and on profitability requirements. As in the rest of the Western world, there was growing opposition to the consumer society, to commercialism and to capitalism.

Back to basics

In September 1971 KF held a membership congress with the aim to increase members' influence and to let them make known their views on the movement. The congress was preceded by extensive prior discussion. Tens of thousands of members took part in study circles while more than five thousand resolutions were submitted. At a mega level there was fierce criticism of the cooperative movement which was accused of behaving in just the same way as any privately owned company.

A large proportion of the resolutions had to do with the range of goods stocked by the stores, in particular clothing. Great and small were discussed. Everything from how seams were sewn in stockings to the lack of black garments for people in mourning. In fact the range of goods available was understood as a matter of democracy and of gender equality. All members of the movement – plump or slender, young or old – should have the same possibility of finding suitable clothing in KF's stores. Many were critical of the fact that short-term trends had found their way into the shops.

At the same time the congress decided that KF should develop a series of basic clothing designs for women. The basic idea was to launch an alternative to the fashion industry's trends that 'fool' consumers to constantly buy new clothes as well as their fixation on bodily ideals. The basic garments were developed by KF's purchasing department and the programme started with a survey of existing ranges with the intention of determining which models had continued to be offered over the years.

Ten types of garments were selected: skirt, dress, jacket, trousers, pinafore dress, shirt dress, blouse, polo jumper, long cardigan and long jacket. In due course a range of gents' clothing was added. The idea was that change should be allowed, but only when there was a real need for improvement. If a new model absolutely had to be included in the collection then another item should be taken out Henell 1976). The project was characterized, in other words, by the notion of a sort of timeless basic model and cut that would be immune to trends and changes in fashion.

Even the colours were determined. The starting point for this was a belief that demand of basic colours is stable. The colours chosen were white, black, brown, green, red, blue and beige. As regards the materials there was no such variation. In principle, all of the garments were made of polyester. That this material was the best possible for the purpose had been determined by KF's laboratories where technical quality, ease of maintenance and durability were decisive (Henell 1976).

Cotton was dismissed with the motivation that cotton fabrics lose colour at different rates. With garments in polyester, for example, a worn pair of trousers can be replaced with a new pair without the colour clashing with a top bought at some earlier time. The synthetic material was easy to launder. Polyester fabrics do not need to be ironed and if the garments are stretched they quickly regain their original form. Polyester garments can be machine-washed and they dry quickly (Henell 1976).

The value of the garments in terms of price in relation to usage over time was stressed. The idea was that the collection of basic garments should be financially advantageous. Since they were designed to last for season after season, expenses in the form of sales and clearances would be avoided. And instead of investing money in designing new models resources could be used for quality control and technical development (Henell 1976; Boman 1976).

That the talk is of garments or clothing rather than fashion is no accident. The project was infused with an almost hostile attitude towards the phenomenon. The range of basic clothing guaranteed you a trouble-free wardrobe. It was intended to solve the problems of 'consumers who do not any longer need to make as many decisions as people who are interested in fashion' (Palmgren 1977, translated by author). The deep suspicion towards fashion is typical of the period and KF has its predecessors.

In the 1960s people questioned accepted notions, not least those pertaining to fashion where a younger generation broke with conventional dress codes. For some of them clothes became a political project. In Sweden young textile designers founded a group and a company called Mah-Jong which expressly separated itself from the commercial fashion industry, wanting to create clothes for the 'people': models that would continue to be available year after year and that required a minimum of care and maintenance.

They were also concerned with women's liberation. Women were not to be dependent on the whims of the market and should be able to dress in a relaxed manner. But the company failed to reach the working classes. The style was seen as eccentric and the garments were relatively expensive (Hallström 2003).

For the cooperative movement life was rosier. Thanks to being made in long series the unpretentious basic garments were cheap and in 1976 some 1.3 million items were sold. The basic collection was responsible for about 20 per cent of the company's total sales of clothing. The models, colours and materials remained basically unchanged, as did the underlying philosophy (Boman 1976).

In the same year work started on KF's basic furniture designed in collaboration with Svensk form (formerly the Swedish Society of Crafts and Design), an organization with which the cooperative movement had previously collaborated in educational campaigns. The range of furniture available in the department stores had long been accused of being flashy and ostentatious. Critics claimed that the market for furniture was dominated by heavy, plush sofas and they asked where the social and aesthetic ideals of the cooperative movement had disappeared to. The debate led to the furniture range being examined with the intention of reducing the number of products and ensuring that half of the range consisted of light, blond items. Big floral patterns were discontinued in favour of monochrome or small-patterned variants (Larsson 1978).

Quite simply, it was a matter of re-establishing the cooperative movement's original profile and a guiding principle of the project committee's work had been to consider such basic functions as sitting, socializing, eating, working, sleeping and storing things (Boman 1976). By creating simple and functional furniture that was hardwearing and easily maintained in an anonymous, neutral and timeless aesthetic, the aim was to re-connect with a Swedish tradition.

The collection was first presented in 1978 and it consisted of a dining/work table, chest of drawers, gate-legged table, coffee table, sofa and a Windsor chair. Later a bed and an armchair were added. The furniture was unassuming and unsophisticated in a straightforward style. There were no unnecessary details but there was fitness-for-purpose and character. The range was, rather, the result of considerations of functional, material and manufacturing aspects with high demands on durability, practicality and flexibility.

That the furniture was tested at Möbelinstitutet, a national organization concerned with assessing furniture was natural. The institute, which was active from 1967 to 1995, was partially state-funded. Furniture that reached the rigorous standards of the institute was awarded a certificate or protocol listing its qualities. All the tables in the range as well as the Windsor chairs were made of birch which is durable and is claimed to be easy to combine with other species of wood. Even the sofa's visible framework was made of birch. The cushions were loose and were fitted with removable and washable covers. But it was not just durability that determined the use of birch. Its ancient Swedish heritage fitted in with the ambition of returning to a Nordic tradition (Boman 1976).

When the basic furniture was presented in KF's furniture catalogue, 1978–1979, in realistic settings a poster from the 1930 Stockholm Exhibition hung on the wall of one of the living rooms. The poster is no accident. In both the preceding debate about the cooperative movement's appalling furniture and in the launch of the basic furniture, as we have noted, there were powerful echoes from KF's educational aspirations and the modernist heritage.

No logo

KF's range of 'non-branded' convenience goods that was introduced in 1979 is a sort of logical endpoint for the basic goods project. The products lacked brand names and the packaging was uniform and factual: white packages only reveal the contents by means of a blue plaque (Figure 5.1). The idea was to offer a constant range of low-cost products, an alternative to artificially

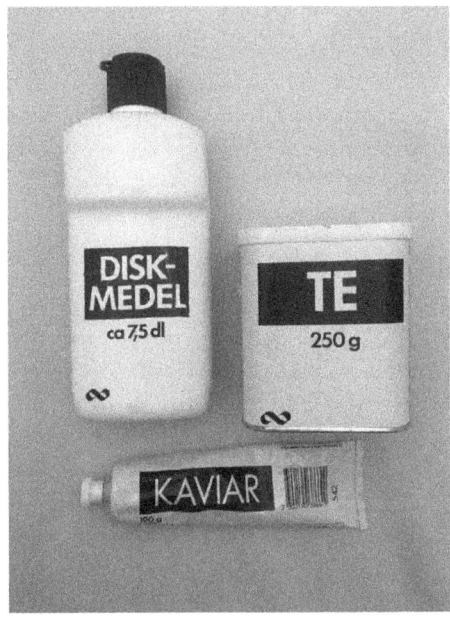

FIGURE 5.1 *Non-branded convenience goods, Swedish Cooperative Union, 1979.*

reduced prices and special offers. By not advertising – except in the initial period – and by using the simplest form of packaging it would be possible to reduce prices. The products were made in KF's own factories and prices were printed on the items at the factory (KF Massmediakontakt 1979).

The project was not unique. The inspiration came from Carrefour, the French chain of food stores which, three years earlier, had launched its 'free products', *produits libres*, under the device 'without a name, equally good, cheaper' (Consumer Report 1978). Like the project undertaken by Carrefour, KF's range should be understood as a contribution to a contemporary discussion about product aesthetics, advertising and packaging.

Thanks to the packaging the products could be protected, stored and distributed in an efficient manner. During the first decades of the twentieth century most items from the food industry were sold in bulk over the counter. Working in a food store was mostly a matter of weighing and measuring, packaging and adding up the bill. Rationalization gradually replaced this manual labour with ready-packaged items. In the self-service shops that grew up after the Second World War, displaying the goods became all the more important; but the packaging also answered new needs. Formerly the staff had informed customers and had launched new products. Now the packaging itself had to do this. Packaging was not just concerned with telling consumers about the product, its qualities and character, but also aimed to stimulate consumption. And so packaging naturally varied depending on the type of product.

Central to packaging of dairy products is information about expiry date, fat content and nutritional value. Images of animals and nature would be unthinkable on packaging of medical products. There is absolutely no room for suggestive elements and the design is strictly regulated. The aim is that the packaging should have a factual character and it has long been customary to use a geometrical design with primary colours and white surfaces. Another category altogether is represented by so-called luxury goods like perfumes and toiletries in which the actual ingredients make up just a small part of the price (Brunnström and Wagner 2015).

During the 1960s more and more critical voices joined the movement against excessive consumption, and commercial forces including advertising. Surface presentation, appearance and packaging are central elements of competition that cost money. In the choice between different types of shampoo it is seldom the contents that determine the outcome. Rather the bottle. In order to create and stimulate demand renewal or 'aesthetic innovation', to borrow a term from Wolfgang Fritz Haug, is required; that is to say a seductive surface that is replaced from time to time (Haug 1986).

In Sweden, criticism of marketing was vigorous and led to comprehensive government reports. KF's new non-branded goods were precisely in line with the times as though answering this criticism. Paradoxically, the campaign can also be seen as a form of brand profiling if viewed from a marketing perspective. True, the aim was to reduce the costs of advertising and the renewal of packaging design. But in retrospect, the minutely planned launch seems just like a hugely effective marketing campaign. KF simply invested in publicity rather than traditional advertising. Even before the products were actually in the shops Sweden's national news agency, TT, reported on the forthcoming campaign. Some eighty daily newspapers reported positively on the campaign as a critical initiative in the face of the consumer society and both radio and TV reported enthusiastically (Protocol KF 1979).

The blue-and-white 'non-branded' brand is something of a contradiction since most purchasers are aware of the fact that KF is responsible for the products. And the products stand out from the other items in the shop through their packaging: their very simplicity makes the packaging highly noticeable. The original blue-and-white packaging continued to be used for ten years. In 1995 'Blåvitt' [Blue and White] was established as a brand and the new name was added to the packaging. This was, of course, a step that broke with the original idea of a non-branded range.

The final chapter in the Swedish story

KF is usually defined and discussed in terms of a democratic popular movement as well as a business (Hwang 1995). But the movement is also a brand. Indeed it may well be the strongest Swedish brand of the twentieth century, associated as it is with values like democracy, justice, solidarity and social responsibility, together with the growth of the Swedish welfare state.

Basically the cooperative movement's history has been a story of success. This success continued for seven decades. But in the 1970s KF lost market shares and financial losses grew. Nothing seemed able to change the downward spiral, neither organizational changes, changes to the name or clearance sales. Seen from today's perspective, the investment in basic and non-branded products can sound like the death knell of the cooperative movement. The initiative broke with the usual marketing strategies and was part of a larger wave of consumer criticism but should also be understood in relation to KF's educational heritage with regard to taste, as well as ideals of thrift.

The campaign fits into a public, normative tradition in Sweden in which function and need have represented what is true and good, while excess and gluttony represent what is vacuous and immoral. In the rhetoric there is a strong moral and normative element. All sorts of excess decoration were dismissed with disdain. Just as with the reformers of the 1930s there is a lack of awareness of the highly differing preferences of taste and of conditions of existence. Material and functional characteristics can, of course, be measured and tested, but taste and appearance are something highly subjective and a matter of social differentiation.

The design of the basic wares was defined as neutral, anonymous and timeless. The language used to describe the project is interesting in that it reveals underlying concepts and ideology. The question is, of course, whether the aesthetic really was neutral. The scaled-down style rather had roots in a modernist world of ideas and a tradition of dreams of an objective and universal aesthetic. From the horizon of the present day the basic products' 'timeless' aesthetic seems somewhat comic and highly typical of the period: polyester reeks of the 1970s and the design of the garments now seem dated.

The concept could not survive the reality of the market economy. If the 1970s are the era of idealism and anti-commercialism, then the 1980s are the heyday of materialism; at least as regards the consumer culture, and the Swedish virtue of thrift was abandoned.

There are many reasons for the fact that KF lost its dominant position. That the decline coincided with the transformation of Sweden's welfare state is, on the other hand, interesting. During the 1980s notions like the welfare state and the planned economy were seriously challenged. And in due course important aspects of the social models that had been built up after the war were abandoned. Central governmental control and regimentation were exchanged for freedom of choice and individual solutions.

From this time onwards it was not KF that furnished the Swedish home. Two companies that succeeded in doing this were H&M and IKEA. The former was introduced on the stock exchange in 1974 while, at the same time, IKEA was planning its international expansion. There are no visions or ideals attaching to these global corporations; rather hard-headed financial calculations. But the question as to what one can learn from the decline of KF and the success of H&M and IKEA is not easily answered.

Still, KF's programme of basic goods shows light on contemporary design culture. However, the ideas from the 1970s continue to play an important role in present critical design discourses regarding sustainability and consumer society even though the institutional foundation has changed.

References

Aléx, P. (1994), *Den rationella konsumenten. KF som folkuppfostrare 1899-1929*, Stockholm: Symposium.
Björkman, J. (2007), 'Rätten till det goda hemmet. Om bostadsinspektion i 1930-talets Stockholm', in C. Florin, E. Elgán and G. Hagemann (eds), *Den självstyrande medborgaren? Ny historia om rättvisa, demokrati och välfärd*, Stockholm: Institutet för framtidsstudier, 107–29.
Boman, M. (1976), 'Den vanligaste vanligheten', *Form* (8).
Brunnström, L. (2004), *Det svenska folkhemsbygget*, Stockholm: Arkitektur.
Brunnström, L. and Wagner, K. (2015), *Den (o)hållbara förpackningen*, Stockholm: Balkong.
Compilation of motions from the Consumer Congress, KF Archives, Stockholm.
Consumer Report (1978), 'Big Savings in Small Packages', June.
Giertz, E. and Strömberg, B. (1999), *Samverkan till egen nytta*, Stockholm: Prisma.

Göransdotter, M. (1999), 'Smakfostran och heminredning. Om estetiska diskurser och bildning till bättre boende i Sverige 1930-1955', in J. Söderberg and L. Magnusson (eds), *Kultur och konsumtion i Nordon 1750-1950*, Helsingfors: FHS.

Hallström, S. (2003), *Det är rätt att göra uppror*, Stockholm: Modernista.

Haug, F. W. (1986), *Critique of Commodity Aesthetics: Appearance, Sexuality and Advertising in Capitalist Society*, Cambridge: Polity [1971].

Henell, O. (1976), *Företagens reaktioner på konsumentpolitiken med sju praktikfall*, Stockholm: Rabén & Sjögren.

Hjalmarsson, H. (1967), 'Foreword' in the manual for programme, KF Archives.

Hwang, S. (1995), *Folkrörelse eller affärsföretag. Den svenska konsumentkooperationen 1945-1990*, Stockholm: Stockholm University.

Larsson, G. (1978), 'Äntligen – nu kommer basen', *VI* 34–5.

Massmediakontakt, K. F. (1979), *Varor till ständigt lågt pris*, Document, KF Archives.

Mattsson, H. (2012), 'Designing the "Consumer in Infinity": The Swedish Cooperative Union's New Consumer Policy, c. 1970', in K. Fallan (ed), *Scandinavian Design. Alternative Histories*, London: Berg.

Palmgren, C. (1977), 'Vad ska vi ta på oss Risto?', *VI* (2).

Protocol meeting, 24 January 1971, KF Archives.

CHAPTER SIX

Buying into the future:

A case study of a Danish brand of fashionable children's clothing

Trine Brun Petersen

In the first decade of the new millennium the Danish children's clothing industry experienced unprecedented growth and prosperity as a number of new fashion-oriented brands were launched. This chapter sets out to explore the character of Danish fashion and dress for children as a specific design cultural configuration through a case study of one particular brand, Katvig, which was founded in 2003 by Katrine Collette and Vigga Svensson. Katvig was characterized by its retro-aesthetic reminiscent of the 1970s, thus drawing both on parents' nostalgia for their own childhood and the vibe of recklessness and anti-establishment associated with the youth rebellion and its aftermath. Later Katvig became a pioneer in sustainable clothing, featuring activism and a politically tinted engagement in changing production and consumption patterns. In doing this, they used their marketing materials to conjure up a number of gloomy scenarios designed both to enlighten their customers and to prompt them to change their sartorial behaviour in a more sustainable direction. The production processes required for making conventional textiles were represented verbally and visually in order to impact the consumer's attitude towards children's clothing. In doing this, Katvig constituted a design cultural node, in which the perceived interaction between the sphere of production and the sphere of consumption was unusually tightly woven.

Framing the field of enquiry

The subject of this study is children's fashionable clothing as part of design culture (Highmore 2009; Julier 2014; Munch, Skou and Ebbesen 2015). This implies seeing fashionable clothing as part of a network made up of professional, institutional and commercial actors (Munch 2015: 10) as well as focusing on how the objects involved – the actual garments – are part of a larger design cultural network. As a discipline, Design Culture has tended to focus mostly on product design and design systems. The present study tentatively sets out to study fashionable clothing from the perspective of Design Culture.

Providing growing children with appropriate garb was once a constant concern to all but the most affluent families (Torell 2007). However, in the modern Western world children's clothing is now part of the fashion cycle with biannual collections, specialized media such as *Vogue Bambini* and trade fairs such as the Danish CIFF Kids. But even though children's fashion is organized much like fashion for adults, several differences still exist, especially in the design of the garments and their patterns of use and re-use. While children's garments are often marketed as fashion, the majority of the models remain the same season after season with only minimal adjustments being made such as changes in colours or patterns. In comparison with adults' fashion, the freedom of expression remains more limited for children's garments; probably in large part due to its vicarious nature, which allows parents to construct an idealized vision of childhood and generally rules out ambiguous and disturbing registers of meaning. Finally, the rapid growth of small children means that the child will often outgrow the garment before it is worn out, thus creating a vivid second-hand market and leading to informal circulation systems among friends and family members (Laitala and Klepp 2017). This creates a tension between children's garments as a durable consumer good and children's garments as fashion.

Studying children's fashionable clothing through the lens of Design Culture entails being mindful of both the commercial systems, which produce a sense of currency, and the cultural notions, which govern the children's sartorial expression. The present study does this by combining fashion scholarship with discourse analysis (Entwistle 1997; Torell 2007), which brings the culturally constructed notions of children and childhood to the fore. Design Culture acts as a flexible frame of enquiry, in which both the commercial and the cultural layers of children's fashion are addressed.

In the present study, Katvig is considered a 'design cultural configuration'. This is addressed on three levels: as an individual actor, that served as a hub for new sustainable production and consumption patterns; as part of the field of fashion (Bourdieu 1993; Bourdieu 1997; Entwistle and Rocamora 2006); and as an integral element of Danish design culture, particularly in relation to sartorial traditions, family structures and the discursive construction of childhood. The main focus is the company's efforts to influence their customers, the fashion industry and the political system to change their attitudes towards sartorial consumption. The study deals exclusively with the first ten years, when Katvig existed as an independent brand, and the material consists of: catalogues and other marketing material from 2004 to 2013; press coverage; and interviews with one of the founders, Vigga Svensson and one of the company's designers, who worked in the company from its seminal years to its sale in 2013.

The founding of Katvig

In the first years of the new millennium, a large number of brands offering children's wear emerged, the most high profile of which were Miniature (2002), Holly's (2002), Molo (2003), Småfolk (2004), Ej Sikke Lej (2004) and IdaT (2005). The trend was possibly sparked by the increase in the number of urban, double-income families with children. These brands constituted a new wave of fashion-conscious children's wear aimed at middle-class parents. Although catering to slightly different segments of the market, these brands were remarkably alike in the structure of their collections, their pricing, their models and their aesthetics (Figure 6.1).

The garments would generally be made in natural textiles, primarily cotton, often in stretchy qualities to afford the child full freedom of movement. In this sense, these brands would draw on a long Scandinavian tradition of providing children with practical, uncomplicated clothing (Torell 2007), which would support and promote the child as an active,

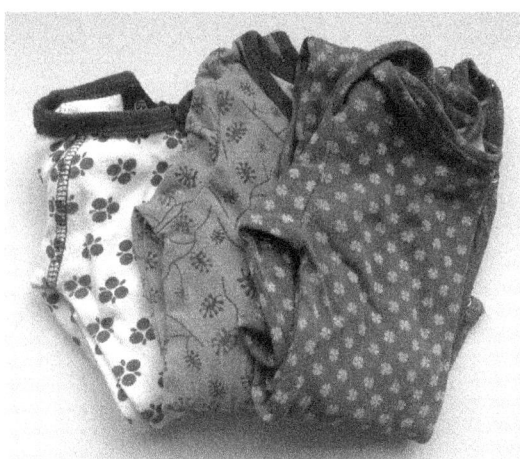

FIGURE 6.1 *A new wave of brands offering fashionable clothing for children aged 0–12 years entered the Danish market in the early noughties. The brands were generally characterized by their use of colourful patterns. Shown here are: Ej Sikke Lej, Katvig and Holly's. Photo by the author.*

autonomous being, whose self-directed development and explorative nature should not be hindered by formal or constricting garments. This attitude meant that the models would generally be rather simple in their cut and detailing, so much of the distinctiveness of the different brands originated from their use of lively, colourful patterns.

Katvig was a part of this wave of new, fashion-oriented children's wear. The company was founded in 2003 by Katrine Collette and Vigga Svensson and named after them both in a contraction of their first names. In 2003 the two founders had recently had a child each and found nothing in the market that appealed to their taste. Instead they decided to take matters into their own hands. In this process, they researched the state of the market for children's clothing, only to be convinced that it contained untapped

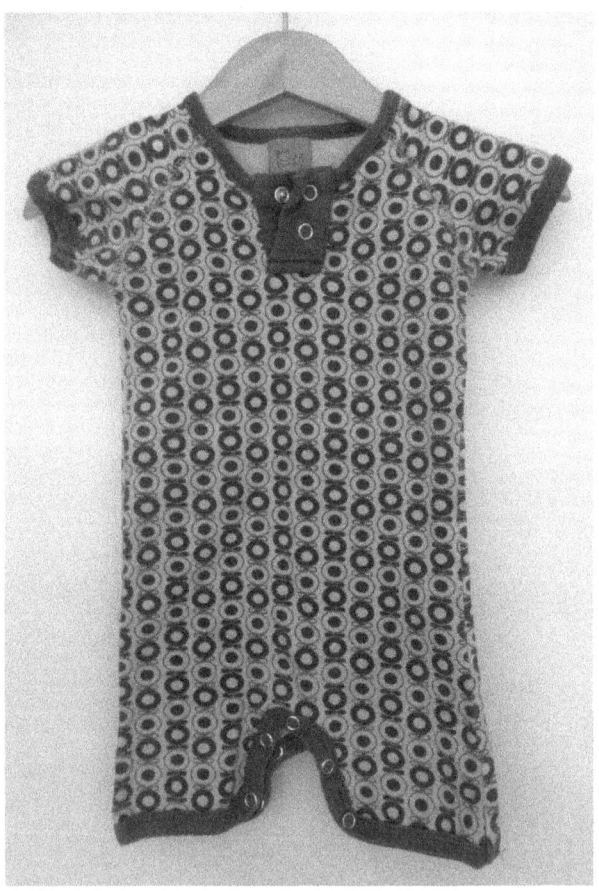

FIGURE 6.2 *Summer romper suit with the Katvig apple pattern. The apple was used in many sizes and combinations and became the trademark of the rm. Photo by the author.*

potential for the kind of clothing, which they had in mind. Following this realization, they decided to start their own company, even though neither of them had any formal training or experience in the fashion business. Initially they designed the garments themselves, but as the company experienced rapid growth, the production processes became more professionalized. Although the link to professional design discourses may have been informal, one of the founders had a background in media and communication. The flair for storytelling turned out to be one of the company's central assets and was essential throughout the company's existence.

This talent was evident from the 'founding myth', which eventually took shape and was recounted by the firm both in the press and in its marketing material. According to this narrative, the idea of starting a new brand of children's wear arose when Vigga Svensson came across an old piece of fabric in her mother's attic in her old Swedish farm. The fabric was printed with an apple pattern, featuring a simple, somewhat naive style (Figure 6.2). This apple was a recurring theme in Katvig's collections and was to become its trademark. The narrative of accidentally finding an old fabric struck central themes such as rural idyll, anti-commercialism and nostalgia, which remained prevalent during Katvig's years of existence and the story was often recounted by the firm both in the press and marketing material. In 2006 Vigga Svensson became the sole owner, and with time she came to play a prominent role as the company's public face, as an advocate for children's right to appropriate clothing and as an environmental activist pushing the boundaries for green transition.

Katvig as sartorial discourse

In terms of cut, materials and colour scheme, the overall aesthetic of Katvig drew heavily on the 1970s, a period of time generally appraised for its subversion of social standards and its vibe of recklessness and anti-fashion (Steele 1997). The brand offered two lines: Katvig Basic consisting of basic cotton models with either the apple pattern or stripes; and a fashion-oriented collection, in which the styles changed twice a year or more. Both lines were, however, generally simple, easy-to-wear and made to withstand the wear and tear, to which active kids subject clothes. The catalogues frequently emphasized this aspect by showing the clothing on children in motion: for example, jumping up and down on a trampoline (Katvig 2005) or in the gym (Katvig 2011b). The garments were typically made of soft, stretchy materials, which afforded full freedom of movement and were stripped of any frilly details such as ruffles, lace or bows. While the garments would generally construct the child as a self-directed, autonomous being, they were also carefully adapted to the conditions of modern double-income families. Thus all garments were machine-washable and made into materials that would render labour-intensive practices such as ironing superfluous. The clothing was not gender-neutral as such, but gender stereotypes were generally avoided. Colourful patterns were part of the core repertoire: especially the above-mentioned apple pattern, which was used in a wide variety of sizes and colour combinations. The inspiration from the 1970s was particularly evident in the choice of styles (e.g. overalls and parkas), materials such as denim and velour and the colour scheme, which consisted of orange, purple and brown. The catalogues espoused the same sensibility, using graphics, colours and locations reminiscent of the 1970s.

In doing this, Katvig was a part of a general retro-movement in fashion and design, which had been going on at least since the 1990s (Mackinney-Valentin 2010). Retro can be defined as a predilection for objects and styles from the recent past (Thorlacius 2009: 253) and can be found in many forms: from a somewhat eclectic taste for all things old to a systematic idolization of particular decades (Jenss 2004). In the case of Katvig, it was consistent inspiration from the 1970s, which allowed parents to commemorate their own childhood, while also providing high-standard, fashionable clothing for their children. The 1970s aesthetic was particularly predominant in the beginning, but started to wane as the aesthetic became more contemporary.

Towards sustainability

Katvig's formula of fashionable, yet practical clothing proved hugely successful and the brand quickly increased in size and turnover. The company gradually grew from a small, niche-brand to selling internationally with agents in Sweden, Norway, Iceland, the UK, the Netherlands, Belgium, Italy and Japan. This development demanded an increased professionalism in all areas of the company: from design and production to marketing. As the management gained more insight into the terms of production in the fashion and clothing business, it decided to take the company in a more sustainable direction.

The turning point for re-organization to sustainable production was in 2008, which was both the company's best year financially and the year when the new sustainable product lines were introduced. Initially the focus was on developing more sustainable production in terms of textile production, packing and shipping. The conversion from conventional to ecologically grown cotton was one of the main focus points, as was the use of recycled polyester in the company's performance wear. At this point, the information was rather technical, explaining the details of different eco-labels, how items were shipped or the chemical composition of different types of plastic.

In a Danish context, Katvig was a pioneer in sustainable clothing production, and therefore made considerable efforts to convince the retail sector, the consumers and the political establishment of the need for a more sustainable approach to fashionable clothing. The catalogues played a vital role in this, as they were used to announce the new sustainability initiatives to both dealers and end-users. In doing this, Katvig worked to create a sense of interest and concern among their consumers that this was in fact a problem worth both their attention and their money. This was done through visual and textual representations of conventional garment production, showing the harmful consequences to both nature and people: for example, deformed children or desolate landscapes ruined by the poisonous substances used to grow cotton. Images were often in the form of hand-drawings and small cartoons. The main point of this material was to link the abstract and distant processes with the consumer's everyday life, and to illustrate how seemingly innocent choices such as shopping for baby clothing, would have perceptible consequences on the other side of the planet.

This endeavour was particularly evident in a small leaflet titled "Katvig. A Story About the Time Vigga Wanted to Make Clothes that Didn't Make

FIGURE 6.3 *In 2010 Katvig published a small leaflet called Katvig. A Story About the Time Vigga Wanted to Make Clothes that Didn't Make Anyone Feel Bad. The story was published in a small, square format reminiscent of a well-known series of inexpensive children's books, widely available in the 1970s. The decision to tell the company's story as a cartoon and the somewhat naïve, simple text seem to suggest that the intended readers were children, but the sombre messages and gloomy scenarios (as well as the fact that the leaflet was published in English) indicated that the intended audience was more likely the parents. Photo by the author.*

Anyone Feel Bad" (Katvig 2010), which told the story of Katvig from the initial idea to its restructuring to sustainable production (Figure 6.3). The story was told as a cartoon, which showed Vigga as an advocate for children and an untiring champion for the environment and social justice. The leaflet emphasized the geo-political injustice in conventional textile production, showing the harmful consequences of modern, effective farming methods. One drawing showed a cotton field being fertilized with a poisonous substance, while two dark skinned children with physical birth defects were playing nearby. The cartoon drew attention to global inequality and how this affected the children of the world, and this fundamental conflict was solved by Vigga's ingenuity as she figured out how to make fashionable clothing without harming anyone. This geo-politic perspective was, however, combined with information, which focused on the comfort and health of the consumers' own children, and the term 'detoxed fashion' was coined (Katvig 2012: 6–7). The geo-political and the intimate perspective converged in an appeal to save the planet 'so our kids can have their own kids too' (Katvig 2007: 4).

As the financial crisis hit the Danish children's clothing industry hard in late 2008, Katvig also felt the economic hardship and the comprehensive, costly restructuring to more sustainable production and distribution were placed under pressure. This was evident from the 'editorial' of the Autumn/Winter 2009 catalogue, almost prophetic in its tone, which compared the strained economy to the much more fateful state of the planet:

> 2009 will be like a nightclub when they turn the volume to maximum. Those who cannot take it go elsewhere. The credit crunch is the great test that separates the sheep from the goats in the fields of fashionable sustainability. Katvig has one answer to starving Mother Earth that has been exploited by a crisis that has not lasted a couple of months, but a couple of centuries: we shall not let you down. ... If we, manufacturers, dealers and customers do not join forces, the nature will pay a price that in the end will cause a bankruptcy of such dimensions that the current financial crisis will look like an ant circus. (Katvig 2009: 3)

Thus Katvig advocated for focusing on the well-being of the planet rather than short-sighted economical concerns in accordance with the long-term, trans-generational perspective of its customers. In reaction to the imminent crisis, Katvig decided to take a more radical path in moving focus from the production chain to how the users would acquire, use, maintain and dispose of the garments, rather than compromising on their green transition.

Fashioning new patterns of consumption

Eventually, the rather technical approach to sustainability, which focused primarily on the production of ecological textiles and a green production chain, was superseded by an interest in the consumer's handling of the clothing. The ambition of influencing the consumer's behaviour after the garment had been bought represented a radical approach to the green transition as this demanded a transgression of the boundaries between corporate culture and the private sphere of the consumer. This was evident in Katvig's attempt to influence how the user would handle the ongoing maintenance of the garments. In the Autumn/Winter 2011 catalogue, Katvig focused on laundry processes. The consumer was told that laundry processes cause up to 85 per cent of a garment's impact on the environment, and Katvig offered advice on eco-friendly maintenance such as washing on low temperatures, using eco-friendly soap, omitting fabric softener, but retaining the labour-intensive practice of line-drying (Katvig 2011a: 26). In the same vein, Katvig also recommended a more thrifty approach to garment ownership by suggesting that users should repair torn garments rather than just throw them out (Katvig 2012: 6).

In an interview conducted in 2014, Vigga Svensson explained:

> After having worked with this for many years there is no doubt in my mind that a green supply chain ... that is important of course, but it won't save the world. It is not until you turn towards the world, of which the product will be a part, and you try to develop some sustainable solutions there, that things will start happening. I mean ... to be able to regulate behaviour and those things. That's where you will be able to really make a difference. (interview with Vigga Svensson 2014, translated by the author)

The need to educate consumers about the harmful consequences of conventional textile production resulted in the launching of a series of 'sustainability schools'. These were educational sessions, in which Vigga taught consumers about sustainable textile production, such as growing methods, water consumption, chemicals and different eco certificates. The schooling sessions were held in shops carrying Katvig garments, which could be bought afterwards. The sustainability schools were thus both an educational and a commercial initiative.

The sustainability schools were Katvig's first attempt to reach out to consumers through means that were more direct than the information campaigns in the catalogues. Katvig's next initiative focused on extending the life of its garments. Small children typically outgrow their garments before they are worn out, which can result in a structural problem of underuse. This structural problem is especially pertinent for children's fashionable clothing as the physical growth of the child and the processes of rapid stylistic obsolescence together make garments practically and culturally unfit before they are worn out. Having witnessed this dilemma, Katvig decided to focus on keeping their garments in circulation. To this end, they launched a number of swap parties, in which customers could swap out-grown clothing for new, pre-owned items. The invitation stated that:

Katvig's clothing is made to be worn. And as Katvig fans know, our clothes are almost impossible to wear out. So it is such a shame to think of the millions of pieces of clothing that have been sold by Katvig in our 9 years history, that might just be lying around in a box somewhere feeling lonely. (Katvig 2013: 6–7, translated by the author)

This passage emphasizes both the utility value and the enduring qualities of Katvig's garments and personified them, suggesting that they were feeling 'lonely', thus spurring parents to take action with a mixture of thrift and compassion. The swapping took place at an event, where users could bring their out-grown garments, which were converted to so-called swap-coins, which could then be used to buy new items. The concept aimed at creating more controlled, more effective processes for the circulation of used children's wear in order to extend the garments' effective service life. Katvig planned to take this idea even further by developing a fully circular system of children's wear, in which pre-packaged wardrobes for children could be rented and returned when no longer needed. In 2013 they received the Danish Ministry of Environment's CSR Environment Prize for this initiative.

However, it was never realized, because in 2013 Katvig was unexpectedly declared bankrupt, allegedly due to an old debt to the bank. While it is tempting to interpret this as an indication that Katvig's activistic approach was not financially viable, this would probably be too simplistic. Although its cultural impact may have exceeded its economical significance, its demise was most likely a convergence of circumstances rather than the inevitable result of an overly idealistic business strategy. After the bankruptcy, Katvig was taken over by JOHA, an established actor in the Danish children's wear industry. Meanwhile the founder of Katvig, Vigga Svensson, went on to launch a subscription service for baby and children's clothing, which would further develop the idea of circulating used clothing among multiple users (Petersen and Riisberg 2017).

Shrinking the design cultural circuit

Throughout its ten years of existence as an independent brand, Katvig evolved from being a fashionable retro-brand to an advocate for sustainable fashion, both in terms of production and consumption. During this period, Katvig offered a mix of staple garments, which remained the same season after season, while also offering more current models to reflect changing fashions. Katvig also struck a careful balance between appealing to parents with an urban progressive life style and educating them about the harmful consequences of the fashion industry. In this process, the owner, Vigga Svensson became a prominent public activist, who tirelessly fought for the rights of the children, the workers in the textile industry and the planet. The company did this by skilfully mastering the objects themselves, the textual representations and the images, each of which offered different potential for conveying meaning. The garments themselves evoked the idea of childhood as an unspoiled realm of freedom and happiness, while the more unsettling messages of social injustice and impending ecological catastrophe were present only in the marketing materials' textual and visual representations and directed to the adult customers. Thus the vicarious nature of children's fashionable garments was evident in Katvig's efforts to endow their products with notions of nostalgia and freedom, while also influencing the fashion industry and consumers in general.

Through the years, Katvig gradually changed from being a traditional fashion brand to being a politically tinted movement, mobilizing progressive parents to act on behalf of the environment and their children's future. This was done by working through all levels of the products' life cycle: from how the cotton was grown and the distribution to patterns of use and re-use. Through the use of dystopic representations of traditional garment production, the sphere of production and the sphere of consumption were brought to influence each other in a contraction of the different nodes of the products life cycle. This contraction was tailored to provide the customers with a sense of insight into the production processes; an insight, which would counteract the neo-liberal conditions of modern-day design culture by fostering a sense of geographical proximity, emotional closeness and trust in the production system on which they relied. Essentially, Katvig worked to visually and mentally shrink the distance between production and consumption by constructing Vigga Svensson as a guarantor for a fair and responsible production process. By doing this, Katvig offered parents a sense of control: not only in terms of how the garments were produced, but also a much further-reaching notion that their consumer choices would be enough to ensure a safe, fair and pleasant world for their children to grow up in. No attempts were made, however, to move production back to Denmark or in other ways change the geographical circumstances of the modern fashion industry.

Children's clothing is a particularly intimate and emotional field of consumption, but the cultural ideal of close-knit, simple and transparent production systems, which the case demonstrates, seem to be a general feature of current design culture. While many design companies, whether renowned, start-up and craft-like enterprises, have moved their production to low-income countries outside Europe, their marketing materials or branding strategies rarely highlight that fact. The case has demonstrated that while close-knit production systems may be economically outplayed, they nonetheless remain a cultural ideal that can be employed to gain competitive edge.

Katvig was characterized by a far-reaching ambition of commercial success and cultural impact, which makes it a rich case for the study of fashion as part of design culture at large. This study has shown that fundamental fashion issues, such as the body, self-presentation and temporality, can readily be integrated into a Design Cultural framework, and has demonstrated that fashionable garments share many concerns with other parts of the design culture. The company's commercial and cultural endeavours have served as the focal point for an exploration of the practices, norms and values of contemporary design culture. The case has yielded insight into the production and consumption patterns of children's fashionable clothes and the attempt to counteract the alienated nature of modern, neo-liberal design culture by shrinking the design cultural circuit.

References

Bourdieu, P. (1997), 'Haute couture og finkultur', in P. Bourdieu (ed.), *Men hvem skabte skaberne? - Interviews og forelæsninger*, Copenhagen: Akademiske håndbøger, 200–09.
Bourdieu, P. and Johnson, R. (1993), *The Field of Cultural Production: Essays on Art and Literature*, Oxford: Polity Press.
Entwistle, J. (1997), 'Power Dressing and the Construction of the Career Woman', in M. Nava, A. Blake, I. MacRury and B. Richards (eds), *Buy this Book. Studies in Advertising and Consumption*, London: Routledge, 311–23.
Entwistle, J. and Rocamora, A. (2006), 'The Field of Fashion Materialized: A Study of London Fashion Week', *Sociology. The Journal of the British Sociological Association,* 40(4): 735–51. doi:10.1177/0038038506065158.
Highmore, B. (2009), *The Design Culture Reader*, London: Routledge.
Jenss, H. (2004), 'Dressed in History: Retro Styles and the Construction of Authenticity in Youth Culture', *Fashion Theory: The Journal of Dress, Body & Culture*, 8(4): 387–403. doi:10.2752/136270404778051591.
Julier, G. (2014), *The Culture of Design*, London: SAGE Publications Ltd.
Katvig (2005), *Fall/Winter 05*, Copenhagen: Katvig.
Katvig (2007), *Katvig Autumn/Winter 07*, Copenhagen: Katvig
Katvig (2009), *Katvig Autumn/Winter 09*, Copenhagen: Katvig.
Katvig (2010), *A Story about the Time Vigga Wanted to Make Clothes that Didn't Make Anyone Feel Bad*, No Place: Katvig.
Katvig (2011a), *Autumn/Winter 11*, Copenhagen: Katvig.
Katvig (2011b), *Spring/Summer 11*, Copenhagen: Katvig.
Katvig (2012), *Autumn/Winter 12*, Copenhagen: Katvig.
Katvig (2013), *Katvig Spring/Summer Pre-autumn*, Copenhagen: Katvig.
Laitala, K. and Klepp, I. G. (2017), 'Clothing Reuse: The Potential in Informal Exchange', *Clothing Cultures*, 4(1): 61–77. doi:10.1386/cc.4.1.61_1.
Mackinney-Valentin, M. (2010), 'Old News? Understanding Retro Trends in 21st Century Fashion', *Multi: The RIT Journal of Plurality & Diversity in Design*, 3(1): 67–84.
Munch, A. V. (2015), 'Designkultur som analyse', in A. V. Munch, N. P. Skou and T. R. Ebbesen (eds), *Designkulturanalyser*, Odense: Syddansk Universitetsforlag, 9–25.

Munch, A. V., Skou, N. P. and Ebbesen, T. R. (eds) (2015), *Designkulturanalyser*, Odense: Syddansk Universitetsforlag.

Petersen, T. B. and Riisberg, V. (2017), 'Cultivating User-ship? Developing a Circular System for the Acquisition and Use of Baby Clothing', *Fashion Practice*, 9(2): 214–34. doi:10.1080/17569370.2017.1313600.

Steele, V. (1997), 'Anti-fashion: The 1970s', *Fashion Theory: The Journal of Dress, Body & Culture*, 1(3): 279–96.

Thorlacius, L. (2009), 'Indie eller klassisk retro? Retromodens værdi og æstetiske status blandt danske unge', in H. D. Christensen and H. Illeris (eds), *Visuel kultur. Viden, liv, politik*, København: Multivers, 252–68.

Torell, V. B. (2007), *Folkhemmets barnkläder: Diskurser om det klädda barnet under 1920 - 1950-talen*, Göteborg: Arkipelag c/o Etnologiska Föreningen i Västsverige.

CHAPTER SEVEN

The Glowing Black of fritz-kola: Aestheticization in design culture

Mads Nygaard Folkmann

This chapter addresses the role of aesthetics and aestheticization in contemporary design culture. Through analysing the case of the German soft drink company fritz-kola, I will discuss how aesthetic elements and mechanisms of aestheticization contribute to constructing the meaning of design in a cultural context. Consequently, I will make a plea for aesthetics as a relevant entry into investigating aspects of design culture, especially how design objects appeal to consumers and how consumers in this process are engaged in the meaning articulation of the actual design.

In its philosophical formulation, derived from Kant's *Kritik der Urtheilskraft* (1790) and further back to the British empiricists of the eighteenth century, *aesthetics* provides a framework for looking into the relationship between a perceiving subject and coded objects with certain qualities or features regarding form, sensory appeal or reflective potential. In a perspective of investigating contemporary design culture, this kind of relationship can be actualized in an analysis of the way the consumer is appealed to through the qualities of specific objects. Furthermore, the aesthetic meaning of design is not only created by inherent qualities in the objects themselves, which may be disclosed when the consumer relates to and engages with the objects, but may be encouraged by the surroundings and contextual setting of the objects – for example by the staging in advertising, shopping environments and brand spaces. With the term *aestheticization*, we can designate the cultural-contextual process of creating new conditions for experiencing aesthetic meaning in a historical perspective, focusing on how form repertoires of art enter everyday culture (Featherstone 1991), and contemporary media culture (Oldemeyer 2008).

In the following, I will investigate how aesthetics plays a role in contemporary design culture when this presents itself not just as a culture of design, but also reflexively as a *designed* design culture' (Julier 2014: 246) aware of its own conditions and opportunities in producing and articulating cultural meaning through design. In particular, I will look into how mechanisms of aestheticization can promote a cultural construction of new conditions for the way consumers experience aesthetic qualities of design. In this, I will look into the *cultural construction of aesthetics* in relation to design.

I will do that in three steps. First, I will present the case of fritz-kola, as the strategies of this company lay the foundation of the analysis. Next, I will analyse how fritz-kola works with means of aestheticization to create a sensually appealing as well as self-reflective profile for the company. The 'dark' universe of fritz-kola contains sensually seductive elements, while also being reflectively 'cool'. Through the analysis, I aim to prove the hypothesis that companies in contemporary design culture may impose perceptual patterns on consumers by aesthetic means. Consumers learn how to perceive the expressions of the companies. Concluding the article, I will discuss the potential of aesthetics as a concept relevant for analysing design in its cultural context within the disciplinary frameworks of Design Culture and Design History.

fritz-kola

fritz-kola was founded in Hamburg in 2002 by the entrepreneurs Mirco Wolf Wiegert and Lorenz Hampel as a project to make a living in a way where the company owners could spent a lot of time in cafés – at least so the story goes, or rather, such is the story put out by the company and reproduced uncritically in a series of media (e.g. Kaiser 2005; Roβbach 2009). The original product was a cola with a high amount of caffeine, 'vielviel koffein', 25 mg/100 ml, and was initiated, again according to the self-representation of the company, through dissatisfaction with existing cola products, especially Coca-Cola which is a large brand on the German market. Since then, the product range has expanded to light and stevia versions of the cola and several fruit flavours. Furthermore, the products are positioned as 'gourmet' products and due to this, they only come in rather small bottles, in a 250 ml German standard bottle, a 200 ml specially designed fritz-kola bottle (since 2008) and a 500 ml bottle with a screw cap (since 2014). The cola is 'gourmet' because of its taste and use contexts, whereas the other products – for example lemon, apple-cherry-elderflower or melons – are 'gourmet' because of having a large content of fruit juice. The claim of being 'gourmet' is one side of the coin; the other side is the attachment to 'coolness' and 'darker' values in relation to party culture, drug use and youth.

Two phases of company development

Since its beginning, the company has grown and at least two phases can be detected in its marketing strategies and market positioning. In the first entrepreneurial phase, the company created its path into the market through provocative campaigns, with ads pointing to systems of meaning in relation to the use of drugs, sexual excess, party and festival culture, youth and subculture. In this way, a continuous slogan has been 'koksen ist achtziger', 'doing cocaine is so 1980s' (Figure 7.1). In its initial setting, the brand colour is black. The colour of the cola functions as a reference for

FIGURE 7.1 *'Doing cocaine is so 1980s'. fritz-kola communicates through provocative statements.*

fritz-kola®

FIGURE 7.2 *fritz-kola logo, 2016. The grinning faces of the founders have been omitted. The logo appears as a clear identification of the brand name.*

the colour of the packaging and the background of the ads, and an abstract graphic representation of the faces of the two company owners is a part of the logo and is displayed on all of the bottles: this personifies the brand and they look at you, grinning ironically, while you drink the cola. In the launch campaign in 2002, a scene of sexual excess is depicted, where fritz-kola is taken to ensure 'long nights', accompanied by a picture of a man with the head of a horse and a woman in an ecstatic mode. This kind of ad not only displays a celebration of sexual excess, but also the kind of reflective language to be found in modern advertising, where consumers are seduced by the visual and linguistic codes of the ads themselves (cf. Leiss et al. 2005), and not by the simple means of identifying, for example with either the man/ horse or the woman of the scene. The launch campaign set the scene for the conscious work of the company with reflective, often ironic, advertising with an explicit reference to excess and party culture.

The second phase was a phase of consolidation; just as the brand has grown and the target audiences have widened from specific groups in subcultures and the nightlife of Hamburg to be more mainstream in Germany and abroad, the brand expression has also changed. In its new version, which in Spring 2018 was not yet fully implemented, the logo features an inversion of colours of the original logo, as the text 'fritz-kola' now appears in black. In addition, the faces of the two founders, the name of the city of origin and the slogan 'vielviel koffein' have disappeared; the company name *is* now the logo (Figure 7.2). The 'darker' tones of party and excess are still a part of the brand values of the company, and 'vielviel koffein' and 'koksen ist achtziger' are still used as slogans in campaigns. But there has been a slight change of tone; as an example, the company doesn't identify itself today with the launch campaign.

Cultural positioning

In another slogan it says that 'feiern ist das neue arbeiten' ('partying is the new work'); the combination of soft drinks and the party culture, which can also be testified to by the visibility of the brand in its local neighbourhoods of St. Pauli and Schanzenviertel in Hamburg, may seem strange, but has its reasons. On a functional level, a cola is not a product to be consumed by children, as also stated by Mirco Wolf Wiegert (Wiegert 2013a). On a level of symbolic meaning, the slogan testifies not only to an exploration of the value universe of partying and so on, but also to the process of attaching this to the brand. fritz-kola is a typical modern company in the sense that the meaning articulation of the products is everything and the generic qualities of each product are not that important. The identity of fritz-kola lies primarily in its symbolic meaning potential.

As indicated by the slogans and the reflexive advertising, fritz-kola aims to engage in a dynamic relationship with its consumers, not only in their minds, but also through social media, where consumers are encouraged to take part in the meaning formulation of the brand. Both in research and in the practice of companies, it is established today as a tenet that consumption is not a pacifying act, as believed in early consumer research, but provides the opportunity for people to engage actively in a process of de-alienating the products and re-formulating and rearticulating the meaning potential of a given product in new and sometimes unforeseen ways (e.g. Miller 1987). While also encouraging the consumers to have active engagement with the brand, fritz-kola aims to provide a controlled framework for this. Consumers can contribute to the brand by, for example, uploading images with a setting of fritz-kola products in staged tableaux using the visual language of the brand, but the company has the power to define and steer this process through its strong visual coding. fritz-kola frames the consumer in a process of *controlled prosumption*, where the brand values never leave the control of the company.

My entry into and interest in the brand universe of fritz-kola took their starting point in its provocative tone, and the subsequent analysis will consequently relate to the related values of the brand, as well as its self-reflective element. I started noticing the presence of the brand in Berlin around 2010 and I have been on a field trip to Hamburg with research assistant Camilla Rothmann Lorentzen to interview Mirco Wolf Wiegert and experience the brand in its original and originating environment (Folkmann & Lorentzen 2015).

Aestheticization

In this section I will ask by which means fritz-kola aestheticizes. What kind of aesthetic meaning does fritz-kola draw upon in order to appeal to consumers? As a starting point, we may talk of aesthetics on three different levels of meaning production in relation to design: (i) as the sensual appeal of the concrete expressions, material or visual; (ii) as the way aesthetic media are not just transparent vehicles for transmission of definite meaning contents, but refract, reflect and challenge meaning; and (iii) in terms of aestheticization, how this process of articulation of aesthetic meaning is being framed by the cultural factors surrounding the design in question (Folkmann 2013). As mentioned, the term 'aestheticization' may in general describe the cultural-contextual process of creating new conditions for experiencing aesthetic meaning. In the company perspective of fritz-kola, aestheticization may describe the process of making something to have an aesthetic meaning content and of positioning and communicating this as having an aesthetic meaning content, whether in relation to being perceived as having a specific sensual appeal or being conceptually challenging.

In a theoretical reflection, aestheticization raises the question of which possibilities of sensual experience are determined by aesthetic media. This approach is represented by cultural theorist Jacques Rancière, who investigates aesthetics as a power issue in relation to the distribution of sensual material. Thus, aesthetics can be seen as 'a delimitation of spaces and times, of the visible and the invisible, of speech and noise' (Rancière 2004: 13). To enter a discussion of aestheticization is to look at how the interface with which we meet the world is changing as a result of strategies of making objects and surfaces more sensually appealing, applying aesthetic coding, and to ask how this process affects experience. Design may be employed to make objects and environments sensually appealing and/or conceptually challenging, and through an attribution of symbolic meaning can play a social and cultural role in people's construction of their identities.

Dimensions of aestheticization

The next step is to look at different strategies in design to contribute to and perform the act of aestheticization and, subsequently, relate these to fritz-kola. In *The Aesthetics of Imagination in Design*, I propose a framework of investigating aestheticization in terms of reflectivity and simulation versus non-reflectivity and realism, while relating these concepts to a span of materiality versus immateriality (Folkmann 2013: 64). The combination of these describes various strategies in the field of aestheticization. With regard to the material dimension of design, a span exists between affirming existing object design (things as they are) and challenging the distribution of the sensual material (things as they could be). With regard to the immaterial, meaning-oriented dimension of design, another span can be detected between distributing, but not creating meaning by means of design (meaning as it is) and challenging meaning and its distribution (meaning as it could be). By this, we may ask how the creation of aesthetic meaning is being framed by processes of distributing not only sensual material in terms of designed objects, but also affiliated discourses pointing to and evoking the meaning potential of the objects.

So how does fritz-kola aestheticize? In its strategies of design and mediation, the company attempts to define the cultural setting and understanding of its products. On this point, the company employs aesthetic means in both its highly reflective ads and campaigns, and also the sensual-tactile appeal of the material and graphic design, which beyond its references to Modernist minimalism, for example in the Bauhaus-inspired typeface employing only minuscules (Wiegert 2013b), creates a product setting stressing the black colour as glowing of dark desire. Just like much of modern advertising, the marketing strategy operates through creating a high degree of simulation, that is, a sense of a reality created by images and 'a generation by models of a real without origin or reality' (Baudrillard 2009: 166). In this way, fritz-kola has created its own environment of a sensual appeal to a never-ending desire, which is marked through-and-through by a reflection of the ads as a site of meaning production in its own right. fritz-kola not only affirms the given, things as they are, but on the level of material appearance, challenges the distribution of sensual material.

Furthermore, fritz-kola *aims* to challenge discourse, in the sense that the impact of the brand not only is the creation of material surfaces of meaning, but even more is a production of a cultural outlook on things. The brand aims not only to reflect culture, but also to evoke new kinds of cultural meaning. The highly reflective ads play a central role in this process of creating 'meaning as it could be'. In their act of communication, they operate on a referential and meta-referential level at the same time. At one level, they often display the product very directly – for example cola bottles – probably in order to make them recognizable for purchase. At another level, the ads offer a reflexive play with the code of creative advertising. The innovative slogans attract attention to themselves as sites of meaning production. This double strategy is a way to meet the challenge that fritz-kola is aiming to advertise to an audience of young and cool consumers who wish to be without advertising (Wiegert 2013a). Paradoxically, fritz-kola's solution is to intensify the communication of the advertising. We are never in doubt that the ads are ads. But even if the ads *qua ads* often display the products, their function is also to be reflective mirrors for the lifestyle aspirations of the young and cool. They are reflexive sites for the construction of cultural meaning. As in a lot of contemporary advertising, the enchantment of the ads is evoked by their reflexive play with the code of communication. Furthermore, words with direct affiliation to being modern, cool, hip, hipster and so on are abandoned in the advertising, as once these words were spoken out, the product would lose its connection to these words (Wiegert 2013a).

Moreover, fritz-kola aims to aestheticize in domains beyond the ads. First, the sensual aspects of the brand and its reflective positioning have a physical and local presence in Hamburg, as the brand is highly visible at bars and cafés in St. Pauli and Schanzenviertel, which – in a strong interpretation of this – may have the character of a brand space for the company. fritz-kola is present through signs and concepts for bars such as ex-sparr (Figure 7.3) and outdoor advertising, often with a provocative tone, like when deliberately making a wordplay of being fucked (',wenn man im arsch ist' literally means being 'in the ass') in a gay area of Hamburg (Figure 7.4).

FIGURE 7.3 *The ex-sparr bar in the St. Pauli neighbourhood features fritz-kola at the façade along with the beer brand Astra. The bar menu next to the entry door is set with the fritz-kola typeface. Photo: Camilla Rothmann Lorentzen.*

FIGURE 7.4 *Provocative presence in the public space in Hamburg; it says that fritz-kola makes you awake when you are 'in the ass' © fritz-kola.*

fritz-kola does not have a brand store of its own, but has (certain parts of) Hamburg. The presence in the cityscape may confirm the shift in branding strategies described by Liz Moor from the 'more obvious cognitive work of persuasion', which also may be an effect of the advertising, to a 'renewed emphasis on the tactility and materiality of communication, and its capacity to affect people at the level of perception and affect' (Moor 2007: 38). By being physically and visually present in the cityscape of not only Hamburg, but also other cities in Germany, fritz-kola aestheticizes by offering a specific context and mode of experiencing the aesthetic qualities of the brand.

Secondly, the aesthetic setting of the company is staged and reformulated by consumers in social media, such as Facebook and Instagram. On Instagram, a complex interplay of production and consumption can be detected: consumers are *active* producers of design mediations and engage in a process of creative prosumption, as they productively co-articulate the meaning of the brand through producing image tableaux (Figure 7.5), while in its strategies of aestheticization, the company defines and controls the frame for this process. This kind of active contribution of the consumer was unknown in the research into the production-consumption relationship until the digital revolution (e.g. McCracken 1988; Walker 1989; du Gay et al. 1997), and is new in terms of design mediations as channels of 'mediating between producers and consumers, and forming consumption practices and

FIGURE 7.5 *fritz-kola on Instagram. Consumers communicate with each other by using hashtags – for example #fritzkola – and produce images clearly within the black-and-white universe of the company.*

ideas about design' (Lees-Maffei 2009: 366). In the social media, a frame is set for a reflective space of creation of meaning simulation, a game with aesthetic signs, originated by fritz-kola, but circulated, reformulated and re-articulated by the consumers. Mirroring the analysis of the relation of things and media in Scott Lash & Celia Lury's *Global Culture Industry*, fritz-kola can be seen as a product that takes place in a 'media-environment' (Lash & Lury 2007: 9). The *thingness* of the product is transformed into media expressions in the form of aesthetic signs, mutable within a fixed frame. In this way fritz-kola is a product created for a contemporary circulation of visual expressions in different kinds of media.

Categories of aestheticization

At a more general level, we may ask how cultural meaning is produced by aesthetic means and what these means are. In her study of contemporary art and culture, *Our Aesthetic Categories*, cultural theorist and professor of English, Sianne Ngai, investigates the categories that frame aesthetic judgements. Her starting point is that 'aesthetic experience has been transformed by the hypercommodified, information-saturated, performance-driven conditions of late capitalism' (Ngai 2012: 1). Quite rightly, she points out the fact that aesthetic categories are variable and she suggests that the major aesthetic categories of the late eighteenth century, such as beauty and the sublime, are in part replaced with the new, minor and more 'trivial' categories of the *cute*, the *zany* and the *interesting*. She talks of a 'commodity aesthetic of cuteness', a 'discursive field of the interesting' and a 'performative aesthetic of zaniness' (Ngai 2012: 1). Basically, these categories are about production, circulation and consumption, where the *zany* is related to production at the interplay of work and play and also to effect and emotion, the *interesting* relates to the distribution of information, and the *cute* deals with a 'paradoxical complexity of our desire for a simpler relationship with our commodities' – for example in terms of intimacy and care (Ngai 2012: 13).

Ngai's notion is that aesthetic experience in our 'hyper-aestheticized world' has changed from deriving its models from art and the beautiful/sublime to being based on 'the stylistic triviality and verdictive equivocality of the zany, the cute, and the interesting' (Ngai 2012: 19). As in tradition, aesthetic experience is no longer about distance, play or disinterestedness. Ngai points out that the aesthetic categories are 'subjective and objective, evaluative and descriptive, conceptual and perceptual' (Ngai 2012: 29), and that they operate both as judgements and as objective styles. Or, to be more precise: styles are culturally produced and codified as such, and they have a bearing on 'our perception of them as stylistic qualities' and, vice versa, our perception affects 'our language of aesthetic judgment' (Ngai 2012: 29). In the end, a style is not just a matter of the object in question, but can be understood as a way of 'perceiving an object' (Ngai 2012: 29),that is, it can be seen as producing a specific perceptual setting.

My point in introducing Ngai into this discussion of aestheticization and fritz-kola is basically twofold. First, with her framework we can clearly see that the aesthetic categories of contemporary design culture, such as in fritz-kola, have changed. Whereas in Ngai's view, 'beauty' tends to mask the dependence of the aesthetic on the non-aesthetic and mundane, 'the interesting, the cute, and the zany make it explicit' (Ngai 2012: 43). Contemporary aesthetics is not niche aesthetics of separate spheres of art, but broadly relates to meaning production in everyday life. In this way, Ngai's approach aligns with the basic thesis in the historical approach to aestheticization that the high culture of artistic expressions has gradually been integrated into the low culture of everyday culture (Featherstone 1991). Something as mundane and commercially oriented as a soft drink brand like fritz-kola may operate through a variety of aesthetic means with sensual appeal in ads and spaces and through self-reflective ads challenging given concepts.

Second, our attention is drawn to learning which aesthetic categories fritz-kola operates through and that the company not only reflects these categories stylistically, but *actively produces their frame of judgement* (see also Folkmann & Jensen 2017). In the visual language of the ads and in the social communication, which actively define cultural parameters, fritz-kola establishes ways of perceiving the products, that is, their style and the reflective judgement of them. As a part of the commodity sphere, fritz-kola could apply to the 'malleable or easily deformable' of the *cute*, but in its reflectivity it rather engages in – and produces – the activity and incessant flow of the *zany* and the temporal-anticipatory of the *interesting*: it is more interesting than cute!

fritz-kola is a company creating a structure of meaning around its products that produces the categories of how to perceive the *relationship* between the brand as an aesthetic product for consumers to engage actively with *and* the conditions of contemporary culture. By this, fritz-kola aestheticizes not only by producing reflective simulation, but also by engaging in a production of the aesthetic categories of the *interesting* and *zany* that frames and stages the perception of its meaning.

Aesthetics and Design Culture

In this concluding section, I will reflect upon the insights gained when engaging with and employing aesthetic concepts in analysing design within a framework of cultural contextualization. Regarding this framework, the focus has been on studying the relationship between production, design practice and consumption, whether it would be in a context of Cultural

Studies (du Gay 1997), the discipline of Design Culture (Highmore 2009, Julier 2014), or Design History (e.g. Fallan 2010).

Remarkably, aesthetics as a concept for entering, analysing and understanding design has often been marginalized within these frameworks. In its formulation as an independent discipline in the 1970s and 1980s, especially in the UK, Design History has primarily promoted the analysis of cultural, social, economic and political contexts for design (e.g. Dilnot 1984, Walker 1989). Within these frameworks, aesthetics has mostly been seen as affiliated with art history and with superficial stylistic changes of form without a connection to context (Lees-Maffei 2014). The reason for this has, in part, been the need for the discipline to find itself at a distance from traditional art-historian approaches. Within the context of Design Culture, aesthetics has primarily been seen as a matter of sociologically based 'taste' in the tradition from Bourdieu, or through Wolfgang Fritz Haug's critical concept of 'aesthetic illusion' (cf. Haug 2009) as a way of describing how the appearance of products makes promises about their performance (Julier 2014: 76). However, in the latest edition of *The Culture of Design*, Guy Julier states that 'studying design culture opens up a potential to vigorously and thoughtfully reintroduce questions of aesthetics into its related academic fields' (250). This reintroduction remains a deficit, as does the investigation of the role of aesthetics in a broader cultural context of design. Attempts to reach a cultural understanding of the role of aesthetics, though, have been made in theories investigating aesthetics in the context of everyday life, for example in the recent movement of 'everyday aesthetics' (Saito 2010; Leddy 2012), or through critiquing the commercial aesthetics of consumer goods (Haug 2009).

I would argue that aesthetics does play a central role in the cultural circuit of design and may function as a mark of quality for designers, manufacturers and consumers. Also, the concept has been highlighted within axiology as one of several values that consumers would attach to goods (Throsby 2001, Holbrook 1999). In consumer studies, aesthetics has gained interest as a motor for consumption practices (e.g. Charters 2006; Venkatesh & Meamber 2008) without, however, a cultural and contextual understanding of design. As an approach to the analysis of design and the cultural settings of design, the interest in aesthetics may methodologically lead to insights into *how objects are coded in order to create appeal to consumers*, how this is evoked by sensual means of for example form and material and/or by means of being conceptually challenging, and how this may be staged in various ways and through various means by different actors in the circuit around the products, for example by companies and consumers on social media platforms. In this cultural understanding of aesthetics, the focus is not on changes in form and style, even if these may play a role, but on aesthetic coding as a vehicle for cultural expressions and framing of experience. As stated in the analysis of fritz-kola, to take an aesthetic approach to the cultural-contextual analysis of design means that the focus is not only on the *aesthetics* of objects, but also on the *mechanism of aestheticization* when actors and media in the circuit of design construct aesthetic meaning to be attached to objects. Not only may the mechanisms of aestheticization by companies be investigated, but also the contribution of consumers when they engage actively through aesthetic means in a process of re-formulating and rearticulating the meaning potential of a given product in new and sometimes unforeseen ways.

In many respects, fritz-kola may not be exceptional as a case of contemporary design culture, as many companies operate with the same means for staging their products in settings that attribute the products with cultural meaning. Entering the analysis of fritz-kola with aesthetic concepts, it can be described *how* the company performs this attribution of meaning. Analysed with concepts deriving from aesthetic theory, the company operates through a reflective aestheticization, carried out in both the physical and the virtual space. In this way, fritz-kola is an example of how a company in contemporary design culture aims to impose perceptual patterns on consumers by aesthetic means. The company creates a reflective simulation which challenges given meaning, while at the same time it challenges this meaning by producing and framing aesthetic categories with which the world is perceived. fritz-kola creates a framework that constructs an *interesting*, that is also reflective, *zany*, that is also provocative, and indeed an *un-cute* product of the Glowing Black.

References

Baudrillard, J. (2009), 'Simulacra and Simulations', in M. Poster (ed.), *Selected Writings*, Cambridge: Polity Press, 166–84.
Charters, S. (2006), 'Aesthetic Products and Aesthetic Consumption: A Review', *Consumption Markets & Culture*, 9(3): 235–55.
Dilnot, C. (1984), 'The State of Design History, Part I: Mapping the Field'. *Design Issues*, 1(1): 4–23.
Fallan, K. (2010), *Design History. Understanding Theory and Method*, Oxford: Berg.
Featherstone, M. (1991), *Consumer Culture and Postmodernism*, London: Sage.
Folkmann, M. N. (2013), *The Aesthetics of Imagination in Design*, Cambridge, MA: MIT Press.
Folkmann, M. N. and Lorentzen, C. R. (2015). 'Med sort som forgrund. Design, subkulturel appel og branding hos fritz-kola', in A. Munch, N. P. Schou and T. R. Ebbesen (eds), *Designkulturanalyser*, Odense: Syddansk Universitetsforlag, 181–204.
Folkmann, M. N. and Jensen, H. C. (2017), 'Design and the Question of Contemporary Aesthetic Experiences'. *Design Philosophy Papers* 15(2): 133–144.
du Gay, P. Hall, S., Janes, L. and Mackay, H. (eds) (1997), *Doing Cultural Studies. The Story of the Sony Walkman*, London: Sage.

Haug, W. F. (2009), *Kritik der Warenästhetik*, Frankfurt a.M.: Suhrkamp.
Highmore, B. (2009), 'A Sideboard Manifesto: Design culture in an artificial world', in B. Highmore (ed.), *The Design Culture Reader*, London: Routledge, 1–11
Holbrook, M. B. (1999), 'Introduction to Consumer Value', in M. B. Holbrook (ed.), *Consumer Value – A Framework for Analysis and Research*, London: Routledge, 1–28.
Julier, G. (2014), *The Culture of Design*, London: Sage.
Kaiser, T. (2005), 'Idealisten gegen Weltkonzern', *Die Welt*, 2005.01.23, http://www.welt.de/print-wams/article120671/Idealisten-gegen-Weltkonzern.html (accessed 2017.03.30).
Lash, S. and Lury, C. (2007), *Global Culture Industry: The Mediation of Things*, Cambridge: Polity Press.
Leddy, T. (2012). *The Extraordinary in the Ordinary. The Aesthetics of Everyday Life*, Peterborough: Broadview Press.
Lees-Maffei, G. (2009), 'The Production-Consumption-Mediation Paradigm', *Journal of Design History*, 22(4): 351–76.
Lees-Maffei, G. (2014), 'Design History and Theory', in M. Kelly (ed.), *Encyclopedia of Aesthetics*, New York: Oxford University Press, 350–54.
Leiss, W., Kline, S., Jhally, S. and Botterill, J. (2005), *Social Communication in Advertising – Consumption in the Mediated Marketplace*, New York: Routledge.
McCracken, G. (1988), *Culture and Consumption*, Bloomington: Indiana University Press.
Miller, D. (1987), *Material Culture and Mass Consumption*, Oxford: Blackwell.
Moor, L. (2007), *The Rise of Brands*, Oxford: Berg.
Ngai, S. (2012), *Our Aesthetic Categories*, Cambridge, MA: Harvard University Press.
Oldemeyer, E. (2008), *Alltagsästhetisierung: Vom Wandel ästhetischer Erfahrung*, Würzburg: Königshausen & Neumann.
Rancière, J. (2004), *The Politics of Aesthetics*, London: Continuum.
Roßbach, M. (2009), 'Mit Koffein, Glück und Geduld', *Frankfurter Allgemeine Zeitung*, 2009.05.04, http://www.faz.net/aktuell/wirtschaft/unternehmen/unternehmensgruender-mit-koffein-glueck-und-geduld-1802401.html (accessed 2017.03.30).
Saito, Y. (2010), *Everyday Aesthetics*, Oxford: Oxford University Press.
Throsby, D. (2001), *Economics and Culture*, Cambridge: Cambridge University Press.
Venkatesh, A. and Meamber, L. A. (2008), 'The Aesthetics of Consumption and the Consumer as an Aesthetic Subject', *Consumption Markets & Culture*, 11(1): 45–70.
Walker, J. A. (1989), *Design History and the History of Design*, London: Pluto Press.
Wiegert, M. W. (2013a), interview 2013.12.16 in Hamburg by Mads Nygaard Folkmann & Camilla Rothmann Lorentzen.
Wiegert, M. W. (2013b), email 2013.12.23 to Mads Nygaard Folkmann.

PART THREE
Positioning design professions

Hans-Christian Jensen

Design is not a profession in strict sense. Occupations that can claim professional status in that respect will have to be characterized by formal academic education, state-granted monopoly of pursuing business in the area, self-regulation of proper conduct by a professional body and a professional ethics founded on altruism. This way law and medicine are among the few classical professions. However the sociology of the professions have pointed to the fact that a wide range of occupations and business pursue a professionalization project and thus display some or several of the characteristics to a greater or lesser extent.

In many countries of the Western world a project of professionalization of design could be said to be taking place. Especially with respect to the existence of formal academic education and the presence of professional bodies and the examples of professional ethics are many. The contributions of this section address different aspects of the ongoing strive of designers to be recognized as a profession. However, from a sociological point of view it is easily observable that the professionalization of design is most likely to never reach far and will remain particularly difficult. In all foreseeable future design is destined to strive for supremacy in business by continuously demonstrating professionalism. It is also easily foreseeable that the situation which has long been the case that 'professional' design is only able to secure a minor part of the total design business for itself will last since the strategies and practices of designers are fairly easily copied or taken over by amateurs or competing professions like engineers. The design profession as a whole is thus bound to be engaged in a game of distinction to carve out a hunk for itself of the total design business, which historically has referred design to the refined and high-end parts of the market.

Design culture in the sense of the superstructure of attitudes values and meanings attached to the business of design by designers then is bound to have a key role in demonstration of aspiration to professional status by the pursuit of altruistic ideals. Once this was thought to be done by modernizing and democratizing industry, later on simply by the endeavour for good design and today the sustainable agenda is prominent in this respect. The common theme across these altruistic commitments is the presumption that design has the ability to civilize what is otherwise left to commercial chaos.

With the article *Design Culture in the Sex Toy Industry: a new phenomenon* Judith Glover recounts the expansion of the professional design realm into formerly uncharted territory around the turn of the millennium by the commissioning of industrial designers by newly established companies or designers setting up alternative product portfolios compared to the established sex industry. The cultivation of this hitherto purely commercial defined and highly primitive design strategy simply mimicking genitals in a naturalistic manner was achieved by utilizing the well-proven formula of sound design intervention of the twentieth century, namely abstraction and infliction of sculptural form to products. Here design culture took on the potential rooted in the ideology of nineteenth-century bourgeois hegemony of enculturation and elevation and setting up a less crude and more refined alternative to the commercial consensus of the form, function and aesthetics of sex toys previously dominating the sex industry. Today many sex toys bear mark of the professional achievement of the design profession and could easily by displayed in design exhibitions in their now sanitized appearance.

In Leah Armstrong's *Working from Home: Fashioning the Professional Designer in Britain* it is shown through a historical case study how carrying the professional activity of designing out in the home has been a long lasting and popular motive in the depiction of designers to the public. Today working from home is a common condition in the creative industries of the late modern era on the whole and thus the ideal of work as leisure and leisure as work in the formation of the professional identity of designers came to prefigure later on generalized realities for good or bad. Maybe even back then it was at question of making a virtue out of necessity, and the question is, if not this in the long run turned out to be a disservice to the design profession itself as well?

Sarah Owens' contribution *On the Professional and Everyday Design of Graphic Artifacts* traces and scrutinizes the investment in fine demarcations of boundaries on behalf of professional towards non-professional practitioners of graphic design since the advent of desktop publishing software and digital printing, that made professional tools available to everyday designers of all kinds. This technological democratization made it even more difficult and acute to the already highly permeable profession to exert the pretension to minimal control of and an aspiration to just the least monopoly on good design practice. Both beforehand and even more so now this could only be attained to minimal degree through exclusionary processes in discourse.

The article *The Fixing I: Repair as Prefigurative Politics* by Gabriele Oropallo thematizes one of the recent activist agendas that attracts interest from and appeal to the design profession profoundly and fundamentally uncomfortable with itself and its role and function in capitalist economies. Oropallo examines the phenomenon of repair activism and the ideology and doctrines it is founded upon that he finds has the same roots as Richard Buckminster Fullers idea of 'comprehensive design' and the North American countercultural movement focused upon self-sufficiency, do-it-yourself, holism and ecological design as expressed in *Whole Earth Catalog: Access to Tools* published between 1969 and 1974. Given that part of the bedrock of the professional ideology of design has its outset in avant-garde movements of the twentieth century seeking for a more democratic faith of industry and eager to reform the alleged chaos of commercialism it is not surprising that the repair movement has already made its entry into key institutions of contemporary design like the Vitra Design Museum.

CHAPTER EIGHT

Design Culture in the sex toy industry:

A new phenomenon

Judith Glover

Introduction

In this chapter, I discuss how the design culture practice of industrial designers is changing the face of the global sex toy industry. I outline the research project that led to this conclusion and the ways in which the methodology of Design Cultural studies has been helpful in unpacking a field and product genre that has traditionally sat outside of mainstream commerce and has been laden with long-standing social taboos around sexuality, gender and sexual practice. The research underpinning this chapter evidences the shift in the meanings and values attributed to sex toys, when designers entered the marketplace as producers and entrepreneurs at the beginning of the twenty-first century in a complex set of changing parameters that the methodologies of Design Cultural studies was able to capture – both socio-sexual and technological spanning 150 years from Victorianism to Raunch Culture. The sex toy industry was unmapped from a design perspective when I became interested in product genre in the late 1990s in my honours year of industrial design. As it was firmly rooted in the values of the pornography industry, it took some convincing to get my Head of Department to let me take on the topic, its reputation for the aesthetic of realistic genitalia firmly etched in the minds of consumers and designers. Ten years later, a PhD thesis and sex toy brand created, it became obvious the research was many stories of social, technological and design history.

One of the key conclusions from the thesis research was the product genre's story can be told as a tale of the social history of the twentieth century based around the emancipation of Western women; one of the key mega-trends of that century. Maines (1999) was right when she said that sex toys represented sexual politics. From the Victorian era through the Sexual Revolution to Raunch culture (Levy, 2005) today, who makes or designs sex toys, owns the means of production and distribution and what values they represent reflect the gender and sexual mores, laws and notions of obscenity of each of those eras (Glover 2013; Maines 1999). Another key finding is how the values of the porn industry dominate sex toy product until the design industry got involved at the turn of the twenty-first century. The values, methods and practices of industrial designers in the first decade of the new millennium start to change sex toy production which opens the industry to more mainstream consumer acceptance (Glover 2013). I argue that the design culture practices of the industrial design profession permeate the porn culture practices of the adult industry and changes the quality of the product genre substantially as early forms of product innovation and competition finally come to the market, which will be discussed later in this chapter.

As discussed in the introduction to this new book, Design Culture as a field or design culture as a practice can be described in many ways – there is a fluidity and flexibility needed to bricolage the complex ways contemporary society (consumer and industry) uses cultural meanings in the production of artefacts. In the context of this chapter and the emerging phenomenon of design culture in the sex toy industry, I argue that the description of Design Culture put forward by the authors that helps understand and unpack this is the ability and necessity for Design Cultural methods to be interdisciplinary. That as a designer and researcher looking into this new phenomenon I needed to access primary or secondary material from fields outside of design to make any sense of what was going on and create links between them because the historical methods of deconstructing individual artefacts, visual material or monographic authorship were inadequate. While my research methodology and methods ultimately resided in design thinking and practice, there was a need to go outside of the design field and engage with epistemology and content of other fields and bring it back to a coherent whole.

A central argument of the research and this chapter is that the socio-cultural meanings around the sex toy industry at the end of the twentieth century, rather than a lack of contemporary technological manufacturing capability, was inhibiting a mainstream commercial acceptance of this product genre and the creation of products more closely aligned with what contemporary female consumers needed or wanted. The research that underpins this chapter had to look at the problem in two different ways.

Firstly, how did we come to this position that sex toys (a vibrator being not that different from an electric toothbrush) resided in the domain of the adult industry at the end of the twentieth century, what where the existing cultural values attached to the artefacts produced by this industry and why where those values inhibiting a greater social acceptance and industry innovation? And secondly if the design culture embedded in the professional practice of industrial design entered the product genre, what were or would be the effects of this and how could these be analysed and mapped? The structure of the 'Domains of Design Culture' map in the first *Design Culture* book (Julier 2014) using the categories of Designer, Production and Consumption allowed for both a historical and contemporary analysis of the industry with the category of Designer being important in capturing the shift at the turn of the millennium in the industry as industrial designers and engineers entered the marketplace with specific intent to create different values. This will be discussed in greater detail later in the chapter.

The following is an overview of the scope of the research and some of its key findings; it is followed by the discussion of how and why the lens of design culture embodied the need for an interdisciplinary approach to knowledge in pulling together the threads of this unmapped topic.

What exactly is the problem with the sex toy industry?

The modern adult industry was historically geared to satisfy male consumers and remains highly male-centric in the types of commodities it produces to this day (Church Gibson 2004; Dines 1998; Glover 2013; Jenson and Dines 1998; McClintock 1992; McKee, Albury and Lumby 2008; Williams 1989). The modern sex toy industry evolved out of the adult industry in the 1960s and 1970s in the United States and has remained associated with pornography, both in public perception and legal definition (Elimelekh 2006; Glover 2013; Klein 2006; Lindemann 2006; McIntosh 1992; Rubin 1984; Schlosser 2003; Sigel 2005). The effect of this relationship has meant products designed for female sexual use have been developed out of a heavily dominated male-centric industry focused on its main target market, the sexual arousal of males not females. However, the perception of sex toys as pornography, or closely aligned with the values or conventions of pornography, undoubtedly reinforced by the continuing association with the adult industry, is also affected by long-standing legal definitions in some jurisdictions still enforced today that continue to define these objects for the sole purpose of arousal as obscene (Elimelekh 2006; Glover 2013; Lindemann 2006). It has not been helped by the conventions, standards and aesthetics embedded in sex toys by the adult industry, with the most classic of images embedded in the public mind of the pink rubber phallus or the fake vagina. Visually literal interpretations of genitalia become one of the key stylistic genres of the industry, helping reinforce the perception of pornography or taboo.

The perception of taboo, and in some cases actual illegality, creates product that must be defined as 'novelties', and retailers and buyers are discouraged from serious discussions of the product's purpose or suitability. This social and legal marginalization created an unregulated industry ignored by governments except for definitions of obscenity. Manufacturers of cheaper product used unsafe materials and flouted laws to protect consumers by failing to label products (Biesanz 2007; Stabile 2013). The type of product produced was affected by two competing forces: the sexual ideals and conventions of its male-focused producers within the adult industry and the long-standing socio-cultural notions of what is considered obscene by national authorities and religious moralists. These socio-cultural notions of sexual ethos are heavily weighted towards a heteronormative male-centric view of sexuality. While one represents sexual freedoms and the other sexual control, both are relatively unconcerned about the real and varied sexual needs and desires of Western women (Glover 2013)

The focus of the thesis on the female consumer related to the evidence of sexual surveys that females are the largest consumer group of sex toys. I questioned the mismatch of values between the adult industry and this group and looked at the opportunities for designers to target in more sophisticated ways large or niche markets of Western female sex toy consumers. A literature review undertaken found a number of sexual health surveys over a 10 year period from 1996 to 2007 on sex toy use, all leading in a similar direction (*Biotech Week* 2004; Davis, et al. 1996; *Durex Global Sex Survey* 2005; Fetto 2002; Michael et al. 1994; Richters et al. 2003; Rye and Meaney 2007). These surveys ranged from highly rigorous surveys by established national health institutes to companies such as Durex harnessing the power of the internet to survey large volumes of respondents. The surveys trend towards recording greater use among women than men, an increase in use comparative to increase in education levels and income, and an increase in total consumption numbers over the last 20 years. There is a broad range of use in age groups, income groups, education levels, sexual orientation groups and marital status. If the average use for couples ranges from 10 per cent of the United States population in the 1995–96 National Sexual Health Institute survey to a much higher use for singles in the 2005 Durex survey of around 40 per cent, then sex toy use, in particular vibrators, is not a fringe recreational or commercial activity (Glover 2013).

The adult industry knew it had both a problem and an opportunity (Comella 2008). Its problem at the beginning of the twenty-first century was declining revenues from its male market and its opportunity was the potential the women's market could bring. That potential for the women's market was a hotly discussed topic at the 2008 AVN (Adult Video News) Trade show in Las Vegas. Comella recounts,

Ask just about any industry insider and they'll tell you the hottest growth market in the adult industry is the women's market. Ken Dorfman, the National Sales Manager for Doc Johnson's, one of the largest manufacturer in the world, explains it in this way in the expo's Show Guide: 'One guy shopping alone – average sale $8. Two guys, $12. But one female shopping alone – average sale $83. Two females shopping together, $170.' (Comella 2008: 62)

But female customers wanted quality, beauty, pleasure, something that worked well and lasted a long time. They want to be educated and access information about sex and sexuality (Comella 2008; Hewson and Pearce 2009). The long-standing embedding of sex toy production in the adult industry created the problem of the mismatch of standards, values and expectations between the biggest users and consumers of sex toys – Western females and the adult industry producers. By the turn of the millennium, this problem created a number of issues, retarding the growth of the industry in regard to these female consumers and a more mainstream commercial acceptance. There was the mismatch of brand values in products, marketing and retail environments depicting women as sluts, vixens, wannabe porn stars and naughty-nurse-type characters; and then there was also a lack of quality, safety, ergonomics and innovation in the products themselves. Normal safety and product design standards applied to most other industries are devoid from nearly every company manufacturing sex toys at the end of the twentieth century.

By the 1970s, mass-manufacturing technologies had moved beyond Bakelite to advanced plastic injection and silicon moulded parts, which were common and of high quality across consumer electronics industries. If you think of the quality of product design and manufacturing in companies such as Braun and Sony since the end of the Second World War (Bürdek 2005; Polster 2009; Sony 2015) – product design by the 1970s could be extremely sophisticated, aesthetically elegant, highly functional and high quality. For the sex toy industry, this was the era of poor-quality and unsafe products, crass designs and a lack of innovation. A small number of porn entrepreneurs and companies dominated the video and sex toy industry (Schlosser 2003). They created a global network of manufacturing and retailing, interconnected and replicating each other in different parts of the world. They were making vast profits out of magazine and video pornography and poor-quality sex toys with huge mark-ups because nobody else would make them (Glover 2013; Schlosser 2003). The playing field and easy profits was theirs, but they were cut off from mainstream commerce and industry – caught by the vast morality wars that waged across the twentieth century about obscenity and pornography (Klein 2006; Rubin 1984).

The industry harnessed the loosening of sexual morals during the Sexual Revolution to make more profits, but they completely missed one of the biggest events of the twentieth century – second-wave feminism. If you took modern pornography from the beginning of porn films in the 1920s with the introduction of stag films into brothels, then it started in an era with many hangovers from Victorian attitudes to female sexuality (Segal 1992; Williams 1989). Pornography tends to start and finish with the male erection and ejaculation and the modern pornography industry seem to start and finish the twentieth century with the same convention. The products at the end of the twentieth century while technologically different still exhibited Victorian values to female sexuality despite second-wave feminism having a profound effect on the way women sexually practiced at the end of the twentieth century and beyond (Glover 2013).

So what did a typical adult industry sex toy from the late twentieth century look like? The genre could be loosely classified into a number of sub-genres. Phallus objects or the literal interpretations of genitalia – both male and female – was by far the biggest category. There were also other types of discombobulated body parts – a fist or a torso or pair of breasts. There were novelty-type objects, either things that took the form of animals – rabbits and dolphins were popular – or blow up dolls or things disguised as other objects like lipsticks. As the digital age slowly took off in the 1990s, so did the fashion for faux technology. The industry's standard practice for innovation was to hybridize existing styles. So the iconic vibrator, the Rabbit, becomes the Techno-rabbit and now the i-Rabbit in the era of the iPhone. The most significant innovation came in the early 1990s when American company Doc Johnson created the Pocket-Rocket which focused on stimulating a woman's clitoris setting off a new sub-genre of smaller clitoral devices. Finally, something reflecting what was then common knowledge of female sexual practice since the 1970s. The clitoris did exist and for 70 per cent of women, it was fundamental to achieving an orgasm (Komisaruk, Beyer-Flores, and Whipple 2006; Whipple 2007).

Before the burst of female-centric retailers after 2005, it was very hard to get quality information on products and in some legal jurisdictions it was illegal to even be selling or giving sales advice on sex toys (Elimelekh 2006; Klein 2006; Lindemann 2006; Loe 1999). While a small number of US manufacturers started to care about safety of materials and quality of manufacturing, as a whole by the end of the twentieth century most products were still overpriced, unsafe, noisy, poor quality and lacking the kind of aesthetic sophistication available in other design genres. The 1990s had seen the rise of Brand and Design Culture with Western manufacturing companies increasingly leveraging design values in their products to remain competitive (Gibney et al. 2000; Gobe 2001; Julier 2014; Glover 2013; Valtonen 2007) and by the 2000s female consumers were becoming increasingly more design-literate and tech savvy with the wealth and capital to buy quality. But the type of sex toys female consumers could buy at the end of the twentieth century did not reflect the changing social and economic landscape for women since the 1970s. By the turn of the millennium, an opportunity existed – a large gap in the market place – that a designerly eye would spot. The adult industry was not producing products or brands to the standard expected of cashed-up, well-educated, professional contemporary Western women that the sexual surveys said were the most likely to consume sex toys.

Design-led companies in the new millennium

A small number of niche producers appeared at the end of the 1990s attempting to provide female-centric brands. Candida Royalle was the first to hire an industrial design consultancy Groet Design Associates to develop the Contours range in 1999. By 2002, Myla, a British start-up lingerie company from the United Kingdom released a small range of sex toys designed by internationally renowned designers Marc Newsome and Tom Dixon. The products while not particularly functional in achieving orgasm were important in challenging the aesthetics of the genre, and the use of such high-profile designers gained much exposure for the new brand and promoting a new type of design-led product. Sexual Health brand Emotional Bliss started in 2002, Lelo in 2003, Jimmyjane in 2004, the Durex Play range was launched in 2005 using consultancy Seymour Powell, Goldfrau, OhMiBod, N-Joy and Jejoue all launched in 2006, WeVibe in 2007 and finally the decade closed with an interesting development as Philips Sound and Vision launched two vibrators onto the European market in 2008. The Hewson Group report (2009) on what they labelled the Erotic Economy discussed the potential for the high-quality, design-led side of the market if companies properly tapped into the needs and desires of their female consumers who were used to the aspirational and lifestyle marketing used by industries such as perfume and fashion (Hewson and Pearce 2009; Hewson and Pearce 2011)

Some of these brands went on to be decent sized players in the market (Lelo, Jimmyjane, Je Joue, Emotional Bliss and WeVibe), some remained niche or cult-ish (Goldfrau, Betony Vernon, N-joy), some failed (Philips foray into the couple's vibrator market) and some later sold out to adult industry companies (Jimmyjane and retailer Coco De Mer). What these brands initially bought to the market were a perspective of the female consumer from outside the adult industry and the culture of design thinking, standards and the ethics of safe manufacture. These sex toy manufacturers either hired industrial design firms or were started by industrial designers or Product Design Engineers (Glover 2013). They moved their product design away from traditional pornography symbols and conventions, creating a choice and variety for female consumers in regard to quality and aesthetics.

The product forms of these new generation companies become simplified and more visually coherent. There was a distinct trend away from literal representations of genitalia and experimentation into materials such as stainless steel, precious metals, jade and ceramic. There was exploration into finishes such as anodized aluminium, the etching of metallic surfaces, the application of decals onto ceramics or the layering of different coloured silicone to create patterns, decoration or detail. The processes varied from high-volume mass-manufactured products to batch-production techniques, some requiring high levels of labour due to attention to detail for high-quality finishing. Some studios such as Goldfrau or Betony Vernon specifically targeted the high end of the market with labour-intensive, high-quality materials and processes in ceramics and metals. Companies promoted their design credentials and discussed themselves as design studios. They became transparent about their manufacturing and material safety designing and manufacturing to common global industrial design standards such as CE, ROHS and WEEE. They started putting their products up for International Design awards and promoting their brands outside of the porn industry into the fashion, lingerie, lifestyle and health media.

Figure 8.1 is an example of the ceramic dildos created for the brand Goldfrau, launched in 2006 that formed part of the design outcomes for the PhD research that underpins this chapter. The creation of the Goldfrau brand provides an example of a possible solution to developing female-centric sex toys that moves away from the historical taboo associations of adult industry products and services. It is an example of how an industrial

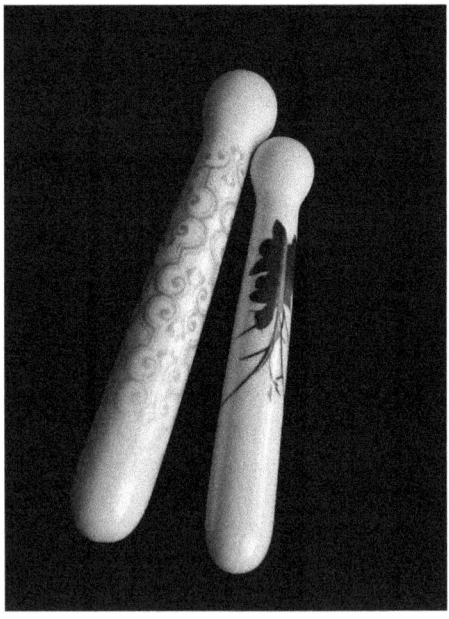

FIGURE 8.1 *Miss Pink large, Miss Saigon classic, Goldfrau Ceramic Dildos, Porcelain Ceramic. Graphics Pandarosa. Source J. Glover, 2006.*

designer can balance the technical design considerations of functionality, manufacturing processes and product quality with the potential female user's emotional and psychological needs in what Norman (2004) calls a Reflective product – one that relates to their sense of self and lifestyle. It is also an example that high tech and advanced manufacturing techniques are not always the solution to a problem as ceramic slip cast production methods are considered traditional forms of batch manufacturing. Porcelain was chosen not only for its high functional strength and low friction (when glazed) but connotations of quality and exoticness and the ability to layer decoration and ornamentation through glazing and graphic decals.

Other companies initially aligned to the adult industry such as Funfactory became consistent innovators and remain high-quality producers. Once competition in the form of higher quality products hit the market the adult industry producers were forced to provide better quality and safer products. The rising tide lifted the industry as a whole. Concurrently a boom occurred in the female-centric retail side of the market enabled by advancements of internet commerce through personal computing devices (Glover 2013). Women were able to buy sex toys off internet retailers offering them safe, higher quality products with sexual advice and good quality product information. The restrictions and embarrassment of physically going to a traditional bricks and mortar sex store was gone. Quality product brands could sell directly to customers or through retailers aligned with their values. The ability of selling directly from business to consumer via the internet had disrupted the old business model of the adult industry reliant on franchises of adult stores geared to male consumers, a few international trade shows and the industry being run by a small number of powerful pornography companies.

Design culture in the context of this emerging phenomenon

The 'Domains of Design Culture' map from the first design culture book (Julier 2014) was of huge value in helping unpack the problems and issues of sex toy product as it stood at the turn of the new millennium. I have re-drawn that map in Figure 8.2 to outline the main areas of the research that fall under the different headings of designer, production and consumption and will explain why the triangulated approach of these three categories was necessary to capture the bigger picture, the combination of all three gives, and why that was valuable.

The initial research into the sex toy industry in the late 1990s started with the question 'How do you make a better sex toy?' This was a Designer question born out of the standard design process of initial investigation – how should you make something better and why should you do it? But how do you improve something if you do not understand its conditions?

- Values and Professional Standards Industrial Design Industry
- Industrial Design methods and processes
- Examples of Industrial Design influenced production twentyfirst century

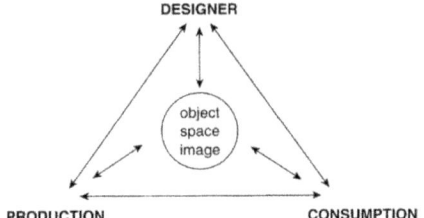

- Manufacturing processes (Victorian to contemporary): who owns and produces
- Manufacturing and safety standards (or lack of) in adult industry sex toys
- Marketing and distribution: Global Trade shows/ historical structure of marketplace
- Branding and marketing: values of adult industry/ values of design culture
- ICT and Digital disruption: how it changes consumption and marketplace
- Retailers: traditional adult industry to new female centric

- Evidence of use and consumption through sexual surveys
- Values of the adult industry: analysis of branding, marketing material and products
- Values of the adult industry: historical symbols and conventions
- Evidence of social changes for women across twentieth century: social and financial empowerment
- Evidence of attitudes to sexual beliefs and mores across twentieth century
- Evidence of the effects of 'morality wars' on the sex toy industry: legal and morality restrictions late nineteenth centuryto late twentieth century

FIGURE 8.2 *Domains of Design Culture: Mapping of the socio-cultural, marketplace and industry interactions in the sex toy industry late nineteenth century to early twenty-first century. Constructed from Julier, G. (2014).* The Culture of Design. *3rd ed. London: Sage Publications. p.11*

And while you can as an industrial designer or engineer stick to a strict product benchmarking and technical analysis soon any decent investigation will involve trying to understand the users' needs and the marketplace you are about to enter. And in contemporary society that marketplace is global and it exists in physical space and now virtual space, as product artefacts, as communications material as spaces and brand messages.

What was unusual about the sex toy industry is it resided in the broader adult industry which at the end of the twentieth century seemed to be devoid of design culture practice – that is it was lacking production companies that described themselves as design-led business or affiliations with design-led businesses. What is interesting about the sex toy industry is we are able to see what an industry is like without the practices of design culture active in the industry and then what happens when designers intervene and become actively involved as entrepreneurs and producers. The adult industry seemed stuck in some land time forgot cut off from the normal processes of global innovation and manufacturing and not through a lack of co-opting new technologies. The industry was quick to jump into any new technology of the twentieth century in communications and manufacturing; however, while the products displayed current technological advancements the socio-cultural values lagged. By the end of the twentieth century, the values embedded in the sex toys of the adult industry where still Victorian in regard to the attitudes and perceptions of contemporary female gender and sexuality. There was a mismatch in the values contemporary females expected of product design, branding and marketing and what the adult industry was producing. One of the key findings of the research was that the design culture practices of the industrial design profession fundamentally changed the way sex toys were manufactured, made and marketed in the first decade of the twentieth century. This is because industrial designers are taught that product design is a combination of many things. It is not just a technical exercise that must satisfy functional and safety requirements – it is about value creation – and those values must match the expectations or lifestyle aspirations of the consumers you want to attract to your products or brand. The objects we create embody many layers of meaning both intentional (and sometimes unintentional) and it is role of the designer or design team to curate and create those meanings using function, form, material, colour and finish in an often complex ecosystem of physical and virtual retail environments, brand material and marketing communications.

Using the 'Domains of Design Culture' map, I describe the set of practices common to industrial design process and methods under the Designer heading as shown in Figure 8.2. As an industrial designer, I could perceive a mismatch between the lifestyles of contemporary women and the values portrayed about women by the adult industry at the end of the twentieth century. I had also been trained to consider and aim for safe products, quality manufacturing enabling long lifespans, products fit for purpose functionally and ergonomically with values that reflected the beliefs, behaviours and lifestyles of the consumers I thought I was designing for. So when I started looking at the product genre in the late 1990s, all I could see where poorly manufactured, unsafe, noisy, inelegant and pornographic products branded and marketed to women as though we all aspired to be porn stars in a retail ecosystem still geared to the traditional male consumers of the adult industry. By the end of the research I had been able to document how and why cultural and professional practices of the industrial designer had started to transform the product genre.

Industrial designers entering the marketplace as producers or entrepreneurs is a strategy for improving and mainstreaming the genre but in the context of PhD-level research the question of 'How did we get here and where exactly is here and why is that important at all?' the evidence that needed to prove an adequate and reliable argument fell under the other categories of Production and Consumption. In this particular case of 'How to design a better sex toy', the methods lie largely in the application of industrial design practices through our process and methods but Production and Consumption will give bigger, more detailed and nuanced sets of information that can be used into the decisions made into the design process. Also if a designer is also taking an entrepreneurial attitude and wants to develop their own brands a realistic understanding of the marketplace and where they wish to situate themselves is important. Who are the consumers they wish to reach and what values, behaviours and beliefs do they have? How much are they willing to spend at what frequency and for what type of products from what kinds of services? These fall largely under the Consumption category although designers also have various methods that sit between social science and business methods to investigate a marketplace or consumer/product category as part of the design process.

Under Production the understanding of the larger structures of the global marketplace and the way technology intersects with that is also important. These things can be looked at in the present and provide valuable information, but they still do not tell us 'How we got here' and why is that an important question to keep asking. The answer lies in Maines' description of sex toys and their precursors being all about sexual politics (Maines 1999). That these are not discreet technological or specifically functional objects but embedded with each generations views, laws and beliefs on the gender and sexual rights of females. What gets made and by whom, in what forms and what values these objects and their eco-systems exhibit tell us much about where we are in regards to sexual freedoms.

To understand why this genre gets stuck in the adult industry and what the effects of that are is very important as it relates to long-standing and very powerful socio-sexual and cultural beliefs around sexual practice and sexual taboos and if you want to create an new set of sexual artefacts – call them sex toys if you want – with a new set of standards and values that honour and celebrate female sexuality in all its gloriousness then you need to understand you are up against thousands of years of misunderstanding and misogyny. You need to look at if the social conditions for women have changed since (at least) Victorian times and in what ways. If you are asking someone to invest in your ideas or you are investing yourself, are the conditions right for new classes of products? Are the conditions right to create high-quality, transparent female-centric sex toys brands and retail environments in the twentieth century? As the research findings evidenced, substantial social change has happened and sex toy designers can now decide whether they want to throw their lot in with the greater adult industry or develop design brands that sit outside of the industry yet still reach consumers easily through the internet and social media.

Conclusion

In 2016, while undertaking research for a sexual health project for a client, I had to benchmark the standard quality of sex toys available 15 years after my honours project. Those companies and products in the design-led end of the market now as a whole conformed to the manufacturing norms of global product design. Companies follow tech trends looking to the CE industry rather than the porn industry for innovation and standards. Some companies, notably new player Iroha, bring a sophisticated Japanese design sensibility with some well-needed innovation in silicon manufacturing creating a functional softness to their products long overdue in the market (Iroha Website, Products 2017). Anecdotal evidence from female-centric retailers confirmed that consumers have finally gotten used to paying higher prices for quality. However, the changes and growth of the design-led end of the market in the last 15 years has only bought the standards of the best sex toy companies up to an acceptable base level of safety and product design. The best companies now need to understand what Design Research is and how it can help them become true innovators. More research needs to focus on users' needs functionally, emotionally and physically across the whole of their lives.

Women are the biggest group of discretionary spenders globally and three-fourth of the Western female economy have mid to high incomes or wealth (Silverstein and Sayre 2009). Much of this group is now retiring and so many opportunities arise to develop products for older men and women with different issues as they age. Long-lasting sexual health should be seen as a part of overall well-being in ageing for both men and women. I am working on a number of cross-disciplinary projects with colleagues that tackle difficult issues within the sexual health space such as prostate cancer, pelvic floor pain and sexual practice and disability. The commonality to the sex toy industry's story is that these fields of health or medicine also suffer the same socio-sexual taboos preventing quality product or service development. There are still so many contemporary hangovers from the attitudes of the Victorian era to sexuality.

In two decades the area of design research has greatly developed inside and outside of academia. Those design-led companies that have mastered good product design need to now move to design research approaches to push innovation and quality with user-centred methodologies at their core. As the fascination increases for new areas of technology such as applications, big data, robotics, virtual or augmented reality – female-centric sex toy companies need to be mindful that women want good quality orgasms first and layers of more tech is not necessarily the solution. Needlessly adding tech is not a solution or useful strategy to new product development. Adding an app does not necessarily make a product better. Do we really need big data in the bedroom or just a reliable and high-quality orgasm from a well-designed and safe product? The design-led sector of the industry needs to keep focusing outside of the adult industry for inspiration and innovation.

My approach to this is to continue to apply the research methods and methodologies of design to these socially taboo topics – to apply the rationality of design research inquiry with the creativity of design thinking and practice to enable product and service innovation. To bring these topics into the academy and to apply a cross-disciplinary and user-centred approach where health professionals, patients and designers can all work towards better outcomes. However, the design culture practices of industrial designers are now embedded in the sex toy industry with many great exemplars. Designers, entrepreneurs and start-ups can decide whether to be design-led companies and continue pushing to higher standards of product quality and innovation started by a small number of maverick design companies at the turn of the twentieth century.

The 'Domains of Design Culture' map was a useful model when mapping the unchartered territory of the sex toy industry. It allowed for the multiple perspectives of producer, consumer and designer across multiple histories and the examples of both the past and present to inform one another. Most of all, it allowed for the stories and experiences of contemporary designers to be heard and recorded so that they might influence the next generation of designerly producers and entrepreneurs.

References

Biesanz, Z. (2007), 'Dildos, Artificial Vaginas, and Phthalates: How Toxic Sex Toys Illustrate a Broader Problem for Consumer Protection', *Law and Inequality*, 25: 203–26.
Biotech Week. (13 October 2004). Study on Female Sexuality Reveals Increased Use of Sexual Aids by Women, 1132. Retrieved 20 July 2008, from Health Reference Centre Academic database.
Bürdek, B. (2005), *Design: History, Theory, and Practice of Product Design*, Boston: Birkhäuser.
Church Gibson, P. (2004), *More Dirty Looks: Gender, Pornography and Power*, London: British Film Institute.
Comella, L. (2008), 'It's Sexy. It's Big Business and it's Not Just for Men', *American Sociological Association Journal Contexts*, 7(3): 61–3.
Davis, C., Blank, J., Lin, H. and Bonillas, C. (1996), 'Characteristics of Vibrator Use Among Women', *The Journal of Sex Research*, 33(4): 314-320.
Dines, G. (1998), 'Dirty Business', in G. Dines, R. Jensen and A. Russo (ed.), *Pornography: The Production and Consumption of Inequality*, New York: Routledge, 37–64.
Durex Global Sex Survey. (2005), Durex Website. Last viewed 6 May 2006, http://www.durex.com/cm/gss2005result.pdf
Elimelekh, S. (2006), 'The Constitutional Validity of Circuit Court Opinions Limiting the American Right to Sexual Privacy', *Cardozo Arts and Entertainment Law Journal*, 24(1): 261–96.
Fetto, J. (1 May 2002). Let's get it on! *B-net Business Library On-line Source*. Last viewed 31 July 2011, http://findarticles.com/p/articles/mi_m4021/is_2002_May_1/ai_88679446/

Gibney Jr, F., Luscombe, B., Rawe, J. and Gribben, S. (20 March 2000), 'The Redesigning Of America', *Time Magazine On-line Source*: 1–5. last viewed 31 July 2011, http://www.time.com/time/magazine/article/0,9171,996372,00.html

Glover, J. (2013), *Taboo to Mainstream: An Industrial Design Solution to Sex Toy Production*. PhD thesis. Swinburne University of Technology. Available at: https://researchbank.swinburne.edu.au/searching.do

Gobe, M. (2001), *Emotional Branding: The New Paradigm of Connecting Brands to People*, New York: Allworth Press.

Hewson, J. and Pearce, J. (2009), *Women, Sex and Shopping: The Future for the Women's Pleasure Goods Sector*, London: Hewson Group.

Hewson, J. and Pearce, J. (2011), *Women's Pleasure Goods: The Future Global Market*, London: Hewson Group.

Iroha Website (2017), Products Page. Last viewed 6 September 2017, https://iroha-tenga.com/en/plus/

Jenson, R. and Dines, G. (1998), 'The Content of Mass-Marketed Pornography', in G. Dines, R. Jensen and A. Russo (eds), *Pornography: The Production and Consumption of Inequality*, New York: Routledge, 65–100.

Julier, G. (2014), *The Culture of Design*, 3rd ed., London: Sage Publications, 11

Klein, M. (2006), *America's War on Sex*, Westport: Praeger Publishers.

Komisaruk, B., Beyer-Flores, C. and Whipple, B. (2006), *The Science of Orgasm*, Baltimore: John Hopkins University Press.

Levy, A. (2005), *Female Chauvinist Pigs: Women and the Rise of Raunch Culture*, New York: Free Press.

Lindemann, D. (2006), 'Pathology Full Circle: A History of Anti-vibrator Legislation in the United States', *Columbia Journal of Gender and Law*, 15(1), 326–46.

Loe, M. (1999), 'Feminism for Sale: Case Study of a Pro-Sex Feminist Business', *Gender and Society Journal*, 13(6), 705–32.

Maines, R. (1999), *The Technology of Orgasm: Hysteria, the Vibrator and Women's Sexual Satisfaction*, Baltimore: John Hopkins University Press.

McClintock, A. (1992), 'Gonad the Barbarian and the Venus Flytrap: Portraying the Female Orgasm', in L. Segal and M. McIntosh (eds), *Sex Exposed: Sexuality and the Pornography Debate*, London: Virago Press, 111–31.

McIntosh, M. (1992), 'Liberalism and the Contradictions of Sexual Politics', in L. Segal and M. McIntosh (eds), *Sex Exposed: Sexuality and the Pornography Debate*, London: Virago Press, 155–68.

McKee, A., Albury, K. and Lumby, C. (2008), *The Porn Report*, Carlton: Melbourne University Press.

Michael, R., Gagnon, J., Laumann, E. and Kolata, G. (1994), *Sex in America: A Definitive Survey*, New York: Warner Books.

Norman, D. (2004), *Emotional Design: Why We Love (or Hate) Everyday Things*, New York: Basic Books.

Polster, B. (2009), *Braun: Fifty Years of Design and Innovation*, Edition Axel Menges.

Richters, J., Grulich, A., de Visser, R., Smith, A. and Rissel, C. (2003), 'Autoerotic, Esoteric and other Sexual Practices Engaged in by a Representative Sample of Adults', *Australian and New Zealand Journal of Public Health*, 27(2) 180–90.

Rubin, G. (1984), 'Thinking Sex: Notes for a Radical Theory on the Politics of Sexuality', in C. Vance (ed.), *Pleasure and Danger: Exploring Female sexuality*, Boston: Routledge, 267–319.

Rye, B. and Meany, G. (2007), 'The Pursuit of Sexual Pleasure', *Sexuality & Culture Journal*, 11(1): 28–51.

Schlosser, E. (2003), 'Empire of the Obscene', *Reefer Madness*, London: Penguin Books, 109–210.

Segal, L. (1992), 'Sweet Sorrows, Painful Pleasures: Pornography and the Perils of Heterosexual Desire', in L. Segal and M. McIntosh (eds), *Sex Exposed: Sexuality and the Pornography Debate*, London: Virago Press, 65–91.

Sigel, L. (ed.). (2005), *International Exposure: Perspectives on Modern European Pornography 1800-2000*, London: Rutgers University Press.

Silverstein, M. and Sayre, K. (2009), 'The Female Economy', *Harvard Business Review*, 87(8): 46–53.

Sony Design: Making Modern (2015), Editor: Ian Luna, New York: Rizzoli.

Stabile, E. (2013), 'Commentary: Getting the Government in Bed: How to Regulate the Sex-Toy Industry', *Berkeley Journal of Gender*, L.aw & Justice, 28(2): 161–84.

Valtonen, A. (2007), *Redefining Industrial Design: Changes in the Design Practice in Finland*, Helsinki: University of Art and Design.

Whipple, B. (2007), *Female Orgasm: Transcript of Interview with Professor Beverly Whipple*, ABC Health Report. Last viewed 21 March 2007, http://www.abc.net.au/rn/healthreport/stories/2007/1878728.htm

Williams, L. (1989), *Hardcore: Power, Pleasure, and the 'Frenzy of the Visible'*, Berkley: University of California Press.

CHAPTER NINE

Working from home:

Fashioning the professional designer in Britain

Leah Armstrong

This chapter examines the representation of the home as a working environment for two Consultant Designers in the formative years of the design profession in Britain, 1950–60: Gaby Schreiber (1916–91) and FHK Henrion (1899–97). The primary focus is on the fashioning of the home as a setting for work in the design profession, as portrayed through fashion and lifestyle media of the time. It argues that this cultural representation was adopted to position the Consultant Designer as a taste-maker, occupying an elite status within the profession. It further suggests that this representation of design work within the home marked the erosion of cultural space between professional and personal life, setting the precedent for the precarious *24/7 culture* that increasingly defines work in design and the creative industries. The chapter is structured in three parts. The first section explores the historiography of the relationship between work, home and artistic professions. The middle section identifies the representation of FHK Henrion and Gaby Schreiber and the last section compares, contrasts and reflects upon the representation of both in relation to the contemporary theorization of design as a sociologically determined practice. Reflecting on the value and meaning of historic and contemporary instantiations of the home as a work environment, the chapter considers some shared characteristics, as well as important distinctions, in representations of the home as a working environment for the designer, past and present.

As anthropologist Christina Nippert-Eng has argued, there is much to be learnt through the exploration of spaces between seemingly distant cultural categories, like work and home. On her book on the subject, *Home Work: Negotiating Boundaries through Everyday Life* (1996), she shows how these apparently oppositional spaces are in fact 'inextricably conceptually defined with and by each other' (Nippert-Eng 1996: 4). She uses the term 'boundary work' to refer to the 'strategies, principles and practices we use to create and maintain and modify cultural categories' (Nippert-Eng 1996: 7) in everyday social behaviour. This chapter uses the concept of boundary work to examine the representation of the Consultant Designer, considering the significance of the home as a representative site through which to mediate the distance between work and home, labour and leisure, production and consumption, to produce a fashionable, stylized image of design work that persists in twenty-first century Design Culture.

Contemporary fashion and design media discourse regularly engages in 'boundary work'. Writing in 2014, British *Vogue* editor Alexandra Schulman presented a special issue on contemporary fashion designers' homes as a method of explaining the creative process, since 'all designs are almost always rooted in a personal mash up of experience and environment' (Schulman 2014). This environmental reading of creativity and the 'pleasure culture' of work has a long history in the creative industries (Nixon and Crewe 2004). For sociologists David Wang and Ali O'Ilhan, it is this quality that gives the creative professions a meaningful professional identity. Writing of the contemporary design professions, they argue that without a knowledge-based professional status, designers can be distinguished from their fellow professionals by the types of cars they drive and the style of their home interiors (Wang and O'Ilhan 2010). This chapter finds historical context for this contemporary reading.

As design historian Zoë Thomas recently discussed in an article in the *Women's History Review*, the tradition of 'At Home with…' first emerged in the artistic press as early as 1901 in the *Art Record: A Weekly Illustrated Review of the Arts and Crafts* (1901–02). Here, male artists were interviewed in their homes, revealing a 'broader public captivation in how the lives of male artists were acted out'. Thomas claims that through the 'home studio', the domestic environment thus enabled female artists in London to negotiate a space in which to construct an identity as professionals (Thomas 2015: 957). In this sense, Thomas importantly establishes a distinctive history of the home that is shared between male and female artists, as a productive setting through which to construct personal and professional imaginaries.

Working from home is now a common practice in many industries, due to the increase in freelance contracts and flexible working hours, but it is a particularly notable feature of the contemporary design profession in the UK (Design Council 2015).[1] Images of the artist or designer working from their kitchen table or home-studio circulate frequently in digital and print media and work to produce an alluring image of the creative professional that is 'unmistakeably in fashion' (Armstrong and McDowell 2018). Recent theorists, including Jonathan Crary, have argued that this fetishization of work is a signature feature of 'Late Capitalism', where productivity is of premium value in the cultural economy (Crary 2012). Referring specifically to design practice, Guy Julier has written of the specific value of performative cultures of work in the design industries, where design is 'sociologically determined', as a lifestyle choice, or a 'routinized behaviour' rather than a technical form of professional expertise (Julier 2014: 54; 2007: 43).

Important socioeconomic factors underpin the changing value of the home as a cultural setting for different types of work and labour. As Angela McRobbie argues, the notion of precarity has been particularly important in the shaping of identities in fashion and other creative industries (McRobbie 1998; 2015). This notion is primarily rooted in what sociologists and cultural economists describe as 'the new economy', linked to market de-regulation in the 1980s (Julier 2010; 2017). Here, the practice of working from home, is revealed to be an inevitable feature of work under the conditions of neoliberalism, where de-regulation loosened the bind of labour contracts and triggered a soaring property rental market, reshaping the individual's relationship to work and, as consequence, their working identities (Crary 2012; McRobbie 2015; Julier 2017; see also Harvey 1991).

The pages of fashion media in post-war Britain examined in this chapter offer a view onto the social construction of the Consultant Designer as a public figure for a new profession. Fashioning an aspirational image for the designer formed an important part of the project of professionalization, where design work was aligned with the values of idealized living. In this sense, it shows how fashion media discourse performs a function in defining what Stuart Hall has termed the 'aesthetics of existence'; a 'deliberate stylization of daily life in practices of self-production in specific modes of conduct' (Hall in Hall and du Gay 1996: 13). As the case studies examined in this chapter will suggest, the identity of the designer acts as an intermediary for the valorization of cultural work.

Questions of cultural identity at work and at home are particularly pertinent to the study of Design Culture. As Guy Julier states 'the site of the domestic has long been the traditional setting for design history and material culture – particularly in its early years' (Julier 2014: xiii), but the point of Design Culture, as it diverges from these fields, has been also 'to understand design at a range of levels' (Julier 2014: 4), whereby the 'qualities' by which design is practiced, performed and perceived, take on significance alongside the material objects produced. In this sense, the intermediary role of the designer in the network of production and consumption, is of critical value. Recent sociologists and design theorists have drawn attention to the formative, constitutive and representative role of work for designers as creative professionals (Elfline 2016; Wang and O'Ilhan 2010). More specifically, dealing with visual representations, architectural historian Andrew Saint has argued that portraiture not only plays an important representative role in the image of a profession for public audiences, but also in the construction of a 'self-image', held within the profession (Saint 1984). As such, the staging of such photography is rarely incidental, but carefully constructed. This chapter focuses on the cultural production of work in the design industry by focusing on its representation in fashion media at a critical period in the professionalization of design in post-war Britain.

The period after the Second World War in Britain marked the intensification of professionalization in many facets of working life. Perhaps one of the most visible shifts occurred in the expansion of the service industries, through the proliferation of new specialized work tasks including advertising, marketing and design. These newly formed professions took on a separate status to the older professions in Britain and worked according to different logics and cultures of professionalism. While professional bodies in design in Britain, including the Society of Industrial Artists (SIA) (1930–) tried to mimic the codes established in architecture and engineering, they were commonly represented, especially within media discourse, alongside the artist. As such, the image of the designer was a composite of artist and professional, forming the basis for what would later be loosely held together under the rubric of 'creative professional' (Armstrong 2017; Armstrong and McDowell 2018).

The representation of the designer in Britain was aligned with the broader project of design promotion taking place in America and Western Europe, particularly pronounced in Sweden, Denmark, Germany and Britain, in the early twentieth century (Woodham 1997). In these places, professional organizations in various forms were set up to represent and promote the practice of design as an industry distinct to craftsmanship. The designer held an 'anonymous' status in Britain before the Second World War (Armstrong 2014; Woodham 1997). Partly in response to this relative anonymity and obscurity, designers and design organizations, including the SIA (1930–) and the Council of Industrial Design (1945) began to promote the profession through a range of media that included public exhibitions, television and the broadsheet and tabloid press. The Consultant Designer became a familiar protagonist of these promotional efforts.

The term 'Consultant Designer' was not used in Britain until the early 1950s, but was a position occupied by American designers from the 1940s, many of whom had achieved great social and material success, including industrial designer Raymond Loewy who featured on the cover of *Time Magazine* in October 1949. There, the consultant designer could be differentiated from his colleagues by the fact of his independence from the organization staff, whether working on an individual basis or as the head of a consultancy. The American Society of Industrial Designers (SID) (1944-) defined the consultant designer as a person who had specialized in at least three design areas and who now took on 'the entire scope of machine design by virtue of his broad knowledge and his ability to integrate the specialized work of others' (Marsh Bennett 1947).

Design historian Penny Sparke has argued that the emergence of the Consultant Designer in Britain was evidence of a 'more clearly defined' design profession there (Sparke 1983: 3). The special status of the Consultant Designer was formally recognized by the SIA in 1953, when it established a group for the 'General Consultant Designer' to 'bring together for purposes of discussion, exhibitions of work, public relations generally and for the formulation of Codes of Conduct, those members of the society, who, having had specialized experience in one branch of design are in practice as both general and consultant designers' (*SIA Journal*, October, 1953). They held their meetings at the Royal College of Art, followed by a lunch at the Arts Club, Soho, London. Members of the group were Fellows of the SIA, the highest level of status within Society's membership structure. Only two were women.[2] As such, they were not representative of the profession as a whole, but of a particular group within it. As leaders of their own consultant businesses and active members of professional organizations, these designers were invested in the promotion of design as a profession. Membership included Misha Black, Milner Gray, FHK Henrion, Jacqueline Groag and Gaby Schreiber.

In February 1960, the *Observer* newspaper stated that 'the emergence of General Consultant Designers as a group in Britain within the past year is an indication that we are slowly coming round [*sic*] to the idea of design as a necessary element in daily life' (*Observer,* 1960). The *Sunday Times* stated in 1960 that 'industrial design has developed into one of the glossiest of the professions and the most quasi-scientific of the applied arts and acquired a truly Hollywoodian glamour' (Harling 1960). The following two sections of this chapter focus on case study examinations of two prominent members of the SIA General Consultant Designer Group: FHK Henrion and Gaby Schreiber. As will be discussed, both designers were frequently photographed and represented to the public in their home-studio environment, even though both ran successful design consultancy offices in central London. The final section of the chapter reflects on how and why the home was used as a setting in which to represent these two designers and suggests some of the ways in which this functions in the production of contemporary design culture.

FHK Henrion: 'The Home of an Artist and Designer in Pond Street, Hampstead'

FHK Henrion, graphic designer and General Consultant Designer, came to London via Paris, in 1939 as a Jewish refugee. Having been trained under Paul Colin in Paris, he first worked with the Modern Architectural Research Society, the Ministry of Information and then on the South Bank exhibition of the Festival of Britain, 1951. Throughout his professional life, he was 'deeply concerned to advance the status of his profession' (Artmonsky 2011: 10), serving as President of Alliance Graphique Internationale in 1972, the Society of Industrial Artists and Designers (SIAD) in 1963–4 and the International Council of Graphic Design Associations, (ICOGRADA) 1968–70. He also taught at the Royal College of Art and the London College of Printing throughout his career. In 1951, he formed Henri Design Associates, one of the most prolific and highly respected design consultancies of the period, with clients including British Airways, KLM and the General Post Office.

Henrion was photographed extensively by staff photographers of the British media and for organizations including the Council of Industrial Design and Royal Society of Arts, as evidenced in the volume of press clippings he organized in folders now held within his archive at the University of Brighton Design Archives, UK. Henrion was self-conscious of the value of the media in representing the role of the designer to the public. In 1966, he referred to the public interest in the figure of the Consultant Designer in Britain in a lecture as follows:

> Design has become fashionable. The leading Sunday papers devote two to four pages to it and even some of the serious weeklies feature design from time to time with critical appraisals of design problems. Hollywood produced a film where the hero was an industrial designer and even some public schools' career-masters consider it a possible profession for some

FIGURE 9.1 *Portrait of FHK Henrion at work in his studio, Undated, Photograher Colin Tait, FHK Henrion Archive, University of Brighton Design Archives.*

of the boys leaving, not necessarily restricted to those who are otherwise hopeless and have merely a faculty for drawing (Henrion 1966).

For Henrion and others invested in the promotion of design as an aspirational profession, this media coverage and public interest was complimentary to the project of raising the status and esteem of the profession in Britain more generally.

In 1958, *Homes and Gardens* magazine featured an article entitled 'The Home of an Artist and Designer in Pond Street, Hampstead'. The article focused on Henrion's personal taste, noting the 'cleverly chosen colours' of the Henrion home, stating that 'the Henrions are experimenting all over the house with every kind of indoor plant from cactus to creeper' (*Homes and Gardens*, 1958). Every stylistic detail of the designer's home was reported to the reader. In March 1960, *Tatler* Magazine published a double page spread on the Hampstead home of FHK Henrion. It read:

> Both of the Henrions work at home; so she has a studio (off the garden) and he has two offices and a studio, a conversion done last year. His office is divided into working and reception areas by a long sofa (modern). Behind his desk (Danish teak) and chair (Victorian) is a wall of revolving bookshelves (his own design) (Tatler 1960).

This idealized description of the artist-designer couple reveals the positioning of the home as a fashionable setting for the practice of a new, modern working arrangement, whereby work and home, labour and leisure, found an easy and pleasurable coexistence. The writer's explicit reference to Henrion's 'own design' suggests to the reader that personal taste and intuition were integral to the Consultant Designer's expertise and could be viewed in the context of other design styles: 'Danish' and 'Victorian'. Henrion's Hampstead address was also an important feature of his cultural capital as a designer in this period. As is well known, Hampstead was the London address for a network of eminent artists, designers and architects, including eminent sculptor Barbara Hepworth and architect Erno Goldfinger, who socialized and worked together professionally (Kinross 1990). Henrion's association with this important network was clearly implied in discussions of his home. For these journalists, Henrion's cosmopolitanism, as an éimgré, was presented as a contributing factor towards his authority as a consultant designer and a figure of British society.

Gaby Schreiber: An Eaton Square home

Gaby Schreiber, originally Austrian, moved to England in the late 1930s, to embark on a highly successful career as an interior and product designer, producing the first examples of moulded plastic cabinet furniture for British manufacturer Runcolite Limited. In 1943, she set up Gaby Schreiber and Associates, based in Chelsea, London, where she led a design consultancy, working on interior design for British Overseas Aircraft Corporation (BOAC) 1957–63, to cabin cruisers, ocean liners and department stores. In the 1960s, she became director of Convel Ltd and subsequently Convel Design International. Like Henrion, Schreiber was committed to the promotion of design as a profession and was active in a number of professional design networks, through her involvement as Fellow of the SIAD, a member of the General Consultant Designers Group and International Council of Societies of Industrial Design (ICSID). She also sat on the jury for the CoID's Duke of Edinburgh Award for Elegant Design in 1960 and 1961. From the immediate post-war period until the end of her career in the 1980s, Schreiber attracted an unusually high volume of media interest both in her public appearance as a professional designer, especially in lifestyle and fashion media with a predominantly female readership. Schreiber's vivid presence in this forum is particularly interesting given the relative 'invisibility' of women designers in Britain at this time (Seddon 2000). As cultural historians have established, professionalism and femininity were categories generally held apart in this period (Hall and Davidoff 1991). Schreiber's archive, therefore, provides a fascinating glimpse into the 'boundary work' involved in constructing professional identity as a woman. For Schreiber, the visual rhetoric of the home-office frequently served a mediating function in the maintenance of these boundaries.

Like Henrion, Schreiber kept meticulous records of her public appearances in the popular press, now held in scrapbooks at the V&A Archives of Art and Design. Schreiber came under particularly intense scrutiny within the pages of fashion and lifestyle press between 1958 and 1966, at the peak of her career. This includes interviews and special features in *Punch, Tatler, House and Garden, The Birmingham Mail, Vogue, The Times, Evening Standard, Harpers Bazaar, Sunday Telegraph* and *Daily Mail*. Like Henrion, Schreiber was also extensively photographed by photographers for design organizations including the Council of Industrial Design and the ICSID. Throughout, it is especially striking to note how Schreiber is shown working from the desk of her home-office in Eaton Square, London. This is the setting for her portrait, taken by the Council of Industrial Design in 1948 (Figure 9.2).

This portrait presents a fascinating image of a designer negotiating the boundaries between professionalism and femininity, with the home-office serving as a setting through which to mediate these cultural gaps. In a brief overview of Schreiber's career in a collection of *Women in Design*, Liz McQuiston states that Schreiber projects 'qualities of sophistication and professionalism' in her physical appearance (McQuiston 1988). This forms a recurrent feature of the representations of Schreiber at home published in *Vogue, Harpers Bazaar, House and Garden* and *Tatler*. Even though Schreiber ran her own consultancy office, it is notable that the magazine chose to represent her within her home setting. While it would be possible to view this representation as an indicator of the limited movement of women beyond

FIGURE 9.2 *Portrait of Gaby Schreiber, Photographer: Gee & Watson, (1948),* Design Council Archive, University of Brighton Design Archives. Original reference: GB-1837-DES-DCA-30-1-POR-S-SC-48-1874.

the domestic sphere, this would be to overlook the similar representations of her male contemporaries. For both Henrion and Schreiber, the domestic setting served a symbolic function in representing and positioning their work as Consultants. It depicted their independence from the factory floor and their position as 'objective', 'free-thinking' individuals, qualities often associated with the position of the Consultant Designer in these years (Dreyfuss 1955; Henrion 1959).

Nevertheless, Schreiber's gender was an important feature of her representation in other ways, as she was idealized for an emergent readership of aspirational career women in Britain. Historian Cynthia White, in her landmark examination of women's fashion magazines, argued that from the early 1950s, both *Vogue* and *Harpers Bazaar* championed the image of the 'New Woman', presenting the career girl as an (often unattainable) aspiration for their reader (White 1970). Media portrayals of Schreiber certainly convey a fascination with her ability to combine qualities of femininity, glamour and work. In 1951, *The Evening News* marvels at her ability to combine 'femininity and efficiency', evoking an idyllic domestic scene: 'The slim, elegant woman of 35 with red gold hair and glowing dark eyes believes she is the only industrial consultant in London. While we talked, Ninotschka, her poodle dozed off in front of a log fire in Mrs Schreiber's office with its white walls, blue curtains and claret coloured chairs' (*The Evening News*, 1951).

In 1956, Schreiber's status as a taste leader was underlined in an advertorial style feature in *Vogue*, in which she is shown test-driving the new Mark VII *Jaguar* car. In this piece, *Vogue* describes Schreiber as a 'capable woman of affairs', again underlining her uniquely desirable career status. The article focuses on her 'designer's eye', positioning Schreiber as an expert in matters of cultural and aesthetic judgement: 'As a designer whose time is devoted to making decorative a wide range of objects and backgrounds for daily work, Gaby Schreiber naturally demands a high standard of looks from her car and those of the Mark VII Jaguar had quite a part in influencing her choice' (Jennings, *Vogue*, 1956). Here, *Vogue* directly implicates the role of the designer in the 'symbolic work of creating needs' (Bourdieu 1984). In 1958, Tatler Magazine featured an article on Schreiber placing greater focus on her home-office. Entitled 'Comet Designer', the article described Schreiber's role as a consultant designer, making particular reference to her fashionable lifestyle:

If Mrs Schreiber were asked which of her many achievements she takes most pride in, she would probably point to her collection of drawings. This ranges from Constantin Guys to Picasso and Marini and includes an unusual Van Gogh and Matisse. The collection decorates the immense top-floor drawing room (which she designed herself) of her Eaton Square home. (*Tatler*, September 1958).

In a similar fashion to the representation of FHK Henrion, the interior decoration of Schreiber's home was used to position the role and expertise of the Consultant Designer as a figure of unquestioned taste. Like Henrion, Schreiber's status as an émigré was not incidental to her media persona. Media profiles frequently drew upon Schreiber's cosmopolitanism as a point of distinction that endowed her with the requisite sophistication and refinement to practice as a Consultant Designer. This outsider status was a feature of émigré culture mobilized by many designers working internationally at this time (Clarke and Shapira 2017).

Working from home

The case studies presented in this chapter offer a view onto the relationship between home and work at a critical period in the formation of an identity for the Consultant Designer in Britain. It argues that the image of working from home served several rhetorical functions for the profession at this time. It presented the values of personal taste and stylized living that gave authority and legitimacy to the designer's claims to expertise in matters of taste. It celebrated the Consultant Designer's elevated professional status and freedom from the factory floor or the corporate office, setting them apart from the everyday 'staff designer' and emphasizing their authority as individuals. Henrion and Schreiber's representations further promised a new vision of work that was modern, pleasurable and seductive. Whereas women artists in the early twentieth century, as discussed by Zoë Thomas, had previously been restricted to the home-studio as a means of negotiating the male dominated work environment (Thomas 2015), Schreiber's office offered something new and exciting; the promise of work and home life. If the maintenance of boundaries between work and home have presented an obstruction imposed through the division of labour since the industrial revolution (Nippert-Eng 1996), then these representations of Schreiber and Henrion suggested that it was possible to move between them. Working from home in this period thus offered a highly alluring and compelling vision of the future of work for aspirant readers of fashion and lifestyle press, a significant portion of which was female and largely excluded from professional culture.

Nevertheless, the convention of presenting the designer in their home-office also established boundaries around the public image of the designer. Focusing on the interior design choices of the designer reduced the image of the profession from a scientific problem-solving activity to a superficial practice largely concerned with questions of styling. Given that neither of these designers were exclusively involved in interior decoration, the continued focus on their choice of furnishings seems reductive for a profession that was seeking to establish a serious self-image alongside the architect and engineer. Nevertheless, as suggested earlier in this chapter, this stylistic concern was not incidental, but connected to the intermediary position the designer held in managing the cultural distance between production and consumption (Bourdieu 1984; see also Negus 2002).

In a contemporary context, the image of the designer working from the café, home-studio and other informal spaces, holds strong in media representations, and has been celebrated as a signature feature of the so-called creative class (Florida 2002). Instagram has become a platform for creative professionals to fashion visions of their working practices. While these contemporary representations share some of the qualities of the working lifestyle represented in Schreiber and Henrion, there are also important historical distinctions to make. Where the glamourization of work in the 1950s served a promotional role in advancing the status of a designer, the contemporary designer's situation, as McRobbie has persuasively argued of artists and designers in London and Berlin, is steered by the logics of the market economy. The invention of digital platforms as sites for work and creative labour, such as blogging, also puts further pressure on the boundaries between work and home, labour and leisure, making them more blurred than ever (Crary 2012; Rocamora 2018). For many contemporary designers, the decision to work from home is not a choice, but an economic necessity.

For Gaby Schreiber and FHK Henrion, working from home served a rhetorical function as a representative setting for a practice that had not yet found a visible identity in the industrial economy. Their representations show that the design profession was defined and represented through a visual language rooted in the domestic rather than industrial environment, planting an early precedent for the 'glamourization of work' and the erosion of boundaries between work and leisure (Wissinger 2015). The case studies discussed in this chapter opened up a specific moment in the re-invention of what it meant to be 'at work', a cultural category that continues to evolve and change over time. If, as Guy Julier states, the 'self-image and status of designers is sociologically determined' (Julier 2014: 54), then this chapter suggests that the home can be a surprisingly productive and revealing site on which to view the changing self-image and status of the design profession.

Notes

1 According to a Design Council report in 2015, 22.3% of the current workforce in design are working freelance. This is in comparison with 13.8% of the UK workforce as a whole. (Design Council, 2015).

2 They were Jacqueline Groag and Gaby Schreiber. This low representation of women was proportionate to the Society in general as female membership of the SIA was roughly one-third of the total.

References

Armstrong, L. (2014), Unpublished PhD thesis, 'Designing a Profession: The Structure, Organisation and Identity of the Design Profession in Britain 1930–2010', University of Brighton, 2014. AHRC Collaborative Doctoral Award with the Chartered Society of Designers.

Armstrong, L. (2016), 'Steering a Course between Professionalism and Commercialism: The Society of Industrial Artists and the Code of Conduct for the Professional Designer, 1930–1970', *Journal of Design History*, 29(2): 161–79.

Armstrong, L. (2017), 'A New Image for a New Profession: Self-Image and Representation in the Professionalisation of Design in Britain, 1945–1960', *Journal of Consumer Culture*, Online First, 20 July 2017

Armstrong, L. and McDowell, F. (eds.) (2018), *Fashioning Professionals: Representation and Identity At Work in the Creative Industries*, London: Bloomsbury.

Artmonsky, R. (2011), *FHK Henrion: Design,* London: ACC Art Books.
Bourdieu, P. (1984), *Distinction: A Social Critique of the Judgement of Taste*, translated by Richard Nice, Harvard: Harvard University Press.
Clarke, A. and Shapira, E. (2017), *Émigré Cultures in Design and Architecture*, London: Bloomsbury Press.
Crary, J. (2012), 24/7: *Late Capitalism and the End of Sleep*, London: Verso.
Design Council, (2015), The Design Economy, the Value of Design to the UK.
Dreyfuss, H. (1955), 'Profile of an Organisation, Transcript of a Talk given at Harvard University Graduate School of Business Administration', Cambridge, MA. Cooper-Hewitt Design Library, Rare Books, TS171.4 D7451955 CHMRB.
Elfline, R. (2016), 'Superstudio and the Refusal to Work', *Design and Culture*, 8(1): 55–77.
Florida, R. (2002), *The Rise of the Creative Class*, New York: Basic Books.
Hall, C. and Davidoff, L. (1991), *Family Fortunes: Men and Women of the English Middle Class, 1780–1850*, Chicago: University of Chicago Press.
Hall and du Gay (1996), *Questions of Cultural Identity*, London: Sage.
Harling, R. (1960), 'Stylists of Industry', *Sunday Times*, (7 February 1960).
Harvey, D. (1991), *The Condition of Post-Modernity*, London: Wiley Blackwell.
Henrion, (1966), 'The Designer as a Problem Solver', FHK Henrion Speeches, Henrion archive, University of Brighton Design Archives.
Henrion, (1959), *DIA Yearbook*, (1959), DIA Archive, V&A Archives of Art and Design, AAD/1997/7/120.
Henrion, FHK (1959), *DIA Yearbook*, DIA Archive, V&A Archives of Art and Design, V&A Archives of Art and Design, AAD/1997/7/120.
Henrion, FHK (1966), 'The Designer as a Problem Solver', FHK Henrion Speeches, University of Brighton Design Archives.
Jennings, M. (July 1956), 'The Woman at the Wheel, *Vogue*, Gaby Schreiber Archive, V&A Archives of Art and Design, AAD/2009/7/7.
Julier, G. (2007), 'Design Practice within a Theory of Practice', *Design Principles and Practices: An International Journal*, 1(2): 43–50.
Julier, G. (2010; 2014), *The Culture of Design*, London: Sage.
Julier, G. (2017), *Economies of Design*, London: Sage.
Kinross, R. (1990), 'Émigré Graphic Designers in Britain: Around the Second World War and Afterwards', *Journal of Design History*, 3(1): 35–57.
Marsh Bennett, R. (1947), 'The Education of the Industrial Designer', in Walter Dorwin Teague, Richard Marsh Bennett, and Edward S. Evans, Jr. (eds), *Good Design is Your Business*, Buffalo, NY: The Buffalo Fine Arts Academy.
McQuiston, L. (1988), *Women in Design: A Contemporary View*, London: Random House.
McRobbie, A. (1998), *British Fashion Design: Rag Trade or Image Industry?*, London: Routledge.
McRobbie, A. (2015), *Be Creative*, London: Polity Press.
Negus, R. (2002), 'The Work of Cultural Intermediaries and Enduring the Distance Between Production and Consumption', *Cultural Studies*, 16(4): 501–15.
Nippert-Eng, C. (1996), *Home Work: Negotiating Boundaries through Everyday Life*, Chicago: University of Chicago Press.
Nixon, S. and Crewe, B. (2004), 'Pleasure Culture at Work? Gender, Consumption and Work-based Identities in the Creative Industries', *Consumption, Markets and Culture*, 7(2): 129–47.

Rocamora, A. (2018), 'The Labor of Fashion Blogging' in Armstrong and Mc Dowell, *Fashioning Professionals*, London: Bloomsbury Press: 65–85.
Saint, A. (1984), *The Image of the Architect*, Yale: Yale University Press.
Schulman, A. 'Editor's Letter', *Vogue*, April 2014.
Seddon, J. (2000), 'Mentioned but denied Significance: Women Designers and the Professionalisation of Design in Britain c.1920–1951', *Gender and History*, 12(2): 425–47.
SIA Journal, (October 1953), Box 95, CSD Archive.
Sparke, P. (1983), *Consultant Design: The History and Practice of the Designer in Industry*, Oxford: Pembridge Press.
Tatler, (September 1958), No.2983, Gaby Schreiber Archive, V&A, AAD/1991/11/14/3.
Tatler, (March 1960), FHK Henrion press clippings, University of Brighton Design Archives.
Thomas, Z. (2015), 'At Home with the Women's Guild of Arts: Gender and Professional Identity in London Studios, c.1880–1925', *Women's History Review*, 24(6): 938–64.
Wang, D. and O'Ilhan, A. (2010), 'Holding Creativity Together: A Sociological Theory of the Design Professions', *Design Issues*, 25(1): 5–21.
White, C. L. (1970), *Women's Magazines 1963–1968*, London: Josephs Press.
Wissinger, E. (2015), *This Year's Model: Fashion, Media and the Making of Glamour*, New York: New York University Press.
Woodham, J. (1997), *Twentieth Century Design*, Oxford: Oxford University Press.

CHAPTER TEN

On the professional and everyday design of graphic artefacts

Sarah Owens

Introduction

Graphic design is – in contrast to more rigidly controlled occupations in fields such as medicine or law – a highly permeable profession. It allows flexible career paths, and is more often than not open to outsiders or self-taught designers. Although there exist numerous professional organizations in design, the field lacks strict licensing procedures or those of penalizing misconduct that may end careers (Julier 2008: 44). In graphic design, this circumstance grants employers and clients a relatively high level of freedom when hiring or commissioning. Thus, even the non-formally trained designer, if applying with an interesting portfolio, has a real chance of entering the professional sphere.

An increased access to professional tools, such as desktop publishing software, has also made it easier for non-formally trained designers to enter the profession. At the same time, it has allowed everyday (i.e. non-professional and non-expert) designers to produce graphic artefacts on their own and for their own use. These technological changes are accompanied by a more general opening up of design towards other disciplines and the public, as evident in the participatory design movement since the 1970s, or more recently through design thinking and design for social innovation. Our visual world thus always contains both professional and everyday design, and the forms in which everyday design has become visible are multiplying to include signs, forms, posters, advertisements, flyers, brochures, business cards, greeting cards, stationary, invoices, slide presentations, websites, blogs and various other types of graphic artefacts.

Such production has been fostered not only by an increased accessibility to tools and services that ensure a mode of production and presentation that looks more finished. It has also been aided by templates or pre-produced graphic elements (likely produced by professional designers) that tie in with contemporary aesthetics and thus allow an everyday designer to achieve results that appear more current. Where typewriters and copiers had, in comparison with letterpress, phototypesetting or offset printing, clearly signalled informality and possibly a non-professional production, digital printing that is affordable and easily adaptable graphic elements in current fashion can assign everyday design into the semi-professional category, even if it can still be distinguished from professional design. The way in which everyday designers deal with design tasks has in the past years also been influenced by the visibility of graphic design (e.g. as topics of films such as *Helvetica* (2007) by Gary Hustwit, or interdisciplinary exhibitions such as *Can Graphic Design Save Your Life?* at the Wellcome Collection in 2017), as well as an interest in gaining access to graphic design knowledge (e.g. through online tutorials or magazines focusing on typeface design or hand lettering). Still, the graphic design profession tends to draw a strict boundary between what it considers professional design and what it considers 'amateur'. For instance, Steven Heller and Teresa Fernandes in their book *Becoming a Graphic Designer*, warn that 'anyone sitting at a computer loaded with a page layout program and a newsletter/periodical/flyer template can pretend to be a graphic designer. ... Today, all the tools of editorial design are at the amateur's disposal, which opens up unfettered access to every possible mistake' (Heller and Fernandes 1999: 9).

When this boundary is drawn, there are certain ways in which an 'us' (professional designers) and 'them' (non-professional designers) are positioned against each other. On a general level, and as the quote by Heller and Fernandes illustrates, there is often no finer distinction made between various types of non-professional designers, which in effect homogenizes this group and renders differences, for instance in status or skill, invisible. Thus, there is no distinction made between everyday designers – non-professional, non-expert designers who have a concept of design but little further interest – and amateur designers, who might possess a significant level of skill and might orient themselves towards professional design, striving to achieve recognition for their work among peers. This chapter views the relationship between professional and everyday designers as particularly interesting, as they could be seen as constituting two ends of a continuum. Consequently, the professional reactions towards everyday designers appear more intense, both on the negative and the positive side.

At the heart of a mainly negative reaction lies the belief that everyday design poses a threat to professional design: by being able to produce graphic artefacts themselves, everyday designers stop hiring professional designers, and at the same time 'pollute' the visual world with unskilled design. Professional designers then understandably reject everyday design, even if this results in denying these artefacts the status of having been designed at all. Here, the boundary between professional and everyday design seems clear-cut: everyday design can allegedly be identified quite easily through typical mistakes that betray even a glossy finish achieved through a high production quality.

In contrast, the highly positive reaction views everyday design as a source of inspiration. Painted signs, handwritten price tags or symbols on transport crates (e.g. Lutz 1990) show peculiarities that deviate from the professional norm and therefore pique the designer's interest. Worth is attributed to this type of design due to its perceived authenticity, spontaneity and purity. It is seen as an expression of raw creativity and thus can be set as an effective counterpoint to a design which is too market-oriented, or too self-referential and elitist. But within this approach, everyday design is also not on a par with professional design. If it cannot be used by professional design as inspiration, it is useless. The specific conditions that lead to everyday creative production, the goals it aims to fulfil, and the functions it can fulfil are here not considered.

A notion of what everyday design is arguably follows from a definition by professional designers, meaning that it is a result of negotiations within a professional design discourse. The design profession is shaped by its discourse, as well as by its active promotion and protection of the tasks it has assigned itself. It also shapes itself through an ongoing differentiation from other professions. There are several lenses through which these mechanisms may be viewed, for instance, by conceiving of professional design as a field of cultural production (Bourdieu 1984), or as part of a system of professions (Abbott 1988). In the following, however, I approach the graphic design profession by discussing how discursive statements contribute to the setting of boundaries between professional design and everyday design, drawing on Michel Foucault's discussion of the order of discourse (Foucault 1981). In outlining three processes by which discourse is contained, 'tamed' and structured, Foucault provides insight into how a field deals with the possible danger of being flooded by its own statements – by the uncontrolled proliferation of utterances, subjects, objects, institutions. These processes run parallel to official means of creating order such as licenses, and their description therefore seems especially valuable for examining graphic design. The examples discussed are taken from observation or from interviews with everyday designers (Owens 2012).

The order of graphic design discourse

In his book *L'ordre du discours* (based on an inaugural lecture 1970 at the Collège de France), Foucault emphasized how discursive statements wield power by establishing and prescribing certain forms of practice and ways of thinking (Foucault 1981). They separate what is to be regarded as part of the discourse from that which is to be regarded outside of it. Those who obtain the power of making these types of distinctions by being considered experts or qualified members (e.g. of a profession) are at the same time bound by their discursive statements. They cannot move outside a distinction they themselves have created. Thus, the notion of who is 'us' and who is 'them' cannot suddenly be overthrown, and even if such a change is gradually effected by exterior forces (e.g. technological change), there appears a renewed effort in reinforcing a boundary that has become blurred. The fact that there has to be an 'us' and a 'them', an 'inside' and 'outside' is not up for debate. So even if a boundary has dissolved due to radically altered conditions, it is instead drawn elsewhere. In graphic design, this process takes place less by means of licensing or official regulations and more through a continuous re-definition of what the graphic design profession considers its main tasks, who it considers as possessing the necessary qualifications or ability to deal with the defined tasks in order to lead to the desired outcomes, as well as which outcomes are desired and which are not.

In design, discursive statements such as design objects, artefacts, texts or debate are the basis of descriptions that govern the behaviour, thoughts and feelings of those involved in professional design, since in order to be recognized as a professional designer, one must act, think, know and talk in ways that are viewed as being appropriate or typical of the profession (Gee 2005). They could therefore be said to create the subjects, objects and places associated with design, and in so doing, they produce knowledge about them. What we know about graphic design, what it is and what graphic designers do, is determined by the currently dominant discourse within graphic design.

The currently dominant discourse within a discipline must protect its ability to classify, judge, issue forth new or render obsolete old statements, and does this mainly by portraying its knowledge, procedures and principles as true (Foucault 1981: 54–5). Graphic design has no choice other than to declare that the only true knowledge about graphic design is that which the domain itself possesses, otherwise its claims would be dubious. It would be highly unsettling should clients, viewers or audiences entertain the thought that the experts have no clear grasp on what design is, how it is done or what it can do. Validity and legitimacy are furthermore achieved by three specific mechanisms outlined by Foucault: *external exclusion, internal exclusion* and the *rarefaction of speaking subjects*. Through these procedures, a discourse artificially restricts itself, thereby corroborating its claim of truth.

Good design

External exclusion governs *what* may be said (verbally or materially), determines what is completely forbidden to be said, and assigns statements either as belonging to the discipline or as situated outside it. Statements that are thought to belong outside the discourse are rejected or ignored. Inside is 'design', 'good design', or more specifically, 'expertly made professional design' while outside is 'not design', 'bad design' and more specifically, 'amateur design'. On a more general level, the distinction that is made can be said to be one between statements that are 'reasonable' and those which are 'unreasonable'. This distinction surfaces whenever assumptions are made that everyday designers create 'unconsciously' or when everyday graphic artefacts are said to be 'ugly' and 'non-functional', or are thought of as being results of merely a whim or personal preferences. It is therefore not enough to draw a line between the inside and outside sphere. That which is thought to belong outside also must be rejected and labelled as 'unreasonable'. Such statements are also shut out of official histories and canons. They serve not as viable models, but are seen as curiosities.

As Foucault notes, the 'unreasonable' may however also be seen as holding a deeper truth, just as a court jester may be the only one who is allowed to voice the unspeakable. This idea is evident in the aforementioned view of everyday design as inspiration. The graphic designer Tibor Kalman, for instance, who was known for his love of vernacular graphics, has stated: 'I am interested in imperfections, quirkiness, insanity, unpredictability' (Bader 2013: 74). Everyday design is 'unreasonable', but it is precisely because of this that it can reflect a 'true' and untainted creativity. Here however, the main function of the 'unreasonable' is to play the counterpart to the 'reasonable'. Definitions of what 'good design' is and how it may be achieved are still reinforced.

The use of the typeface Comic Sans is a telling example. While initially regarded simply as a fun and unspectacular typeface, its use became unacceptable among the graphic design profession due to its extensive usage by everyday designers. Comic Sans was originally designed for a software package aimed at children and novice users. It used comic-style illustrations to create a less inhibiting mode of interaction. Comic Sans was designed by Vincent Connaire to accompany these illustrations. The typeface later became part of the Windows 95 operating system and through this, achieved a widespread usage in desktop publishing by everyone who sought an informal, playful look. Soon, the typeface gained the reputation of an 'amateur font' and for professional designers, there seemed to be no plausible scenario that would warrant its use (Helfand 2006). While some in their argumentation tried to explain why this typeface was badly (or too quickly) designed and why it is predisposed for improper usage, others indulged in emotion-filled tirades (e.g. Holly and David Combs with their 'Ban Comic Sans' initiative). The debate also flared up recently in the public chastising of the CERN research institute for announcing the discovery of the Higgs Boson particle on slides that contained Comic Sans (Kingsley 2012). The CERN reacted in 2014 with an April Fool's joke, claiming that it had adopted the typeface for all of its communications (O'Luanaigh 2014).

This criticism, however, does not consider why the typeface is being used by everyday designers. The argument of improper usage is telling in this respect – it implies that there is a proper way to use the typeface, but that everyday designers do not possess the required skill and judgement. In this sense, the criticism aimed at Comic Sans is a veiled critique of the perceived lack of skill and knowledge on the part of everyday designers. And the reasoning is circular: Everything everyday designers produce is 'bad design'. Since they use Comic Sans, and since Comic Sans has been badly designed, anything using Comic Sans is bad design. A bad design is easily identifiable by its use of Comic Sans.

As soon as the typeface was considered *taboo* by professional designers, alongside other 'don'ts' such as stretching or distorting typefaces, a niche within the profession discovered its subversive potential. In deliberately pursuing 'ugly design', some professional designers began to imitate everyday design, in the knowledge that this affront or rule-breaking would have the effect intended (Asensio and Lorenz 2012). Alongside 'ugly design', Comic Sans (re-)entered the design discourse. Strictly speaking, using Comic Sans in a subversive manner did, however, not suddenly render it acceptable. It was within this context and for this intention a useful means of creating a stir. What is also important to note here is that these designers did not imitate actual forms of everyday design. Instead, they drew mainly on an abstract notion of it. As a result, 'ugly design' does not replicate everyday design, but instead is made up of renditions or stereotypes that assemble formal characteristics attributed to everyday designers by professional designers (e.g. clip art or drop shadows). By containing merely stereotypes, 'ugly design' eschews a meaningful dialogue with everyday design and therefore neither can account for its actual function nor understand its conditions. A subversive use of Comic Sans by a professional designer also drains it of its original connotations. Rather than being a playful typeface intended for informal and friendly messages or dialogue, it instead begins connoting a radical stance from within the profession. A commentary of this kind can be limited. In the case of Comic Sans, it has been restricted to certain domains, such as design for cultural institutions, self-initiated or personal projects, or satire. Even proponents of 'ugly design' will find it difficult to recommend it as the main typeface for a large corporation.

Simultaneously, everyday designers have become aware of the portrayal of Comic Sans as 'unprofessional', and therefore some have begun avoiding it. There are also more and more typefaces offered by operating systems and software, thus presenting many viable alternatives. This could mean that in everyday design, the use of Comic Sans has been decreasing or that, should it be employed, this is done in a more strategic manner and in awareness of the debate surrounding the typeface. This development shows that a discursive statement possibly intended only for the discipline or profession can travel, it can influence the 'outside'. To the profession then, rejecting Comic Sans is the proper thing to do, while for everyday designers, rejecting it becomes a mark of distinction for those who have gained some form of insider knowledge against those who remain uninformed. External exclusion in this case governs both the inside and outside, professional rules are here applied to non-professional circles.

Good designing

The second mechanism sketched by Foucault is that of *internal exclusion*. This process governs *how* things may be said and aims to limit chance and arbitrariness. It classifies and arranges. It separates discursive statements according to whether they refer to the dominant discourse, are attributable to certain authors, result from the use of certain tools or equipment, follow certain rules or methods. For graphic design, this means that there are not unlimited ways in which a graphic artefact can be made and still be considered a valid part of the discourse. Internal exclusion is not only a distinction between outstanding and acceptable work, the former of which is canonized, but also between work that is recognizable as graphic design as it adheres to the standards and principles set by this particular discourse, and work that cannot demonstrate the necessary links – via citation, author and/or method – to this domain.

In graphic design, the process of rule-following is interesting in this respect. Publications that list current do's and don'ts appear quite regularly, especially in the area of typography. The rules that are formulated can be very specific, for instance, the rule that during typesetting, one should 'avoid more than three consecutive hyphenated lines' (Bringhurst 1999: 42) and thus demand precise adherence. In the typography community, perceived transgressions are rapidly brought into debate and sides are taken. But a peculiarity within this discourse is the formulation and repetition of a rule that states that 'all other rules should be broken'. An action that in other areas could lead to the work being perceived as invalid is here portrayed as desired behaviour. Purportedly, what rule-breaking does is show how far the design student or novice has come in mastering the activity in order to be able to leave the basics behind. However, at the same time, rule-breaking is not permitted if the designed artefact reflects that its designer has not mastered the rules. In ambiguous cases, further cues (e.g. designer, audience, quality of material, contained information, situation in which encountered) are taken into consideration to determine whether the statement is valid.

Some graphic design rules are of a relatively fleeting nature. Rules requiring the designer to refrain from using certain typefaces or graphic elements have a surprisingly short turnaround time, and in this differ from rules that aim to ensure that a designer applies skill, care and diligence. Due to their quickly shifting nature, temporary rules may appear arbitrary, and in the ongoing stream of digital influences, navigating what is permissible and what is not has become more difficult. Still, such rules need to be considered at least somewhat important in order for a non-adherence to acquire any significance. Otherwise, the rule-breaking becomes a mere quirk, a feeble form of eccentricity. More permanent rules, however, involve apart from aesthetic concerns long-term notions such as legibility and readability, forms of appropriate representation and so on. Following these rules can function as an important marker of skill, craft, ethos and responsibility; it confirms and substantiates the commitment of the professional designer to her profession. Hence, breaking more permanent rules requires highly favourable conditions that guarantee that the resulting discursive statement can be understood as an effective antithesis within the discourse, and that it does not run the risk of being assigned to the sphere of the 'unreasonable'. Flouting rules can be more easily tolerated and lauded as unconventional and exciting when it remains contained – when it addresses a very specific audience, at a certain point in time, within a smaller area of graphic design – and therefore functions as a contrast to the more dominant and widespread acceptance and adherence to these rules.

It is sometimes assumed that everyday design can be characterized by a non-observance of rules. This assumption grows more complex when acknowledging the acclaim given to some forms of rule-breaking as outlined above, and when recognizing that rules that are not known cannot be broken. Whether this assumption is true also hinges on what rules are considered. Particular typographic rules that, if observed, bespeak the mastery and finesse of the typographer (e.g. using ligatures or adjusting kerning) form part of a specialist education and are therefore difficult to access for an everyday designer. Gaining access to this knowledge, as well as trying to follow methods or aiming to understand established ways of thinking within professional design can therefore be a challenging undertaking for someone who has not been formally trained in design or who does not possess extensive practical experience. Very general rules, for instance, those concerning the direction of writing or basic hierarchical structures are in everyday graphic artefacts usually observed, since they form part of a general education in reading and writing. Thus, they are part of everyday knowledge that informs everyday designing. In a domain that, however, avoids notions of *best practice*; of thinking that there is only one correct way to design, a sense for the appropriateness of methods, for the relative weight of certain names, or for the currently permitted ways of referencing and commenting history and the present, is for the everyday designer difficult to obtain.

Good designers

The third exclusionary process active within a discourse *restricts the number of subjects* who are allowed to contribute. This process positions qualified individuals against unqualified ones, and assigns them roles. While qualified individuals may create, classify and prescribe, unqualified ones can merely listen, consume or follow. Qualified subjects must however first conform to certain standards and satisfy certain demands; they must have overcome typical obstacles and must appear credible, be it through having acquired a reasonable amount of experience or acceptable modes of education, or through showing the accepted kind of talent or promise.

Equally important is the acquisition of what Foucault terms 'rituals' (Foucault 1981: 64). These are certain sensibilities, forms of behaviour and ways of expression, as well as interpretative schemata that aid in deciphering meanings attributed to these expressions. Members of a profession can be seen as being disciplined by adopting specific phrases, mannerisms, assumptions and principles, the cornerstones of which are provided by a specialized education that controls knowledge and imparts certain ways of seeing, thinking, sensing and acting. Descriptions of these specific ways of perceiving and interacting with the world surface, for instance, in designers' accounts of their professional development. Vince Frost recollects that: 'I think I've always been a designer. I was always inquisitive. Even when I was delivering newspapers I wanted to do it quickly, accurately, and make sure the paper landed on the doorstep in a nice line' (Bader 2013: 8) and with this, attributes certain characteristics (efficient, diligent, neat) to himself as a professional designer. In a specialized design education, the focus lies on the acquisition of an awareness of the values and beliefs of the discipline, an orientation towards its subject matter, questions and methods, and the ability to distinguish between 'good' and 'bad' statements. Rituals show how the discourse is internalized.

Everyday designers are, in this sense, unqualified to contribute to the graphic design discourse. It is not only that they are denied the possibility of contributing meaningful statements, but that within the discourse, it becomes unthinkable for an everyday designer to achieve importance and therefore to hold definitional power. While some professional designers may concede that everyday design is indeed design, there is no possibility for everyday designers to tell professional designers how to design. The speaking is done internally and outward: professional designers judge their own discursive statements and assess everyday design, but the latter is not a two-way process. The assertion of expertise ensures that this process stays unilateral.

As shortly mentioned previously, a restricted access to knowledge may also enforce the boundary drawn between 'us' and 'them'. Foucault argues that some part of this restriction is always deliberate on the side of those who count themselves as members of the discipline. In effect, there is some degree of secrecy surrounding vital or foundational aspects of disciplinary knowledge. In graphic design, this applies for instance to initiatives that aim to educate everyday designers. These may declare that they disseminate expert knowledge to the benefit of everyday designers, but the distributed knowledge is often only a watered-down version, consisting of simplistic do's and don'ts or tutorials that aid imitation rather than acquisition of method. With their guarantee of outcomes that require little technical knowledge or experience, they hardly resemble the practical and theoretical knowledge employed by an expert designer in a tricky design situation. These initiatives appear progressive and inclusive, and thus it remains unquestioned what type of knowledge is in these cases actually offered to 'outsiders', and how this offer mirrors or distorts what everyday designers think expert designers do. Upon being confronted with such a limited portrayal of design knowledge, everyday designers might have good reason to ask: Is this all there is to it?

The keeping of secrets is, however, also partly unintentional. Some aspects of practical knowledge, gained through experience and reflection, cannot be transmitted. For instance, practical knowledge about what constitutes an appropriate curve on the serif of a single character, or about the appropriate measure between a block of text and the corner of the page on which it sits, both of which navigate between the calculated and the haphazard, is likely located somewhere in between brain, eye and executing hand. A hand, which, for instance, has repeatedly drawn such curves, or an eye that has repeatedly measured such distances in order to determine what is possible and what is not. It is difficult to transfer such knowledge in verbal form, let alone as simplistic rules that cannot consider the specificity of the design situation. The uniqueness of a graphic artefact, resulting from a distinctive blend of citations, the conditions of the design situation, the ethos of the designer, the particular methods used and intentions realized, make for another type of intransitive knowledge that leads to unintentional secrecy.

Everyday designers in turn are in their approach and self-perception likely influenced by professional notions of what constitutes design (Owens 2012), even if this influence remains veiled. They may be interested in a professional understanding of design, in which case their interest impacts on how they approach and frame design tasks. They might view these as creative tasks that require goals attributed to a professional understanding, such as originality and creativity. Or they might not directly refer to a professional understanding, but still aim to delineate creative pursuits from non-creative ones. They might also fully adopt a professional definition of everyday design (though resulting from exclusionary processes), and thus view themselves as 'non-designers'. This perspective readily links to a portrayal of creative production not as designing, but as simply 'fiddling around', emphasizing a lack of control over the task, even if such control exists. The self-portrayal as 'non-designer' reinforces again a separation between 'creative' and 'non-creative', by hinting at the assumption that some people are innately more artistic or talented in areas conducive to creative pursuits. In so doing, everyday designers disallow themselves any visual competence, practical knowledge or technical skill, even if their work shows a high awareness of functional and aesthetic aspects.

Through particular self-portrayals on both sides that evidence perceptions shaped by rituals and judgements, the sphere of professional design is rendered a highly specialized domain that comprises certain ways of thinking, speaking about and dealing with its subject matter. Even if the everyday designer is interested in the design discourse, she might therefore experience professional design as a domain that is obscured by specialist terminology, irreproducible criteria and phenomena that elude outsider attempts at comprehension.

Conclusion

When professions and disciplines emerge, they rely both on mechanisms of association and exclusion. A process that aims to exclude certain statements, methods, actions and individuals and thus fortify its own requires the *other*, but is not bilateral. The design discourse reserves itself the right to define everyday design, but denies everyday design the legitimacy required for both spheres to meaningfully interact. Instead, it could be viewed as a kind of monologue that is nevertheless able to illuminate how professional designers define tasks, criteria, methods, knowledge and outcomes for themselves by defining what professional design is not. For design culture studies, it is essential to remain aware of these intentions, and to consider alongside what is being excluded by each discursive statement within design. What is furthermore needed is an open and attentive approach to everyday design. What I have found in my studies of this form of designing is that, concerning motivation, methods and perception, they mirror the heterogeneity found in professional design. Accordingly, the distinctions made between professional and everyday design are much less clear-cut than they appear. Both are tightly linked, and with further technological and economic change, are becoming more and more so.

References

Abbott, A. (1988), *The System of Professions*, Chicago: University of Chicago Press.
Asensio, L. and Lorenz, M. (eds) (2012), *Pretty Ugly: Visual Rebellion in Design*, Berlin: Gestalten.
Bader, S. (ed.) (2013), *The Designer Says*, New York: Princeton Architectural Press.
Bourdieu, P. (1984), *Distinction: A Social Critique of the Judgement of Taste*, London: Routledge and Kegan Paul.
Bringhurst, R. (1999), *The Elements of Typographic Style*, Point Roberts: Hartley and Marks.
Foucault, M. (1981), 'The order of discourse', translated by I. McLeod, in R. Young (ed.), *Untying the Text: a Poststructuralist Reader*, Boston: Routledge and Kegan Paul, 48–78.
Gee, J. P. (2005), *An Introduction to Discourse Analysis*, Oxon and New York: Routledge.
Helfand, J. (2006), 'The Global Curse of Comic Sans', Design Observer, 20 July. Available online: http://designobserver.com/feature/the-global-curse-of-comic-sans/4567

Heller, S. and Fernandes, T. (1999), *Becoming a Graphic Designer*, New York: John Wiley & Sons.
Julier, G. (2008), *The Culture of Design*, London, Thousand Oaks, New Delhi and Singapore: Sage.
Kingsley, P. (2012), 'Higgs boson and Comic Sans: the perfect fusion', 4 July. Available online: https://www.theguardian.com/artanddesign/2012/jul/04/higgs-boson-comic-sans-twitter
Lutz, H.-R. (1990), *Today's Hieroglyphs: Imprints on Packaging for Transport*, Zurich: Verlag Hans Rudolf Lutz.
O'Luanaigh, C. (2014), 'CERN to switch to Comic Sans', 1 April. Available online: http://home.cern/about/updates/2014/04/cern-switch-comic-sans
Owens, S. (2012), 'Design is Ordinary: Lay Graphic Communication and Its Relation to Professional Graphic Design Practice', Ph.D. diss., University of Reading.

CHAPTER ELEVEN

The fixing I: Repair as prefigurative politics

Gabriele Oropallo

Introduction

'When somebody uses a tool or piece of equipment', writes Peter-Paul Verbeek, 'a referential structure comes about in which the object produced, the material out of which it is made, the future user, and the environment in which it has a place are related to each other' (2005: 79–80). Verbeek believes that when I pluck the strings of this choral meshwork, relationships are not simply revealed, but actually made: they truly 'come about' in the very moment the hand meets the object. What happens when one of the threads of this meshwork that entangles human hands willing to use and things ready to be activated suddenly snaps?

In this chapter I will examine a series of instances how repair has been reframed in design discourse – the total of the conversations that are had about design – over the decade that followed the 2007 financial crisis. This period saw the launch of a number of initiatives including networks, and regular repair events in which expert 'fixers' meet members of the public to provide both 'entertainment, empowerment … and, ultimately, enlightenment through guided disassembly of your broken stuff' (Fixit Clinic n.d.). Geographically, these initiatives found a hatching ground in Western Europe and North America, even though they celebrated and re-contextualized language and methods adopted from repair traditions that developed over a longer period and in a less vocal fashion in scarcity economies including Cold-War Eastern Europe, Latin America and South

Asia. Their narrative of bettering of the world through repair took new momentum once the cultural milieu of the 2007 crisis in Europe and North America provided the conditions for presenting this practice as providing a sphere of activity that is suspended from the unpredictable and de-personalized arena of market economy.

The chapter is by no means an exhaustive review of all the repair initiatives that have been launched over the decade. In the first part of the text, I examine the theoretical premises to the adoption of repair as a practical and metaphorical element of a programme for social renewal. In this part of the chapter I also trace the genealogy of contemporary repair thinking to ideas of degrowth and conviviality that circulated in Western Europe in the 1970s. In the second part of the chapter, I identify two polarities within the wave of repair initiatives that took place within the timeframe in question. On the one hand, the re-contextualization of repair from the more contained sphere of homes and repair shops to the public sphere and its elevation to spectacle. On the other, the promotion of individual action through consumer choice and a radical approach to property rights in which opening the black box of the technological object equal to re-establishing un-compromising ownership.

I then illustrate them with specific references to two examples in particular: the Repair Manifesto and the iFixit network. To a greater or lesser extent, repair initiatives also share several rhetorical tropes with those that go under the rubric of design activism in their criticism of repetitive consumption and opposition to a policy environment that favours orthodox application of classical economy principles such as the ability of the market to self-manage itself and the neutrality of the state in economic policy matters (Julier 2013). However, they also consistently place a hard emphasis on the opportunity of repair. Repair is presented as a way to unlock resources, and this language of expansionism sometimes seems at odds with a practice that promotes containment.

Broken world thinking

I am borrowing the title of this section from an essay by Steven J. Jackson 'Rethinking Repair' (2014). Between 2014 and 2017, Jackson and Daniela Rosner, who have a background in computer–human interaction and design research, co-led a project on repair, maintenance and sustainability at Cornell University. The project involved an ethnographic study of informal repair sites such as the ubiquitous mobile repair stands in locations like Namibia and Bangladesh and how they function as networking hubs. This work chimes with previous research in which Rosner examined social gatherings in California and concluded a main aim of the groups involved in this kind of activism through promotion of repair was to re-articulate the definition of citizenship while reassembling devices (Rosner 2013).

Jackson's proposal for 'broken world thinking' is a call for reframing repair as a constituent rather than accidental moment of interaction between people and their material environment: 'repair may constitute an important engine by which technological difference is produced and fit is accomplished' (227). Albeit implicitly, Jackson's treatment of repair as re-articulation work seems to me to fit well into a tradition of design writing that looks at the treatment of flaws and inadequacies during the process of design and use, and identifies them as instances of thinking that happens through design (as opposed to through verbal or visual language). In *The Nature and Art of Workmanship* (1968), David Pye, a cabinet-maker and woodworking tutor at the Royal College of Art, London, coined the term 'workmanship of risk' to describe such workmanship in which the quality of the outcome continuously depends on the care and judgement that the maker employs while working. Throughout the execution of a project, there is an ever-present risk that the original design might go wrong. The maker has no previous knowledge of the inner structure of the wood she is working, and cannot anticipate the resistance that the material will put up. So she has to continuously monitor the progress of work and readapt approach, tools and even the whole design to the conditions she will meet along the way. Other design theorists have later elaborated on the negotiation of this friction between intention and implementation to describe designerly ways of thinking and knowing (see for instance Lawson 1980; Schön 1983; Buchanan 1992; Cross 2001).

How does breakdown put me in the condition to recognize connections between people and things that otherwise stay tacit? According to Jackson, a key to understand this is offered by Martin Heidegger's treatment of 'tool-being', which describes the difference in state between tools that are 'ready-to-hand' versus 'present-at-hand' (Heidegger 2008). In the former case, the interplay between me as a subject and the material world as an object happens so seamlessly, that no question about the object needs be asked. Its existence and instrumentality are given for granted. In the latter case, instead, the object in its broken state obstructs or thwarts action, and in the process, it calls attention to itself. In fact, Graham Harman further elaborated on Heidegger's notion of tool-being and pinned down the moment of breakdown as the proof that relations are the basis for the pre-emptive acknowledgement of any object as valid (Harman 2002: 44–9). Thanks to breakdown, light is shed upon the otherwise dark matter that, while not seen because it is given for granted, constitutes the scaffolding of everyday life. As I reach my hand willing to use and encounter an unexpectedly broken tool, I am forced to recognize barriers and figure out how to overcome them in a no longer smooth landscape of interaction. In the process, I acquire knowledge about the layout of a meshwork of which I am both constituent and probe.

Throughout this chapter I refer to a series of initiatives for the promotion of repair as 'repair activism'. I am using this term not for lack of better terms, but because the people involved in these projects actively want to engage with the existent social and economic conditions. They intend to use repair sessions as exercises in prefigurative politics, through which they illustrate their ideas for an alternative way of managing material fluxes. Repair activism grants an effective entry point to those whose agenda has the ambition to critically review the inner workings of the material world. 'Fixing means freedom and independence', argues Ravid Rovner of the Fixperts collective: 'As a fixer, you don't need to worry about wear and tear. Nothing stays new, so forget perfection' (Rovner 2013).

Repair, understood as continuous struggle to make things work, is also a universally empirical strategy. Outside the sphere of ostensibly post-scarcity societies characterized by repetitive consumption and assimilation of durable items into consumables, repair activism would not find enough traction because mending and fixing are widespread modes of interaction with the material environment, and have already their iconography and culture. One example is the *jugaad* culture of India (Julier 2017: 131–3). Repair cultures of the Cold-War Soviet bloc also provide a case for different considerations. Ekaterina Gerasimova and Sof'ia Chuikina examined the social implications of the constant state of scarcity that afflicted the Soviet Union, and concluded that despite the everyday hardship citizens had to endure, the practice of repair offered them the opportunity to develop their individuality outside the state-controlled sphere. They argue that in the specific conditions granted by plan economies, 'permanent repair as a form of creativity and lifestyle' (Gerasimova and Chuikina 2009: 58) came to be 'not the lot of the dispossessed but an experience shared by most of the population. It was a zone where the individual was in control and could create his or her own symbolic arrangements, a sphere of activity that was independent of the state' (Gerasimova and Chuikina 2009: 74i1).

Maintenance as a professional or domestic practice has been the subject of a number of ethnographic studies (Dant 2004; Bond, DeSilvey and Ryan 2013). These studies include Julian Orr's examination of the daily routines of the technicians who repair photocopy machines. Orr's work showed how their knowledge is shaped not only by manuals and formal training, but also decisively by shared oral traditions. As most oral traditions, these pieces of knowledge are held together by a mythological framework of epic battles with troubled machines and dysfunctional moving parts (Orr 1996). In contrast, repair activism is meticulously documented. It is treated neither as a casual part of the trade nor as inside knowledge for a small circle of initiated. Instead, it is widely transcribed in visual and writing. The iFixit organization, established in 2003, presents itself as an 'open repair manual'.

Along with traditional repair crafts and scarcity economy ingenuity, jugaad and other similar examples from Latin America or Africa are routinely celebrated by activists, used for inspiration, and interpreted as living proof of their prefigurative politics. Yet, this very process of re-contextualization of the source material reveals an approach to fixing and mending that is more self-conscious, even designerly in its cultural implementation (Julier 2013). When the Dutch curating collective Platform21 launched their repair-themed programme 'Platform21 = Repairing. Stop recycling, start repairing!' in March 2009 they stated that their aim was 'to raise awareness of a mentality, a culture and a practice that not so long ago was completely integrated into life and the way we designed it'. To this aim, they wrote 'a manifesto describing the benefits of fixing things and calling upon designers and consumers to break the chain of throwaway thinking' (Platform21 2009). Similarly, one of the tenets the Restart network in London lists in its 'Code' is: 'We will take seriously the act of bringing another gadget into the world' (Restart n.d.). This emphasis on needless expansion of consumption and generally on 'enoughness' is reminiscent of the antagonist message of two world views with their roots in the 1970s: alternative technology and degrowth. Throughout the 1970s, the political theorist André Gorz advocated a clean break with the 'ideology of growth', and this is the material culture that he imagines taking place at the other side of this break:

> Imagine a society based on these criteria: the production of practically indestructible materials, of apparel lasting for years, of simple machines which are easy to repair ... Each neighbourhood, each town would have public workshops equipped with a complete range of tools, machines, and raw materials, where the citizens produce for themselves, outside the market economy, the non-essentials according to their tastes and desires. (Gorz 1979 [1975]: 9)

The utopia Gorz imagines is characterized by three elements: shared access to tools, which results in accumulation of social capital instead of profit; life cycles of objects are slowed down, with the objective of emphasizing the phase of use rather than the phase of manufacturing; finally, crafts and repair skills are actively encouraged, with the result of increasing the participation of the user in the design process. Comparable ideas were articulated in the same decade by Ivan Illich who coined the expression 'tools of conviviality' (Illich 1973) to define value exchanges that could be qualified more in social and cultural terms than financial ones. Ideological investment in such a project is a marker of a humanistic posture that aims to re-appropriate technology to man, and make of the alienating industrial means of production a means of post-scarcity self-development.

Repair as a countercultural practice is mobilization of people and things (human and non-human actants) that wants to engage in an immediate manner with the existing human-made environment and the pace at which things enter and exit this very space. Mobilization is triggered by a situation perceived or mediated as critical. From this point of view, the financial crisis started in 2007 offered a favourable environment for repair initiatives.

In 2008–09, 'as the global economic collapse was gathering momentum', the Proteus Gowanus Gallery in New York dedicated a series of exhibitions and other events to the theme of mending in an exploration of 'the disappearing skills and tools of repair'. As part of the programme, the gallery also established the Fixers' Collective, which was presented as 'a social experiment in improvisational fixing and mending' and as 'intentionally aligning itself with forces generated in reaction to the current economic crisis' (Proteus Gowanus n.d.). The collective, whose logo features a red monkey wrench in strong contrast with the ornate lettering of the gallery's logo, kept on meeting weekly on Thursday evenings. The sessions bring together 'Master Fixers' and private citizens, who make an offer of five dollars for each broken object they bring to the session.

In the same period other groups and networks were established, such as the Repair Café, which was originally launched in Amsterdam and then became a not-for-profit franchise, and the Fixit Clinic in Albany, California. Since 2008, hundreds of public sites of repair have emerged globally with members of public bringing their electronic casualties and other broken objects to repair gatherings in the hope to learn how to bring them back to life thanks to the help of an expert fixer. Demand is abundant: manufacturers work to price points and are constantly finding ways to cut corners to bring cost down. Consequently, it is often cheaper or easier to dispose of a device and replace it entirely rather than have it professionally repaired. Two of the latest additions are two London-based initiatives launched in 2012: the Restart Project founded by Janet Gunter, and the Fixperts network, started by James Carrigan and Daniel Charny. The exhibitions dedicated to the subject included 'Fix Fix Fix' at S O Gallery, London, in 2013, and 'Repair!' at the Vitra Design Museum in Weil am Rhein, Germany, in 2014.

In the next part of this chapter, I will examine more closely two initiative for repair promotion that were among the first ones for receive recognition in the timeframe I have chosen for this text: Platform21's Repair Manifesto and the iFixit network. I believe they illustrate two polarities of a large discourse upon which most design activism taps. On the one hand, the appropriation and elevation to spectacle of practices that previously took place within the more domestic sphere of homes or repair shops. On the other, the emphasis on distributed but individual action as agent of change and the attribution of more shares of responsibility on users rather than other sources of agency.

From repair shop to repair show

In March 2009, the Amsterdam-based curator collective Platform21 launched a programme of workshops, an exhibition, lectures and 'repair evaluation clinics' with practitioners, including designers, artists and technologists. Featured participants to this repair-themed programme included id Jan Vormann, Siba Sahabi, and Rachel Griffin. They respectively led workshops on repairing walls with Lego bricks, mending plastic bags, and the versatility of duct tape.

The programme was accompanied by a Repair Manifesto that started with the imperative 'Stop recycling, start repairing!' (Platform21 2011). A copylefted document, the manifesto became immediately particularly popular and has since been extensively translated and readapted worldwide. Remarkably enough, Platform21's repair programme was biased against recycling, perhaps the most symbolically charged practice in sustainability discourse. Recycling, the collective argued, can consume the same or more energy as harvesting the raw materials from the environment, and can sometimes have an even more negative impact from an ecological point of view. This position is grounded. Recycling is certainly today still a better solution than a culture of indiscriminate disposal. Yet, it involves costs and passages that can be drastically reduced when the product is simply not disposed of. Also, the product we entrust to the recyclers only because our brief love affair with it has ended can often be perfectly functional and usable to someone else.

Platform21 itself was a temporary endeavour (2006–09) that was meant to function as an incubator for an Amsterdam design museum to be and the repair programme constituted its grand finale. Its former member Joanna van Zanden continued the experience of the repair programme by founding a new collective of facilitators called Repair Society (RS), which has since led public workshops in cities like Zürich, Stockholm, and Amsterdam, and continues to build an archive of repair stories. In 2014, RS was invited to take part in the Istanbul Design Biennial, which was for that iteration co-curated by Zöe Ryan and Meredith Carruthers, and entitled 'The Future is not What it Used to Be'. In the run-up to the event, RS led workshops with design students and members of the public and installed a 'Repair Room' in the main venue of the biennial, where it exhibited the many repair stories developed by the workshop participants, along with a series of critical texts and artefacts. In the course of the exhibition, visitors were let free to add their own repair stories or instructions, and hang them on the wall alongside the existing posters (Figure 11.1). Through this attempt at collective and generative authorship, RS tried to move from the single tenet-enunciating voice of the manifesto to a multiplicity of perspectives:

> Repair is not just about fixing things. The act of repair has cultural, social, economical effects and benefits. Repairing is about the constant struggle to make things work, from language, to things, to relations between people, to systems in society. In fact, repairing is a way to go forward; it bridges old and new, past and future, and could therefore be seen as a sensitive way of thinking about future forms of society. (Repair Society 2013)

The argument RS puts forward is that repairing does not come after designing. It is an integral part of the same process. They are equal moments of the same operational chain that includes harvesting materials and functions from the environment around us, shaping and combining them into objects, and ultimately activating them through use and handling. The same life chain also includes tinkering, hacking, adapting and repairing: all actions that aim at bringing an object onto a further stage of its active life. A broken thing, RS maintains, is in fact a chance to design and engage with functions and materiality. When users refuse to

FIGURE 11.1 *A participant posts his repair instructions in the 'Repair Room', a project by Repair Society at the 2013 Istanbul Design Biennial.*

engage with design, then they accept design to be imposed upon them in a top-down manner.

This programme is very 'cultural' in the sense that it appeals to a large set of ideas, customs and social behaviour of a society and aims to connect them through a tangible narration. Its political content aims to unlock and mobilize the labour and value capital contained in unused objects. In fact, it is a programme that requires active engagement, pointing as it does to a change in lifestyle that goes beyond the relationships between people and things, for it also includes relationships between people and people. Both initiatives, the Repair Manifesto as well as RS thus ultimately reveal a radical ambition that appeals even farther than the hands-on, small-scale repair sessions of other collectives such as the Fixers' Collective of the Fixit Clinic. The conceptual machinery that powers such a programme is the re-contextualization and elevation to spectacle of practices that previously took place within the more domestic sphere of homes or repair shops.

The fixing I: Individual action through repair

Kyle Wiens and Luke Soules originally established iFixit in 2003. After realizing that repair manuals for Apple devices were not available to the general public, they studied the construction of a series of laptop computers to reverse-engineer their own repair and maintenance instructions. Wiens and Soules initially put the manuals they authored for sale online, but in the face of discouraging sale numbers, eventually changed distribution strategy and made them copylefted, freely amendable and downloadable to anyone. At that point, their website became quickly popular with specialized online Apple forums, and subsequently received wide attention in the press. Wiens, who is the chief officer of iFixit and a prolific writer, in his profile picture brandishes an oversized monkey wrench in an antagonist and almost menacing pose before unambiguously declaring: 'I am fixing the world' (Wiens n.d.). He describes his organization without fearing hubris as 'what the world needed ... an open-source repair manual for everything' (Wiens, quoted in Koebler 2015) that posts free repair instructions for any electronic devices.

The business model of iFixit involves making available 'repair kits' that can be purchased along with the free instructions. The kits include the required materials for any repair job, from spare parts through solvents and glues, to special iFixit-branded tools like the thin plastic cards that serve to pry tightly assembled device parts open – typically laptop or mobile phone LCD screens. These tools are occasionally more and complex and reverse-engineered for the task at hand. The most iconic case is the pentalobe screwdriver. In the 2010s, Apple started to replace traditional screw heads with a new proprietary star-shaped standard that required a tool that was only distributed to licensed repair people. Wiens and Soules prize themselves for being among the first to create a compatible tool and put it on the market. At the time of writing, inexpensive non-iFixit-branded versions of the pentalobe screwdriver made in China could also be purchased online for about 2 euros.

In addition to the manuals, the iFixit website has since inception collected thousands of hours of instructional videos shot by enthusiast repair people. While instructing their neighbour, these enthusiasts accompany their

FIGURE 11.2 *Kyle Wiens of iFixit brandishes an oversized monkey wrench in the profile picture he uses on the website of his organization.*

films with personal commentary on their relationship with the device they are fixing or their lives in general. The iFixit organization and other similar endeavours are thus collecting vast libraries of a novel narration genre, which can potentially function as a reservoir of source material for ethnographic or historical research in a manner similar to product reviews on e-commerce websites.

Wiens defines himself as a 'right to repair activist' (Figure 11.2) who is 'fighting the second law of thermodynamics' (Wiens n.d.). Discontent with industrial practices perceived as deceitful and dishonest is one of the main streams that feeds into this kind of repair activism. For iFixit, Apple represents that epitome of the contemporary corporation that pushes the notion of high technology as hermetic black box to an extreme. Wiens's right to repair activism is meant to extend ownership of the product to the buyer beyond its mere surface. The right to repair activism narrative attributes controlling powers to individual behaviour and strives to retain integral property rights for the buyer on any device, however complex it is. In 2013, he co-founded the Digital Right to Repair Coalition, based in North Haledon, NJ, with Gay Gordon-Byrne. The Coalition actively aligns itself with all campaigns pushing laws to strengthen the rights of product owners (Leibner 2015). An example of the successful campaigning for right to repair issues was the agreement signed in 2014 by a group of important US carmakers to make diagnostic tools and repair instructions available to independent mechanical workshops or directly to car owners upon request, instead of exclusively to franchised dealers. This was the result of a decade-long fight that also involved a referendum in the state of Massachusetts in which 86 per cent of the voters chose to enact a 'right to repair' bill. In 2016, the manufacturer John Deer moved to counteract such opening of the black box and retain ownership of the product beyond the surface by forcing purchasers to sign agreement that forbids nearly all repair or modification to farming equipment. Since most of the last-generation equipment is sold with embedded software, the manufacturer reserves the right to remotely shut down tractors that have been tinkered with. In response, a market emerged for hacking firmware coded in Eastern Europe and traded on invite-only online forums (Koebler 2017).

Conclusion

Breakdown is a state of things at which the forms of entanglement between people and things that otherwise stay tacit are suddenly revealed. After the 2007 crisis and the disillusionment that followed, repair has been invested with a potent symbolism. In this narration, repair can re-establish a balance and unlock untapped potentials. Not only the intrinsic value of unused objects, but also the vanishing knowledge of the repair trades, the bricoleur wisdom of idealized faraway people making do with almost nothing. More generally and conceptually, repair has been elevated and celebrated as a metaphor of a new deal between fellow humans and their material environment.

In contrast with repair practices in scarcity or informal economies, 'repair activism' actually involves acknowledging the value broken things still carry. RS dedicated one of their workshops in 2015 to 'The Life of Objects'. Repair activists seek both the opportunity to reduce the quantity of consumption by avoiding buying new products, and the chance to intervene first-handedly by engaging with an object that would otherwise go on to join the multitude of 'former things' populating the landfill. Repair events are imagined as the emergency room of the sustainable age; things are grabbed hold of at the threshold of their afterlives, and given extraordinary treatments to rescue their functionality along with their symbolic capital.

As I have shown in this chapter, there are two currents that can be seen to sustain the rhetorics that circulate in the landscape of contemporary social and political engagement through repair. On the one hand, the mentioned 'enlightenment through entertainment', I mentioned in the introduction. This is an extension and elevation to spectacle of a practice that previously took place within the domestic sphere to the public one, and the appropriation of space for practice left vacant by the progressive disappearance of the professional repair trade. Repair sessions distil the conceptual content of maintenance work and elevate the practice from the sphere of the workshop and the toolbox into the realms of ethics and moral. On the other hand, in the rhetorics of other repair initiatives, material culture emerges as a field to be negotiated through individual choice. Instead of merely accepting technology as something imposed upon us, citizens are invited to appropriate it as a means of personal development. The sphere of individual choice and behaviour are thus promoted to arena for action and prefigurative politics.

References

Bond, S., DeSilvey, C. and Ryan, J. R. (2013), *Visible Mending: Everyday Repairs in the South West*, Axminster: Uniformbooks.
Buchanan, R. (1992), 'Wicked Problems in Design Thinking', *Design Issues*, 8(2): 5–21.
Clinic, F.c. n.d. 'About', https://fixitclinic.wordpress.com/about/ (accessed on 15 January 2016).
Cross, N. (2001), 'Designerly Ways of Knowing: Design Discipline versus Design Science', *Design Issues*, 17(3): 49–55.
Dant, T. (2004), *Materiality and Society*, Milton Keynes: Open University Press.
Gerasimova, E. and Chuikina, S. (2009), 'The Repair Society', *Russian Studies in History*, 48(1): 58–74.
Gorz, A. (1979), (1975), *Ecology as Politics*, New York, NY: South End Press.

Harman, G. (2002), *Tool-Being: Heidegger and the Metaphysics of Objects*, Chicago, IL: Open Court4.
Heidegger, M. (2008), (1927). *Being and Time*, New York: Harper Perennial.
Illich, I. (1973). *Tools for Conviviality*, New York: Harper and Row.
Jackson, S. J. (2014), 'Rethinking Repair', in T. Gillespie, P. Boczkowski and K. A. Foot (eds), *Media Meets Technologies: Essays on Communication, Materiality, and Society*, Cambridge, MA: MIT Press, 221–39.
Julier, G. (2013), 'From Design Culture to Design Activism', *Design and Culture*, 5(2): 215–36.
Julier, G. (2017), *Economies of Design*, Thousand Oaks, CA: Sage.
Koebler, J. (2015), 'How to Fix Everything', *Motherboard*, 24 November, https://motherboard.vice.com/en_us/article/8q89wb/how-to-fix-everything (accessed on 15 January 2016).
Koebler, J. (2017), 'Why American Farmers Are Hacking Their Tractors With Ukrainian Firmware', *Motherboard*, 21 March, https://motherboard.vice.com/en_us/article/xykkkd/why-american-farmers-are-hacking-their-tractors-with-ukrainian-firmware (accessed on 21 March 2017).
Lawson, B. (1980), *How Designers Think*, Oxford: Architectural Press.
Leiber, N. (2015), 'The Fight to Fix Your iPhone (and Other Stuff)', *Bloomberg*, 10 September, https://www.bloomberg.com/news/articles/2015-09-10/iphone-fix-the-fight-for-your-right-to-repair- (accessed on 15 January 2016).
Orr, J. E. (1996), *Talking about Machines: An Ethnography of a Modern Job*, Ithaca, NY: IRL Press.
Platform21. (2009), 'Platform21 = Repairing. Stop recycling, start repairing!', *Platform21*, http://www.platform21.nl/page/4315/en (accessed on 22 March 2009).
Platform21. (2011), 'Repair Manifesto', in J. van der Zanden, *Curatorial Cookbook*, Arnhem: ArtEZ Press, inside front cover.
Proteus, Gowanus. n. d. 'Fixers Collective', *Proteus Gowanus*, http://www.proteusgowanus.org/proteus-gowanus-archive/fixers-collective/index.html (accessed on 15 January 2016).
Pye, D. (1968), *The Nature and Art of Workmanship*, Cambridge: Cambridge University Press.
Repair Society. (2013), 'About', *Repair Society*, http://www.repairsociety.net/about (accessed on 15 January 2016).
The Restart Project. n.d. 'Code' *The Restart Project*, https://therestartproject.org/code/ (accessed on 15 January 2016).
Rosner, D. K. (2013), 'Making Citizens, Reassembling Devices: On Gender and the Development of Contemporary Public Sites of Repair in Northern California', *Public Culture* 26(1): 51–77.
Rovner, R. (2013), 'Fixing as a Way of Resisting', *Fixperts*, 20 June, http://fixperts-org.tumblr.com/post/53437010372/fixing-as-a-way-of-resisting-ravid-rovner (accessed 15 January 2016).
Schön, D. A. (1983), *The Reflective Practitioner: How Professionals Think in Action*, New York: Basic Books.
Verbeek, P.-P. (2005), *What Things Do: Philosophical Reflections on Technology, Agency and Design*, University Park, PA: Pennsylvania State University Press.
Wiens, K. n.d. 'Kyle Wiens', *Kyle Wiens*, https://kylewiens.com/ (Accessed on 15 January 2016).

PART FOUR

Locating design culture

Anders V. Munch

Where do we encounter and experience design cultures? What are the meanings of places and spaces, localities and regions, nation-states and international networks to design? And at which levels can Design Culture approach and interpret the spatial and geographical environments, as well as the local and global conditions? As we speak of design culture at very different scales – ranging from the culture of a singular firm or local production and up to the global perspective of our current design culture – it becomes very important to locate any design culture in question. This final part of the book contributes to a mapping of how far and widespread the traces and effects of design cultural conjunction are. The chapters in this part contribute by discussing very different cases – not only cases from different countries as Denmark, Turkey, Belgium, the Netherlands and Jordan but also cases that depict the conditions and transformations at local, national, regional and global levels. They sketch very different configurations of levels, spaces and places in this mapping of design culture, and they show differing movements in spatial and geographical fields, such as relocations, expansions, deterritorializations, segregations and Westernization. And they all document the intricate challenges to design culture – that is, of locating design culture.

If we look at the historical development of modern, industrial design as a backdrop of contemporary design culture, it was understood and promoted as universal principles, carried by an international movement originating in the Western world – the UK, Germany, France and the United States – and spread all over the globe during the last century. But this worldwide industrialization was also part the opening of a world market, which ignited an international competition among the nation-states. Each country had to show special capabilities and cultural values to compete. So while modern, industrial design evolved and spread through international activities and global processes, most design histories as well as design policies have been written and announced in more narrow, national perspectives. This nexus of the national and the international that was formed by the global industrialization and commercialization has during the last decades been paralleled by a nexus of the global and the local, produced by globalization and digitalization of a media-driven economy. This is understood as the global production, distribution and consumption of multinational brands provoking counter-movements of enhancing local production and cultural differences.

Something Old, Something New, Something Borrowed: Relocating Kähler's Brand Heritage by Niels Peter Skou addresses the specific case of a Danish ceramic firm, Kähler, that has been revitalized as a brand, but without its original production site, the production is now in Portugal, and none of the earlier products has been continued. This outsourcing of production was nonetheless followed by a rebranding of the firm that has dealt intensively with the history of the lost workshop. The relaunch of the brand, Kähler, has heavily historicized the new activities of the firm in the light of the history of the old workshop that was visited by Danish artists and studio craftsmen through generations. And parallel to this storytelling, Kähler has built up the brand universe with flagship stores and restaurants in another city – to relocate the brand heritage. The irony of this story is that, as the firm later acquired the original workshop, the authentic place of origin, it seemed difficult to fit into their brand spaces, their simulation of brand heritage.

Performing Turkish Design in Products, Collections and Exhibitions: Expanding the Archive, Seeking Depth by Harun Kaygan go beyond the wish for a fixed national style in Turkish design and deals with the question of how 'Turkishness' is performed on different levels of Turkish design culture. It follows motives and ideas in either products or their mediation, through brands, collections and exhibitions, and explains all these elements as the Archive, out of which they can recontextualize and perform as Turkish. Kaygan distinguish between motives of multiple appearance, which might carry references of Ottoman, Anatolian or Islamic origin, but just as well more arbitrarily vernacular, personal or even international inspirations, and designers configuring a depth of meaning to new designs from history and culture. However, in both cases the 'Turkishness' is rather performed on different levels and platforms of design culture, statements, competitions and exhibitions – and often in contradicting ways – than as any identifiable national idiom.

A Theoretical Straddle: Design Culture between National Structures and Transnational Networks by Joana Ozorio de Almeida Meroz and Katarina Serulus, addresses the 'methodological nationalism' that again and again blindly takes the national state as the appropriate context for interpreting design – and in this sense takes the critique of Kaygan a step further. Through a Belgian and a Dutch case, they point to the mesh of national agendas, transnational relations and international frameworks that challenge ideas and historical narratives on national design identity. The first case focuses on transnational relations in design culture governed by international organizations as International Council of Societies of Industrial Designers (ICSID) and linked to national agendas through the rise of 'design centres' in the post-war decades. Despite its role as display of Belgian design, the activities of the Belgian Design Centre mainly fitted into the schemes of international networks and were entangled in transnational exchange. The second case is the Italian design duo, Formafantasma, working in the Netherlands, who has gradually been associated with the core identity of Dutch design, as their installation, *Autharcy*, seems to mirror the 'artificial reality' as a recent interpretation of Dutchness. Both cases – as well as the Turkish cases – show how national design cultures produce meanings, but also that national design histories cannot be written without taking in transnational relations and international frameworks.

The Challenges and Opportunities of introducing Design Culture in Jordan by Danah Abdulla changes the more descriptive focus on design cultures to a discussion of, what future introduction courses in Design Culture might bring into Jordanian Design School programmes. She does describe the situation of the severely segregated capital of Amman, the low status of design educations and the design profession and the lack of esteem of local traditions as well as Islamic art as backdrop for an Arab, or more specifically Jordanian, design culture. But this situation is mostly the product of Westernization both in the universities and design practice that closely follows either Western norms or orientalist clichés of Arab motives. An example from the Amman Design Week 2016 was that a workshop on local crafts, *Designing Contemporary Heritage*, was led by the Dutch Studio Mieke Meijer and sponsored by the Dutch Embassy. There is a lack of professional organizations as well as Arab publications on design, and blind borrowings from Western design and communication in English obstruct a consciousness of the regional conditions and cultural contexts to develop a responsive design culture. Courses in Design Culture investigating local and regional conditions would create an awareness of different kinds of design as answers to challenges in Amman and make both design education as well as practice more relevant, instead of just reproducing universal set of solutions from Western industrial design. In this case design projects needs to be more 'located', and Design Culture as discipline could help to embed practice.

CHAPTER TWELVE

Something old, something new, something borrowed:

Relocating Kähler's brand heritage

Niels Peter Skou

In 2014, the Danish ceramics company Kähler introduced a limited-edition bronze striped vase in their series 'Omaggio' in order to celebrate the company's 175th anniversary. It became so highly demanded that the distributor's homepage crashed, which prompted a storm of complaints on the internet, first by dissatisfied customers, later by people claiming that the fuss over a design object reflected Western materialism and 'first-world problems'. In 2015, a ritual smashing of Kähler vases was even arranged to protest against the alleged indifference of the public towards the international refugee crisis. (TV2, 20/12 2015). Kähler had thus been caught in a heated discussion of materialism, consumption and national identity. This line of events was of course highly unusual for a ceramics company and it illustrates how Kähler had managed to achieve an extraordinary commercial and cultural impact, where its products had become almost omnipresent in everyday Danish home décor. This cultural status was not less remarkable given that Kähler had been reintroduced to the market only 4 years earlier.

What was not questioned, thus, was the company's claim to its 175th anniversary, which may seem a little less clear on closer inspection. The company Kähler was founded by the German potter Hermann Joachim Kähler in the Danish city of Næstved in 1839 as a company mainly producing ceramic stoves (Holst Schmidt 2001: 9). Its heyday was around 1900 when the company's workshop became a centre for Danish arts and crafts/secession movements and featured cooperation with renowned Danish artists like Thorvald Bindesbøll, H.A. Brendekilde and Kai Nielsen. The history of the workshop and the family business came to an end, however, in 1974, when the fourth generation of the Kähler family sold the workshop to the local municipality (Holst Schmidt 2001: 258). After a turbulent period with different uses and ownerships architect and entrepreneur Frantz Longhi acquired the rights to the Kähler name in 2008 and two years later the brand was reintroduced by the opening of a flagship brand store in M.P. Bruunsgade in the Danish city of Aarhus. At that time, however, what was taken over from the old company consisted primarily of the brand name and logo and a few historical objects and images. The historical workshop has later been acquired, not for the purpose of production, though, but as a flagship store and historical exhibition. The new range of products is produced in Portugal, China and Thailand. There has thus been a reconstruction of the company where its historical continuity tied to a specific family and a specific place of production has been replaced by a focus on the construction of brand identity, which has involved an intense staging of the company history in marketing and brand spaces. In a design cultural context, the interesting thing about the revival of the Kähler company is thus the tension between, on the one hand, the discontinuation and de-location of production which was earlier tied to the workshop as a specific Danish location and, on the other hand, the processes of relocation in space, through the design of brand spaces like flagship stores and themed restaurants and relocation in time through the discursive construction of continuity.

In this chapter, Kähler is investigated as a paradigmatic case of the use of history in present design culture. While strategic discourses often link design with innovation, the present design culture is as much about history. In Denmark, there has, in the last 20 years, been a growing tendency to equip design with historical references and predecessors in order to position it as a continuation of the Danish design tradition. This mirrors a general interest in cultural heritage in Denmark in the twenty-first century both as a political agenda and a positively loaded concept in commercial and everyday discourse, a tendency identified and discussed in a British context since the 1980s (Cf. Hobsbawm and Ranger 1983; Lowenthal 1998; Samuel 1999) One of the significant characteristics of the new Kähler is that it introduced a range of newly designed products produced in a globalized chain of production, while at the same time the staging of links between the new products and the old Kähler workshop and product range became the central marketing claim. In this respect, the heritage normally connected with brand identity – name, logo and so forth – and the material remains of the old company in the shape of objects, images and locations were all treated equally as reservoirs of historical meaning to be transferred to the new objects. This process can be described as a process of 'self-historicization'

(Folkmann and Jensen 2015), which indicates that the identification of the new objects as a continuation of the 'Kähler tradition' can be seen as the result of a set of strategies for activating company history in an attempt to control the consumers interpretation of the objects. In this case, this need was enhanced by the fact that the company addressed two quite different groups of consumers, an older segment which had a personal memory of the old Kähler and a target group of younger women who had no knowledge of the company or its history beforehand.

According to Guy Julier, the current changes in design practice and the emergence of design culture as both object and approach of study is linked to the rise of branding (Julier 2014: 13–14, See also Moor 2007 and Munch 2017). Branding in a design context calls for the integration of the design object with the shaping of its representations and contexts in an attempt to control the cultural meaning ascribed to it. 'In this way, the system of branding inhabits much of the space of design culture, turning information into an 'all around us' architectonic form' (Julier 2014: 14). The reverse order in which the company was restructured is thus significant. Traditionally, acquiring a company is connected with taking over a set of production facilities and a range of designs. In this case, however, the actual material and immaterial objects acquired – name, logo, images and historical objects – were acquired mainly for their symbolic and narrative properties in order to stage and support the claim of the continuation of the company tradition, despite the brand-new range of ceramic designs. This should not be considered, however, as Eric Hobsbawm has coined it, as an 'invented tradition' (Hobsbawn and Ranger 1983), but rather as 'appropriated' tradition. The process by which Kähler has gained cultural impact and recognition can be seen as a deliberate endeavour to gain acknowledgement of the new Kähler products as legitimate representatives of the brand in such a way that the continuation between the historical Kähler and the new reconstructed company has become self-evident and unproblematized. This appropriation of history has involved a historical loop in which history has been generative as a provider of forms, images and meanings but also subjected to a strategic activation and rewriting.

In the case of Kähler, the use of heritage must be understood through the simultaneous rise of the experience economy as a model for both the commercial and the cultural sphere (Sundbo and Darmer 2008: 2–3, Pine and Gilmore 1999). In the period in question, a number of historical museums were thus rebuilt and transformed from primarily scientific and educational institutions into experience museums addressing a broader public. At the same time, the emergence of flagship brand stores has implied the transference of a number of terms and techniques from the cultural sphere to the commercial sphere (Chung et al. 2001). Together these parallel developments illustrate the convergence of shopping, cultural experience and public education. Kähler furthermore illustrates how this historical interest has not only concerned historical objects but also produced meanings that may be applied to new objects in a dialectical process.

This chapter will follow these processes of history use by investigating the reintroduction of Kähler as a design brand from 2010 to the present. The material used is primarily concerned with the physical and visual staging that includes product design, commercials, catalogues, homepage as well as brand spaces which gains special interest due to the company's deliberate focus on experience creation. Furthermore, the materials have also included interviews with key designers and company managers.

Brand spaces

Kähler's marketing has been based on a double strategy. The actual products have been priced mid-range in the market and distributed in conventional interior stores. But besides this, the brand has been localized in a number of branded spaces falling into two categories. One is flagship stores, where the first one in Aarhus has been supplemented by one in Oslo and the reconfiguration of the original workshop in Næstved. The other category is a number of restaurants employing the Kähler name and using the products in gastronomical settings. At present, there are three Kähler restaurants placed in Aarhus, where one is in the same street as the first brand store, creating a strong local presence and a coherent brand universe. In 2011 Kähler also opened a highly profiled restaurant in Tivoli in Copenhagen, which was closed again in 2017. Kähler labels itself as a 'design- and food brand' and gives recurring references to the 'Kähler experience', which is characterized as a sensuous experience (Kähler Design 2017a). The basis of the strategy is thus that the diverse range of cultural experiences and contexts, Kähler is affiliated with, creates the meaning that is transferred to the products in the mainstream shops. The importance of the restaurants and brand stores in this strategy is thus not primarily about creating financial turnover, but rather to be a part of the overall production of brand meaning. In this aspect they mirror how marketing researcher Robert Kozinets define the flagship brand store:

> *Flagship brand stores* can be distinguished by three characteristics. First, they carry a single (usually established) brand of product. Second, that brand's manufacturer owns them. Finally, they are operated—at least in part—with the intention of building or reinforcing the image of the brand rather than operating to sell product at a profit. (Kozinets et al. 2002: 17)

Two things are noticeable though. In the case of Kähler, the brand stores are part of a larger network of experience places that combine and break down borders between retail, entertainment, education, dining and cultural activities and institutions. Secondly, they were not – at least at the outset of the reintroduction – tapping into a commonly established brand meaning but rather revitalizing an old company identity as an 'historical brand' understood as a brand that was characterized by its heritage. In the following, we will concentrate on the flagship stores in Aarhus and Næstved.

Shop – museum – theatre

Kähler's flagship stores can be considered with the term of the British historian Raphael Samuel as 'Theatres of memory' (Samuel 1999) in the sense that they present a theatrical staging and re-enacting of the company history in ways where it is interwoven with overarching histories of Danish Design and the growing public as well as political interest in cultural heritage. It is thus significant how the company at the same time makes claims to tradition and authenticity and highlights branding and storytelling as part of the experience. The new Kähler is in its own discourse not just a continuation of the past, it is also a staging of it:

> The company's history and traditions live on in every single hand-made item we produce, and in the modern design that makes up a large part of many people's lives. Because Kähler is now a vital part of the Danish cultural heritage, as well as being one of Scandinavia's most popular and innovative brands, combining authentic history with contemporary design and Nordic restaurant experiences. (Kähler Design 2017b)

The notion of combining tradition and innovation is of course a favourable position and one which is often called upon in marketing discourse. In the case of Kähler, though, the innovation is as much attached to the different forms of cultural marketing as to the products themselves, and the storytelling and staging can be seen as ways to negotiate the paradox of being authentic and modern at the same time.

From a historical perspective Kähler's heyday in the late nineteenth century coincided with the growth of shopping as an activity that incorporated the theatricalization and aestheticization of goods:

> Even the consumer's relationship to goods was changed: he no longer considered an object in its specific utility, but rather contemplated an ensemble of objects, in a coherent vision prompted by the theatre of the shop window, by adverts, manufacturers and brands. (Béret 2002: 69)

French art historian Chantal Béret considers the intimate relationship between the museum and the development of the department store in the nineteenth century as a new way of dealing with and presenting things:

> This new experience was founded on the desire for mass produced objects, and the possibility of its satisfaction; in this it was unlike the experience

of the museum, which the department store so closely resembled, with the same vast spaces, the same division into departments, the same display of objects, for in the museum these remained unique and inaccessible. (Béret 2002: 70)

The present discourse about the 'experience economy', which is mirrored in the recurring mentioning of the 'Kähler experience' can thus be seen as a radicalization of some of the features of the modern consumer society as it was shaped in the late nineteenth century. The tension between the demonstrative way in which sales are downplayed in the Kähler brand stores in favour of the added value of the brand experience and the accessibility of Kähler's products through their pricing and broad distribution in mainstream shops can thus be seen as a continuation of the dynamics of creating desire through cultural elevation while at the same time making its satisfaction accessible.

The evolution of brand stores has given rise to a discussion about the theatricalization of shopping inspired by Pine and Gilmore's influential *The Experience Economy* with the subtitle *Work is Theatre and Every Business a Stage* (Pine and Gilmore 1999; Kozinets et al. 2002: 20). In Kähler's Brand Store in Aarhus, this theatricalization expresses itself both in a form of the interior design which contains references to both the old workshop and a domestic interior, and through visual references to the theatre room positioning the shop as a stage (Skou and Hansen 2015: 116–22). The shop is arranged in a converted butcher's shop from around 1900. The historical character of the room, which did not originally have any connection with Kähler, is in this way used as a frame to add meaning and authenticity to the new products. In the front area, a large table is set using Kähler products. The room is otherwise dominated by a large self-portrait by Karl Hansen Reistrup who was the artistic leader of Kähler from 1888 to 1929 posing self-assured with a cane. The back section is separated from the rest of the shop by a black curtain and an original sign with the inscription 'Hermann A. Kähler'. Here the original terrazzo floors and wall tiles are kept but otherwise the walls are painted black to create an illusion of depth (see Figure 12.1). This section includes another set table, but also shelves with stored products and large prints showing historical photographs of the shaping and painting of ceramics as well as more intimate family photos.

The room thus re-uses and alludes to the traditional bourgeois differentiation between public and private, frontstage and backstage, where the front room refers to representation and socialization and the back room to production and intimacy. In this way, the image of the old workshop as a form of family is evoked as well as the image of a tight connection between art, craft, production and consumption. We enter a historic set piece, which offers us to travel back in time while it, on the other hand, through its references to the theatre room, points at itself as an illusion.

Kähler's flagship brand store in Aarhus this way applies a number of strategies known from culture-historical museums where the displayed

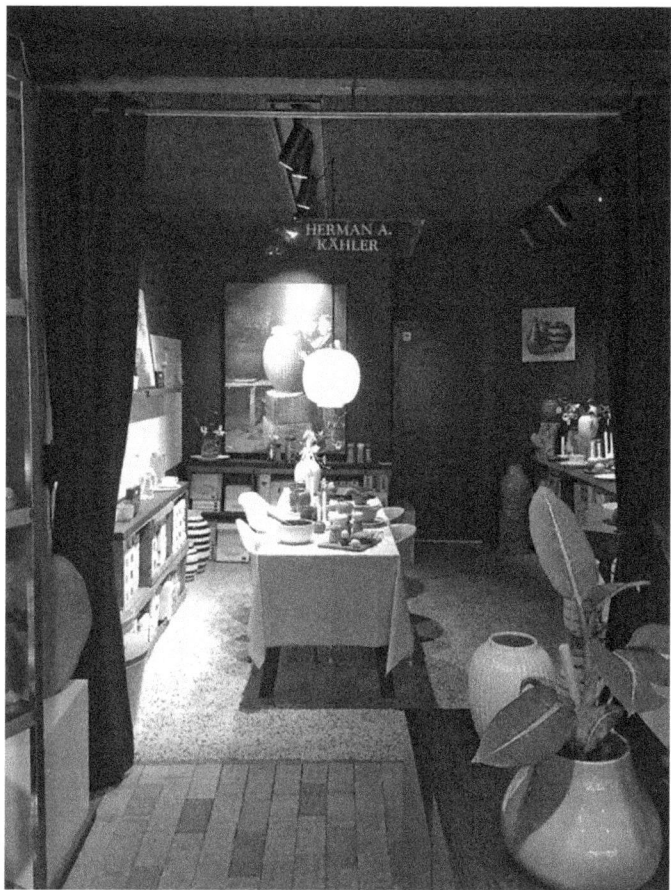

FIGURE 12.1 *Kähler's flagship brand store, Aarhus. The back part of the shop both presents the illusion of entering an old workshop and points at itself as a staged room.* Photo: Niels Peter Skou, 2017.

objects are presented in a historical environment, though not of course with the same demands on historical accuracy. In contrast the flagship brand store at the original Kähler workshop in Næstved more resembles the traditional art historical museum. This brand store was opened in 2016 after an antecedent process of obtaining and renovating the old workshop. The parts of the workshop open to the public consist of a shop and a 'historical exhibition'.

In the exhibition part historical Kähler products borrowed from the collection of nearby Næstved Museum are mixed with new products from the present Kähler selection. The presentation is chronological and singles the objects out using glass cases. (See Figure 12.2) One main effect is that the 'naturalization' of the identity and continuity between the old and the

FIGURE 12.2 *Historical exhibition, Kähler's flagship brand store, Næstved. The objects are singled out and the use of timelines and chronology 'naturalizes' the continuity between the old and the new company. Photo: Niels Peter Skou, 2017.*

new company is fulfilled. At this point the new Kähler had produced its own history, which the exhibition presents as part of a longer unbroken chronological development. A second effect is that the displayed objects are elevated and equalized as objects of art. It is also a little paradoxical, however, that while the location of the shop represents the highest degree of historical authenticity in the Kähler universe the conversion of the workshop has more or less neutralized the rooms, while the objects are singled out as objects of aesthetic contemplation and the historical distance between the objects and the viewer is emphasized. It seems that the space in Aarhus with its more vague historical reference allows more freedom to conjure images and experiences of the past.

Historicizing materiality and materializing history – from Omaggio to Hammershøi

If we turn from the brand stores to the main product series, it becomes clear how the product design in this case cannot be seen independently of the media and spaces surrounding it. During the first years after the reintroduction of Kähler a specific series established itself as 'the Kähler vase', namely the series Omaggio characterized by a stripe pattern, which was also the pattern of the infamous celebration vase mentioned in the introduction. The name of the series 'Omaggio' plays on the Italian word for homage (the new owner has Italian roots) and the whole series is thus supposed to be a celebration of the Kähler tradition. (Skou and Hansen 2015: 126) The link to the tradition is, however, not that obvious since the simple graphic stripe pattern is quite different from the more elaborate colour schemes and glazing traditionally associated with Kähler. In the marketing the link is visually drawn to the so-called Swedish pieces produced in the period after the Second World War often painted by Swedish girls who stayed for the summer and more generally to the female painters doing the actual painting on the old Kähler workshop and in many cases actively developing decoration patterns and techniques. (Holst Schmidt 2001: 210–13) In the 2016 Catalogue, the Omaggio vase is presented as an 'Iconic design vase with history':

> However, not many people know that the iconic Omaggio vase is in fact an interpretation of the historical Kähler vases from the early and mid-20th century. The modern Omaggio vase was inspired by Tulle Emborg, one of the talented women painters in Kähler's workshop in the 1930s and 1940s.
> The Omaggio vase continues some of the handicraft traditions that have been characterizing Kähler for more than 175 years. As in the old Kähler workshop, each and every stripe on every single Omaggio vase has been hand-painted by talented women painters, and the Omaggio vases then go through multiple hand processes in connection with glazing, quality checking and fine polishing. (Kähler 2016: 56, translation by the author)

Tulle Emborg was probably the most profiled of the painting ladies at Kähler working for the company for over 40 years and playing a central part in the development of decoration types and techniques. (Rasmussen 2004: 282–5) In the accompanying pictures she practices the art of cow horn painting, which was a hallmark of the old Kähler, but this is not the technique used today, and the painted stripes play only a small though significant part in the production process. The Omaggio pattern matches a dominant contemporary minimalist aesthetics (See Skou and Munch 2016); it is easy to comprehend and can be transferred through different media. But at the same time the company goes to considerable lengths to locate the design in company history and convince the customers that it represents continuity both in terms of design and in terms of craft-based production methods. This also means that the text carefully omits references to the outsourced parts of the production process that place it in a modern globalized setting. Only the handmade decoration is highlighted and there is a contrast between the personalization of the historical women painters and the anonymity of the present. Another consequence is a form of rewriting of company history where vases, which in earlier historiography plays a minor role made partially out of necessity due to the harsh conditions after the Second World War, are elevated as ancestors of the iconic 'Kähler vase'.

The construction of continuity is perhaps best illustrated by a company ad from 2010 (Figure 12.3) An arrangement of pottery and large photo prints is placed in an open, white room, which associates to a museum room – in retrospect not unlike the design of the historical exhibition in Næstved done later. The gaze of the eye is guided from Omaggio pottery through a picture of the 'Swedish' pieces from the 1940s to a large photography of artist Svend Hammershøi, brother of the famous Danish painter Vilhelm Hammershøi and a renowned ceramic artist in his own right, working on a handmade vase almost as large as himself. The text reads 'Kähler. Master of difficult ceramic crafts'. Visually the ad confirms

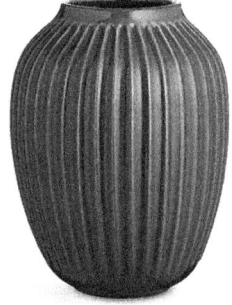

FIGURES 12.3 & 12.4 *From materiality to representation and back. Left: Kähler advertisement equipping the Omaggio vase with visual ancestors. (Boligmagasinet, maj 2010) Right: Modern Hammershøi vase as a reinterpretation of the historic image.* © Kähler Design

a number of preconditions central to the marketing of the new Kähler. It implicitly states that there is a direct continuity throughout the company history where the new products stand on the shoulders of the old, that this continuity maintains an advanced craft tradition and that modern design and designers can be considered as artists in the same way as the artists working with Kähler earlier. A modern Robby and Francesca Cantarutti 'Forest' chair is thus placed at the spot of the custodian's chair. The setting of the ad this way both confirms Kähler's position as part of the art institution and design as an art form. Read in the opposite direction it also illustrates the differences, however. Where the Omaggio pattern consists of painted stripes, Hammershøi worked in his vases with grooves integrated in the clay. On the picture, he measures the quality of the vase with his hand and it is mainly this picture that is supposed to support the claim of Kähler's mastery of advanced craftsmanship.

This specific picture of Svend Hammershøi is perhaps the most frequently used in Kählers marketing and it also has a prominent space in both brand stores treated in this chapter. (See Figure 12.1) Initially the function was to establish links between the new products and the Kähler tradition as we have seen. In 2015 Kähler introduced, however, a new series called 'Hammershøi' inspired by this particular vase. It is not a replica, but rather an updated version adapted to modern taste and mass-production methods. It might seem, thus, that Kähler is moving closer to an actual reestablishment of the old Kähler product line, but it might not be that simple. Prior to the introduction of the Hammershøi line had as we have seen gone a process where Kähler both established their history through storytelling and re-enactment and established their new design line as 'the Kähler vase'. It is thus both a case of the new material objects needing a diverse context of representations to gain meaning and a case of the representations gaining material form. In Kähler's marketing, a limited number of historical pictures (partly due to the limited number of historical pictures available) are used over and over, and in this case these pictures can be said to have materialized themselves in physical shapes. The process can thus be interpreted in the light of Celia Lury's definition of the brand as a 'media-thing' moving back and forth between representation and physical materialization (Lury 2004; Lash and Lury 2007).

Cold Kilns: Design, identity and the relocation of design culture

Looking at the design and marketing strategies of Kähler the main concern has been the construction of identity through the uses of history. In this respect it is quite typical for the ongoing heritage focus prompting companies to tell and activate their own history. What makes the case of Kähler significant, however is the fact that having been dormant for a long period the company was at the outset only history, so to speak, and had to be revitalized or reinvented. In Danish design history, the old Kähler was not only known for their products but also as an example of a locally embedded artistic milieu fulfilling the Arts and Crafts ambition of a tight-knit cooperation between artists and craftsmen. Kähler was reintroduced with a marked ambition of recreating a similar environment and the image of 'the workshop' functions as a recurring metaphor in the company's communication and marketing. As we have seen this has been featured both in texts, images and the design of brand spaces, where the first flagship store in Aarhus contained strong visual references to the old workshop. Though not an actual part of Kähler's own history, the physical location in this case contributed with general historical authenticity. The hand-picking of historical locations has thus enabled the cross between cultural heritage and experience economy and contributed to a historicized brand environment, which is however also exclusively a consumption universe designed to infuse the new products with historical aura. Central to the brand store as phenomenon is the conception that what is important is no longer the concentration of goods but the concentration of meaning. In this sense, the brand space does not end with the store or the restaurant:

> As the ideals of marketspace flagships filter through the world of retail, manufacturers may increasingly recognize that the total packaging of a product ends not with a thing itself, nor its container, but continues to include its position in a store, the entire store environment, the mall, district, city, nation, and in cyberspace. Successful themed retailers will localize, localize, localize their location, location, location. (Kozinets et al. 2002: 26)

The irony is, however, that while Kähler's brand universe in Aarhus approaches the consumer with a promise of experiencing history brought back to life, the actual workshop in Næstved which was acquired at a later time presents itself as a museum. The old kilns are at display as archaeological remains, but they stand cold while only a small new oven is used to allow the visitors to make their own vase and recreate a production process which otherwise takes place far away in a globalized production network.

In this way, Kähler speaks into the current tension between globalization and the rise of branding on the one hand and the focus on national history and cultural heritage as sources of identity on the other. As we have seen, Kähler has very actively activated both local company history and common narratives on Danish design tradition in both product design and the design of representations and retail contexts. The products have thus been infused with meaning in a dialectical play between past and present, representations and materiality even to a degree – as the 'Kähler crisis' initially described illustrates – where the symbolic meanings went out of the company's own control. These meanings can be localized in the sense that the brand space entrench them in a physical space, but the idea of the workshop works, however, today only as simulation. Confronted with the actual workshop it rather points at itself as something lost.

References

Béret, C. (2002), 'Shed, Cathedral or Museum?', in C. Grunenberg and M. Hollein (eds), *Shopping*, Berlin: Hatje Cantz, 69–79
Chung, C. J., Inaba, J., Koolhaas, R. and Leong, S. T. (2001), *Harvard Design School Guide to Shopping*, Köln: Taschen.
Folkmann, M. N. and Jensen, H. C. (2015), 'Subjectivity in Self-Historicization: Design and Mediation of a "New Danish Modern" Living Room Set', *Journal of Design and Culture*, 7(1), 65–84.
Hobsbawm, E. and Ranger, T. (ed.) (1983), *The Invention of Tradition*, Cambridge: Cambridge University Press
Holst Schmidt, A. M. and Holst Schmidt, A. (2001), *Kähler og Keramikken*, Humlebæk: Rhodos.
Julier, G. (2014), *The Culture of Design, 3rd ed.*, London: SAGE
Kähler Design (2016), *Kähler Design Main Catalogue* (Accessed at https://issuu.com/kahlerdesign/docs/k__hler_design_hovedkatalog_2016_is, 26 May 2017)
Kähler Design (2017a), https://www.kahlerdesign.com/inspiration/kahler-flagshipstores (Last accessed 26 May 2017)
Kähler Design (2017b), https://www.kahlerdesign.com/crafts (Last accessed 26 May 2017)
Koolhaas, R. et al. (2001), *Harvard Design School Guide to Shopping*, Köln: Taschen
Kozinets, R. V., Sherry, J. F., DeBerry-Spencea, B., Duhacheka, A., Nuttavuthisita, K. and Storm, D. (2002), 'Themed Flagship Brand Stores in the New Millennium: Theory, Practice, Prospects', *Journal of Retailing*, 78, 17–29
Lash, S. and Lury, C. (2007), *Global Culture Industry*, Cambridge: Polity Press
Lowenthal, D. (1998), *The Heritage Crusade and the Spoils of History*, Cambridge: Cambridge University Press
Lury, C. (2004), *Brands. The Logos of the Global Economy*, London and New York: Routledge
Moor, L. (2007), *The Rise of Brands*, Oxford: Berg.
Munch, A. V. (2017), 'Nærkontakt i Brandspace', in H. Larsen, Ane et al. (ed.), *Visuelle tilgange*, Aarhus: Passepartouts Særskriftserie, 179–95.
Pine II, B. J. and Gilmore, J. H. (1999), *The Experience Economy*, Cambridge, MA: Harvard Business Press.
Rasmussen, P. (2004), *Kählers Værk*, København: Nyt Nordisk Forlag Arnold Busck/Kunstbogklubben.
Samuel, R. (1999), *Theatres of Memory*, London: Verso.
Skou, N. P. and Hansen, K. (2015), 'Kähler. Fra værksted til oplevelsesunivers', in A. V. Munch, N. P. Skou and T. Riis Ebbesen, *Designkulturanalyser*, Odense: Syddansk Universitetsforlag, 110–34.

Skou, N. P. and Munch, A. V. (2016), 'New Nordic and Scandinavian Retro: Reassessment of Values and Aesthetics in Contemporary Nordic Design', *Journal of Aesthetics and Culture*, 8(1): 8/11 2016

Sundbo, J. and Darmer, P. (eds), (2008), *Creating Experiences in the Experience Economy*, Cheltenham: Edward Elgar Publishing.

TV2 (20 December 2015), http://nyheder.tv2.dk/samfund/2015-12-20-efter-smadring-af-kahler-vaser-nu-afsloerer-hun-sandheden-bag (Last accessed 25 May 2017).

CHAPTER THIRTEEN

Performing Turkish design in products, collections and exhibitions:

Expanding the archive, seeking depth

Harun Kaygan

Introduction

I had barely started working on this chapter in November 2016 when a committee representing four ministries of Turkey visited the Department of Industrial Design at Middle East Technical University. On The Tenth Development Plan of Turkey (2014–18), under the Program for Reducing Import Dependency, the Turkish Ministry of Science, Industry and Technology was appointed to work with universities, chambers of commerce and industry, NGOs and government bodies to 'create a platform for universities and design organizations to cooperate and determine the Turkish style in specified sectors'. The purpose of the visit was to start negotiations towards fulfilling the action.

Historically, industrial design has been a medium of international cultural and commercial competition since mid-nineteenth century. The period up to the Second World War was marked by cultural and political nationalism as vernacular cultural elements were utilized, or outright invented, to define and promote national cultures in the form of applied arts throughout Europe (Greenhalgh 1995; Hobsbawm 1983). International exhibitions provided public platforms for the display and comparison of national achievements (Greenhalgh 1988) and helped extend the competition to Europe's peripheries (Yagou 2003; McGowan 2005; Andermann 2009; Bhagat 2011). In the post-war period, concerns for the role of design in economic competition continued (Sparke 1992; Aynsley 1993), while national design styles increasingly became akin to brand names – Italian design as playful, German design as rational, etc. (Sparke 1981) Design historical literature has been generally critical of such discourse, finding it to be overly formalistic and dependent on nationalist rhetoric (Jackson 2006; Yagou 2007; Narotzky 2009). However, a recent paper on how Dutch design has been branded as 'intrinsically open' under government support (Ozorio de Almeida Meroz and Griffin 2012: 414) proves that the discourse on national design styles can still be influential over policy making.

From a historical point of view, then, the committee's mission to describe a national design style does not seem ill-advised; nor is it an anachronism. But how could I explain to a bureaucratic committee the logistical complications of such an undertaking, not to mention its theoretical precariousness? I find it untenable to look for commonalities, however tentatively, among either the aesthetic qualities of a geographically bound set of products, or the design practices that shaped those products, or the professional identities of the designers or other actors involved. At the same time, I find value in mapping out from a design cultural perspective the ways in which claims for common qualities are produced, disseminated and more importantly materialized in design. In this chapter, I examine how various claims in the name of Turkish design – both as a community and as a design identity – are materialized in design products, collections and academic texts, especially via references to national culture. I argue that, rather than an identifiable idiom, Turkish design is better described as changing confluences of statements and anecdotes, forms and motifs, everyday objects and associated practices, design products and strategies. I propose that this aggregate is structured as an unfolding *archive*, a historical repository, shaped by the practices of design and curatorship that borrow from and thus enact it.

To view national design as the performance of an archive, we need to shift our methodological emphasis from aggregation and generalization to movement and multiplicity. In this, I am influenced by Lash and Lury's methodological exposition (2007: 16–33), where they ultimately propose that we follow and map the movements of cultural objects as things and media across diverse sites. Further, in inventorying movements and connections, I am particularly attentive to claims to cultural authenticity and historical continuity that express the teleological characteristics of nationalist histories (Anderson 2006), in other words, claims to *depth*, as opposed to post-modernist and post-structuralist pre-occupations with *surface* (Jameson 1991). Below I present a series of vignettes from the design field in Turkey, building on document analyses and interviews with professionals. Following an introductory overview of recent discussions over Turkish design style, I present two products, *Compass Rose* brooch and *Dervish* coffee cup, then pursue their connections to exhibitions (*İlk in Milano* and *Table of Contents*), a design initiative (*Barbar*), and lastly a collection (Paşabahçe *Omnia*). The analysis proceeds from narrow to wide in scope, from ornament to product to initiative to exhibition to collection. If the scope remains fairly limited to the works of a certain group of designers and their interactions, it is because my objective is not to make a complete review of Turkish design, but to follow and identify the ways in which objects traverse different sites and extents of design culture, and in traversing, articulate with and so enable varied discourses on Turkish design.

Overview of the field

Arguments for a Turkish identity in design go back two decades, concurrent with the rise in public awareness of and industry interest in industrial design in Turkey (Hasdoğan 2009; Balcıoğlu and Emgin 2014). A review of design products in this period finds references to cultural elements associated with Turkishness, such as local customs (e.g. coffee preparation, tea drinking), objects (e.g. water pipe, tulip-shaped tea glass), symbols (e.g. tulip, carpet motifs), and architecture (e.g. Turkish bath, mosque). Many of these are incorporated to high-design products by freelance designers and consultancies, offered in limited production, sometimes only for display in exhibitions. Others are mass-produced consumer products whose association with traditions were underlined in their design and mediation, including electric coffee makers, tea glasses and bathroom tiles (for classifications, see Kaygan 2008; Balcıoğlu and Emgin 2014: 103, note 29).

In addition to novel products and a rich discourse around them in press releases and interviews, the arguments over Turkish style have inspired design initiatives, design collections and several exhibitions in Turkey and abroad, as well as seminars, panels, research papers and theses. In a conference paper in 1996, Oğuz Bayrakçı called for a return to local culture for differentiation in the global market; a decade later at the ADesign Fair 2004, the same argument dominated the panel discussions. At one panel, it was suggested that manufacturers should suspend competition and cooperate towards creating a Turkish presence in the global market, which was characterized as 'a total war' by Güran Gökyay, chairman of the furniture company Nurus. Among the designers speaking at the panel, there was no consensus over how this can and should be achieved. Some advocated the use of cultural elements, albeit carefully. Designer İnci Mutlu criticized designers who merely reproduce 'a Turkish motif ... in plastics' without asking: 'What is in the essence of that object? What are its oriental curves?' Others voiced their opinions against the overuse of Ottoman imagery, or against the idea of a unitary style in general (Art+Decor 2004).

In 2007 design scholar Gökhan Karakuş attempted a unifying reading of around 100 products by 29 designers that were presented at the *İlk in Milano: Turkish Touch in Design* exhibition in Milan Design Week 2007 – arguably the peak in a series of design exhibitions that sought to advertise the accomplishments of Turkish design to audiences in Turkey and abroad (Emgin 2008). In his analysis, Karakuş (2007: 26) outlined a tension between 'universal cultures of rational modernism' and the local, 'autochthonous culture' of Turkey, with which Turkish designers dealt either through a form of 'geometric abstractionism' or by introducing 'Ottoman, Anatolian even Islamic forms' to their work. More recently, Balcıoğlu and Emgin (2014) published a historical review that described an ongoing 'quest for a Turkish design identity', fuelled by the desire for Turkish design to be recognized as an equal yet distinct brand within international competition. My own research demonstrated the 'liberal neo-nationalist' (Bora 2003) basis of such design practices, in which expressions of national pride and responsibility get intertwined with expectations of economic benefit from the successful articulation of Turkish brands to global cultures of design and consumption (Kaygan 2016a).

In these, one can see a shared discourse on local–global interactions, and identify the significance of curatorial and collective work such as exhibitions in the formation and dissemination of that discourse and related practices. I start with a globally well-connected work of design that illustrates these basic observations.

A brooch: Product as multiplicity

Ela Cindoruk's *Compass Rose* series from 2006 consist of brooches and other pieces of jewellery made of white paper doilies, held by red string and gold wire (see Figure 13.1). They were exhibited at the *İlk in Milano* exhibition, and Karakuş's (2007: 88) commentary stressed the way the designer 'appropriate[d] traditional materials and patterns directly into her work, [taking] as her reference paper doilies commonly used as decorative accessories in Turkish homes'. In contrast with the way Karakuş associated her designs with Turkish homes and traditions, Cindoruk typically contextualizes her work with reference to the ubiquity of ornamentation through world history (see Cindoruk in Karakuş 2007: 87). In my interview with her, she narrated her design process similarly in terms of her encounters with ornamentation:

> I was [brought up] wearing crochet collars. (She laughs.) ... In my dowry, underneath all the handmade crochet there were also paper doilies, stored away with care. ... Later I began collecting the paper doilies that

FIGURE 13.1 Compass Rose *brooch, designed by Ela Cindoruk, 2006. Image courtesy of the designer.*

are served under Turkish coffee cups. And one day I put a safety pin through [the doilies] and wore them as a brooch. I thought, this is a good material, and I started experimenting with it. ... One step before that, ... once I was on vacation in Bodrum and I saw people buying plastic cornices at the DIY store. I found it interesting ... that we cannot give up that urge to ornament. ... Since then I have been using that crochet form. (Ela Cindoruk, interview with the author, 7 Feb. 2017; my translation)

In our conversation, Cindoruk insisted that crochet 'has nothing to do with Turkishness'. The international recognition it received was not related to her use of local culture; on the contrary, it was due to its coincidence with global design trends: Her example was Marcel Wanders' ornamental work. The products could not find commercial success in Turkey either, since the white colour and fragility of the brooches scared off local customers.

On a critical note, Cindoruk's account contradicts Karakuş's theory of national style only to offer another narrative, a story of personal experiences and oeuvre that subsumes the meaning and significance of the products. In that sense, *Compass Rose* is a typical piece of *high design*, in which 'conscious designer intervention and authorship, along with the price tag, play a large role in establishing the cultural and aesthetic credentials of an artefact' (Julier 2008: 77), and in which the designer's personal history combined with playful experimentation with forms is used to explain success (Lloyd and Snelders 2003: 243).

Still, as a text, I am inclined to favour the designer's elaborations over the design critic's totalizing formalism – not because the designer relates to the originary event but because her narrative provokes a richer metaphorical space: crochet collars and grandmother's doilies, coffee cups, polystyrene cornices, Wanders's works, and finally her many experiments, from the readymade brooch to *Compass Rose* onto her later newspaper coasters, silver jewellery and similarly decorated cups and glasses. In that sense, we can view Cindoruk's designs not as a series of products that derive their significance from a singular local cultural reference, but as an itinerary of influences and experiments that are only loosely gathered around the idea of the doily as ornament: an unfolding object (Knorr Cetina 2001). To clarify the kind of unfolding the doily presents, we require comparison.

A coffee cup: Product as depth

Dervish cup by Kunter Şekercioğlu, a Turkish coffee cup in white porcelain, evokes the white dress of a whirling dervish with the curls of its saucer (see Figure 13.2). In an interview, he provided me with an account of his inspiration, the story of another unfolding object. Erdem Akan, as the curator of a design exhibition for Starbucks in 2008, asked a group of designers, artists and architects, in Şekercioğlu's words, 'to interpret either the coffee mug or the coffee cup' for rapid prototyping. At the time, Şekercioğlu was producing work as a founding member of the *Barbar* design initiative:

> In those long meetings, in that productive period of the *Barbar* project, ... you know, [discussions on] Islamic enlightenment and Sufism, Haji Bektash Veli, Mevlana, um, Farid ud-Din Attar, their predecessors in Iran ... Once you research a little, you get filled up [with inspiration]. Ideas sometimes just come to you at once, but they still have a strong background. So I was trying to come up with an idea when, I swear,

FIGURE 13.2 Dervish *coffee cup by Zula, designed by Kunter Şekercioğlu, 2010. Image courtesy of the designer.*

the design was finished in 20 minutes. ... So why is [the cup shaped like a dervish]? ... Turkish coffee is the first coffee drink; it's the oldest [technique]. Sufi lodges in Yemen are the first to make it. It fits well, doesn't it? Coffee gives you energy; it helps you resist sleep [during the long religious rituals]. ... [In the exhibition] I wrote under it the popular saying: 'The heart fancies neither coffee nor coffeehouse / The heart fancies companionship [or conversation], coffee is an excuse.' ... So that it became a visualization, umm, that fits well with Islamic tolerance and Islamic esoterism. (Kunter Şekercioğlu, interview with the author, 22 Dec. 2009; my translation; the saying translated by Kafadar 2007: 120)

At the time of the interview, Şekercioğlu had just started working on a prototype with an eye to marketing *Dervish* as what he called a 'designer product'. Unsatisfied with the early results, he was experimenting with the form, and planning user tests.

The designer's account of *Dervish* is comparable to Cindoruk's story, for it builds on a range of citations from a rapid-prototyping exhibition to the meetings of Barbar to historical anecdotes and popular sayings onto ceramic moulds and usability requirements. Nevertheless, *Dervish* is more 'stable' in its materiality (Law and Mol 1995) than Cindoruk's doilies, in which the unfolding takes on a further peculiar character. Some of Cindoruk's experiments navigate close to the actual doily, as in the coasters, whereas others relate to it only via detour, as with her highly abstracted *Doily Moily* bracelets (2012). Especially in the latter, the movement of the doily as ornament comes close to what Lash and Lury (2007: 25) term 'transposition', a process whereby it is not the artistic integrity of the form that brings together the series through purposive production of an identity (as in *Dervish* cup), but singular features (in this case, the vaguely florid ornamentation) that multiply over a range of media. In simpler terms, Cindoruk's work does not seem to finalize in a calibrated expression, as does *Dervish*. The doily seeks expansion through multiplication, whereas *Dervish* moves towards condensation and depth through successive prototypes and a focused discourse.

I showed elsewhere in the case of electric Turkish coffee makers how products can be associated in their design and mediation with traditions to sustain a figure of historical permanence (Kaygan 2016a, b). Here my interest lies in the curation of a style, so in the following sections, I turn to two events: the *Barbar* meetings, which stimulated the idea for *Dervish*, and an exhibition in Helsinki, where it was displayed in 2012.

An initiative: Production of depth

Barbar was a design initiative made up of eighteen designers, predominantly from industrial design backgrounds, who had three exhibitions of rapid-manufactured objects in 2007, 2009 and 2011. Among the designers mentioned previously, Akan, Cindoruk and Şekercioğlu were all members. Their manifesto states that the initiative 'focused on a combination of the environmental, social and mental realities that have existed in Istanbul and Turkey's cultural geography for thousands of years ... to create objects' based on 'the highly conceptual and sensitive term "barbarian"' (Babadağ et al. 2009: 384–5).

The significance of *Barbar* arises less from its exhibitions than from the frequent, sometimes weekly informal meetings in members' design offices. In these, the designers engaged in heated debates over professional issues such as business conditions in Turkey, and academic topics such as what it means to be a barbarian. Not having access to the actual transcripts of the meetings, the following quotation from my interview with Murad Babadağ offers a glimpse:

> What some foreign designers do is ... archaeological theft. They go and see a form; they use it directly or after somehow abstracting it. They won't think about its content, where it comes from. This has always been so in history: ... The tulip is one of the most important of Islamic motifs because in *abjad* counting, the words *tulip* and *Allah* have the same count of 66. However during the Crusades, the knights who saw it, loved the form and brought it directly back to their churches without knowing about its meaning.

Babadağ went on by criticizing some of his fellow *Barbars* for being similarly whimsical in their employment of local resources, his arguments resembling İnci Mutlu's objections I quoted previously. The designer added: 'You cannot have this much whim and arbitrariness. You should somehow justify [your decisions] rationally. So *this* is the sort of discussion we always had. We argued over the very nature, the *essence* of design' (Murad Babadağ, interview with the author, 15 Mar. 2017; my translation).

As Babadağ's and Şekercioğlu's arguments show, *Barbar* initiative seems to have functioned principally as a forum for interpreting the existing conditions of design practice, and developing local expert knowledge in the form of concepts, anecdotes and design philosophies as a response to those conditions. Ultimately, the outcomes were used, or at least expected to be used, for inspiring and justifying design decisions. *Barbar* was foremost a machine that produced depth.

An exhibition: Recontextualization of products

In 2012, Istanbul Technical University Department of Industrial Product Design organized an exhibition in Helsinki in collaboration with Turkish

Ministry of Tourism and Culture and Helsinki Caisa Gallery with the title, *Table of Contents: Contemporary Tableware Design from Istanbul*. The unpublished press release described the selection as 'products with simple and basic forms' from 'the last 10 years [of] Turkish design'. Photographs show objects made of clear glass, white ceramic or plastic with occasional chrome and green, sparsely distributed over white IKEA tables. White panels provide for the objects a background of large blue leaves and petals stylized from illuminations, accompanied with literal translations of Turkish sayings in lightest Helvetica (see Figure 13.3). A member of the curating committee, Hümanur Bağlı, explained that they wished to avoid 'clichés ... like Turkish ornaments, ewers, so on [and] build an alternative image for Turkish food culture', and chose instead of 'exhibiting Turkish, old, traditional stuff, to show that we do produce modern design'. She indicated as an example Homeend *Royaltea* electric tea maker by Designum, which she found modern in style but still related to the local food and drink culture. The white and blue exhibition panels were also her design. In discomfiting contrast was a simultaneous art exhibition at the same venue, titled *Past to Present: Turkish Arts and Culture*. She commented: 'While we were, like, modern Turkish design, a little designer's touch ... where we questioned the traditional; there they had actual *kaftans* and laces' (Hümanur Bağlı, interview with the author, 9 Mar. 2017; my translation).

Another curator, Çiğdem Kaya, named their major criterion as 'mass-accessibility', implying a contrast with high-design objects that have dominated many exhibitions of the last two decades. She highlighted the affordable Üçsan *Zeytin* polypropylene oil bottle by Abluka Design, and a tea glass designed by Defne Koz for a promotional campaign by Lipton (interview with the author, 6 Feb. 2017). With the emphasis on modern, accessible design, the organizers I interviewed recalled their doubts about bringing such a collection to Finland, such as that the glassware 'looked too Finnish', or that the minimalism would not be found interesting by the visitors.

FIGURE 13.3 *View from the* Table of Contents *exhibition, Helsinki, 2012. Image courtesy of Koray Gelmez from the curatorial team.*

Dervish coffee cup was also included, even though both its contextualization by its designer in historical anecdote and religious symbolism, and its status as a design object would be opposed to the curatorial perspective. Within the white and glass simplicity of the exhibition the ceramic cup does not look out of place. As anthropologist Nicholas Thomas put it sternly, with objects, 'what we are confronted with is ... never more or less than a succession of uses and recontextualisations' (1994: 28–9). Yet what we see in this almost frictionless inclusion of design objects to divergent (albeit not adversarial) definitions of Turkish design is not mere interpretive flexibility. These objects from tea makers to brooches are weakly organized as an *archive* from within which practicing designers, design journalists, event organizers and design academics can make a selection. I have shown two types of relations – the expansive connections of the doily and relations of depth in *Barbar* – that make up this archive; one can also discern a common vocabulary that shapes the selections, a vocabulary that revolves around dualisms such as traditional/modern, local/global and ornamental/simple. Star and Griesemer (1989) called 'boundary objects' those objects of collaboration (repositories, standardized forms, etc.) that are structured in such ways that permit diverse parties to cooperate without consensus. In our case the archive allows for, even inspires collaboration in exhibitions and collectives under the umbrella of, or sometimes in the name of, Turkish design. It is not that in each event the object is assessed differently; rather the object travels from one event to the next, gathering connections while remaining recognizable across recontextualizations.

On the other hand, unlike Star and Griesemer's repositories, which rely on standardization, here we find Turkish design to be in a creative flux. With our methodological focus, what we see might not be an archive so much as a series of archivings. To illustrate this point, in the last section, I look at a design managerial practice.

A collection: Building archives

To celebrate its 80th anniversary in 2015, glass manufacturer Paşabahçe launched the *Omnia* collection, comprising 260 new pieces of glassware (133 new glass moulds), designed by 15 freelance designers and consultancies based in Turkey and abroad (including designers from non-Turkish backgrounds) in addition to the in-house designers and glass workers. Akan and Cindoruk were among the contributors. Product manager Müge Bozbeyli explained to me their objective as 'redesigning the future of glass ... without giving up on our traditional values ... [but] to sustain those values and carry them on to the future with courage' (Müge Bozbeyli, interview with the author, 22 Feb. 2017; my translation). The design brief encouraged open-ended experimentation by merely providing a list of glass manufacturing techniques and traditional objects that the designers were expected to study: *çeşmibülbül* (filigree glass), Beykoz style (gilding and enameling), crystal cutting, free blowing, *nazarlık* (evil eye bead), tulip-shaped tea glass and a seventh, free category. All of the design alternatives developed by the designers were accepted without a selection phase, and after being refined for production, all but a handful of conceptual objects were taken up for mass production. Almost a year and a half after the collection was launched, new objects were still being released.

Behind the large number and diversity of designers employed and designs produced, there seems to be a motivation to exhaust the possibilities of traditional techniques and objects: to produce all – hence the title *Omnia*. Indeed, during the interview, Bozbeyli likened the collection to 'a really broad design dossier. It is as if you open the cupboard and you bring [the objects] into life one by one' (Müge Bozbeyli, interview with the author, 22 Feb. 2017; my translation). The printed catalogue shows a huge variety of tableware and decorative objects, and at the extremes, products such as a filigree glass motorcycle headlight by Ali Bakova. One of Cindoruk's contributions is a tulip-shaped tea glass with doily-like patterns. A short text by its designer accompanies each product, indicating wildly diverse formal references: travertines of Pamukkale, a motorcycle exhaust, rose syrup, birds in Beykoz, African culture, trees in one designer's neighbourhood, to name a random few. Any attempt to classify is countered by the Czech designer Rony Plesl's annotation for his contribution, the *Flower Factory* vase: 'A carafe or a vase in the form of a chimney – why not?'

Including non-local designers and a medley of conceptual references, and putting value on the sheer quantity of design outcomes over their consistency, *Omnia* radically extends what I have called an archive, and with that, demonstrates the limits of conceptualizing that archive as a structured and more-or-less stable catalogue of national cultural elements. The resulting collection is a patchwork of transpositions, in which a technique or an object is echoed in formal or conceptual explorations, so that it becomes by itself a critique of the possibility of a Turkish design style.

Conclusion

In this chapter, I have objected to an understanding of national design in terms of common qualities of design objects, processes or people. I suggested that to understand such a variegated design cultural object as national design, we can instead trace the interactions between its various actors and sites and describe the translations that take place. Doing that, I identified two opposing movements. First is expansion through transposition, as in the doily or the glass manufacturing techniques in their many manifestations in

Omnia collection, which proliferates concepts, forms and techniques across sites and modalities of design without concern for maintaining unity in style. It is opportunistic in its inspirations and future-oriented in its experiments. Second is a search for depth, which contextualizes design products with the use of philosophical concepts or historical anecdotes to create a sense of historical continuity and cultural authenticity, as in *Barbar* meetings. It stabilizes meaning as it expands the product's connections; it regulates and authenticates. Unities can also be established via strong attitudes in exhibitions and academic texts, both of which may piece together several products, as well as other media, to set forth arguments for the nature or history of Turkish design. The two opposed trends outline an unfolding archive of heterogeneous elements, from which new explorations can set off in the form of novel products, brand identities, exhibitions, and so on and perform Turkish design differently. Diverging interpretations of existing designs, or projects with divergent approaches can coexist and even collaborate insofar as they translate into the terms of the archive and its dualist discourse on traditional and modern, local and global.

One point is that national design as an imagined community (in this case, imagined as a network of practitioners and organizations that are defined through their interconnected practices) coincides with national design as an idiom (in this case, enacted as an archive, a weakly structured gallery of references, a repository of value) both in discourse and in practice. At the macro level, it is crucial to acknowledge the impact of global neoliberalism and resurging nationalisms on design cultures, as not only ministerial committees at the national level, but perhaps more importantly localities, from neighbourhoods to transnational communities, are pressured to capitalize on their resources (social, cultural, natural, etc.) to the point of depletion by utilizing designerly approaches (Julier 2017). Still we need to document the specific manifestations of those ideologies in different sites of design culture in the form of, for instance, national and international exhibitions and awards that encourage, even impel the search for cultural value, practices of authentication that struggle to regulate local design cultural fields, and sites and media in which designers exchange resources and disseminate sensibilities, nationalistic or otherwise.

A second, methodological point concerns how we can study politically significant (in this case, multiply performed, weakly regulated and potentially exclusionary) design cultural objects such as national design without reifying them, contributing to their ongoing performance as singular and unchanging. We might remember Arjun Appadurai's (1996) warning that *culture* as a noun highlights and in fact substantializes dominant ways of thinking and doing, whereas the adjectival form is capable of bringing differences to the foreground. Design cultures as multiple and changing objects of study may be specifically amenable to analysis in the adjectival form as we direct our attention to *design cultural* flows and exchanges.

References

Andermann, J. (2009), 'Tournaments of Value: Argentina and Brazil in the Age of Exhibitions', *Journal of Material Culture*, 14(3): 333–63.
Anderson, B. (2006), *Imagined Communities*, rev. edn, London: Verso.
Appadurai, A. (1996), *Modernity at Large: Cultural Dimensions of Globalization*, Minneapolis: University of Minnesota Press.
Art+Decor (2004), 'Tasarımın Cazibeli Yolculuğu' [The Seductive Journey of Design], *Art+Decor*, 140 (November), Paneller Konferanslar Özel Eki: 88–96.
Aynsley, J. (1993), *Nationalism and Internationalism: Design in the 20th Century*, London: Victoria & Albert Museum.
Babadağ, M., Cindoruk, E., Gencol, H., Güven, G. and Karakuş, G. (2009), 'Barbarian Rhapsody', *The Design Journal*, 12(3): 383–94.
Balcıoğlu, T. and Emgin, B. (2014), 'Recent Turkish Design Innovations: A Quest for Identity', *Design Issues*, 30(2): 97–111.
Bayrakçı, O. (1996), 'Yerel Ürün Kimliği – Küresel Dış Pazar' [Local Product Identity – Global Market], in N. Bayazıt, F. K. Çorbacı and D. Günal (eds), *Tasarımda Evrenselleşme: 2.Ulusal Tasarım Kongresi Bildiri Kitabı*, 13–15 March 1996, Istanbul: Yapı-Endüstri Merkezi, 93–102.
Bhagat, D. (2011), 'Performing White South African Identity through International and Empire Exhibitions', in G. Adamson, G. Riello and S. Teasley (eds), *Global Design History*, London: Routledge, 72–81.
Bora, T. (2003), 'Nationalist Discourses in Turkey', *South Atlantic Quarterly*, 102(2): 433–51.
Emgin, B. (2008), 'ID-Entity in Question: Turkish Touch in Design in "İlk" in Milano', Master's thesis, Izmir: Izmir University of Economics.
Greenhalgh, P. (1988), *Ephemeral Vistas: The Expositions Universelles, Great Exhibitions and World's Fairs, 1851–1939*, Manchester: Manchester University Press.
Greenhalgh, P. (1995), 'The English Compromise: Modern Design and National Consciousness 1870–1940', in W. Kaplan (ed.), *Designing Modernity: the Arts of Reform and Persuasion 1885–1945*, London: Thames & Hudson, 111–39.
Hasdoğan, G. (2009), 'The Institutionalization of the Industrial Design Profession in Turkey: Case Study – The Industrial Designers Society of Turkey', *The Design Journal*, 12(3): 311–38.
Hobsbawm, E. (1983), 'Introduction: Inventing Traditions', in E. Hobsbawm and T. Ranger (eds), *The Invention of Tradition*, Cambridge: Cambridge University Press, 1–14.
Jackson, S. (2006), 'Sacred Objects: Australian Design and National Celebrations', *Journal of Design History*, 19(3): 249–55.
Jameson, F. (1991), *Postmodernism, Or the Cultural Logic of Late Capitalism*, Durham, NC: Duke University Press.
Julier, G. (2008), *The Culture of Design*, 2nd edn, London: Sage.
Julier, G. (2017), *Economies of Design*, London: Sage.
Kafadar, C. (2007), 'Janissaries and Other Riffraff of Ottoman Istanbul: Rebels without a Cause?', in B. Tezcan and K.K. Barbir (eds), *Identity and Identity Formation in the Ottoman World*, Madison, Wisconsin: University of Wisconsin Press, 113–34.

Karakuş, G. (2007), *Turkish Touch in Design: Contemporary Product Design by Turkish Designers Worldwide*, Istanbul: Tasarım Yayın Grubu.

Kaygan, H. (2008), 'Tasarımda Milli Kimliğin Varoluş Koşulları' [The Conditions of Existence of National Identity in Design], in T. Balcıoğlu and G. Baydar (eds), *Kim(lik)lerin Tasarımı: 4T Türkiye Tasarım Tarihi Topluluğu Bildiri Kitabı*, 12–13 May 2008, Izmir: Izmir University of Economics, 123–30.

Kaygan, H. (2016a), 'Electric Turkish Coffee Makers: Capturing Authenticity for Global Markets', in N. Möllers and B. Dewalt (eds), *Objects in Motion: Globalizing Technology*, Washington, D.C.: Smithsonian Institution Scholarly Press, 92–111.

Kaygan, H. (2016b), 'Material Semiotics of Form Giving: The Case of the Electric Turkish Coffee Pot', *Design Issues*, 32(2): 78–90.

Knorr Cetina, K. (2001), 'Postsocial Relations: Theorizing Sociality in a Postsocial Environment', in G. Ritzer and B. Smart (eds), *Handbook of Social Theory*, London: Sage, 520–37.

Lash, S. and Lury, C. (2007), *Global Culture Industry: The Mediation of Things*, Cambridge: Polity Press.

Law, J. and Mol, A. (1995), 'Notes on Materiality and Sociality', *The Sociological Review*, 43(2): 274–94.

Lloyd, P. and Snelders, D. (2003), 'What was Philippe Starck Thinking of?', *Design Studies*, 24(3): 237–53.

McGowan, A. S. (2005), '"All that is Rare, Characteristic or Beautiful": Design and the Defense of Tradition in Colonial India, 1851–1903', *Journal of Material Culture*, 10(3): 263–87.

Narotzky, V. (2009), 'Selling the Nation: Identity and Design in 1980s Catalonia', *Design Issues*, 25(3): 62–75.

Ozorio de Almeida Meroz, J. and Griffin, R. (2012), 'Open Design: A History of the Construction of a Dutch Idea', *The Design Journal*, 15(4): 405–22.

Republic of Turkey Ministry of Development (2015), 'İthalata Olan Bağımlılığın Azaltılması Programı Eylem Planı, Onuncu Kalkınma Planı (2014-2018) Öncelikli Dönüşüm Programları: 2' [Program to Reduce Export Dependency, The Tenth Development Plan (2014-2018), Priority Transformation Programs: 2], http://odop.kalkinma.gov.tr/dokumanlar/02Ithalata_Olan_Bagimliligin_Azaltilmasi_Programi.pdf, accessed 1 February 2017.

Sparke, P. (1981), *Consultant Design: the History and Practice of the Designer in Industry*, London: Pembridge.

Sparke, P. (1992), *An Introduction to Design & Culture in the Twentieth Century*, London: Routledge.

Star, S. L. and Griesemer, J. R. (1989), 'Institutional Ecology, "Translations" and Boundary Objects: Amateurs and Professionals in Berkeley's Museum of Vertebrate Zoology, 1907-39', *Social Studies of Science*, 19(3): 387–420.

Thomas, N. (1994), *Entangled Objects: Exchange, Material Culture, and Colonialism in the Pacific*, Cambridge, MA: Harvard University Press.

Yagou, A. (2003), 'Facing the West: Greece in the Great Exhibition of 1851', *Design Issues*, 19(4): 82–90.

Yagou, A. (2007), 'Metamorphoses of Formalism: National Identity as a Recurrent Theme of Design in Greece', *Journal of Design History*, 20(2): 145–59.

CHAPTER FOURTEEN

A theoretical straddle:

Locating design cultures between national structures and transnational networks

Joana Ozorio de Almeida Meroz
and Katarina Serulus

Introduction

Historically, one of the dominant modes of categorizing and studying design has been in terms of the nation-state. However, some design historians question whether the nation-state provides the most suitable framework for the historical study of design, particularly given the challenges posed by globalization (Adamson, Riello and Teasley 2011). Nevertheless, given nation-states' enduring relevance to the development of design practices, it might be too early to overthrow the national framework altogether. Indeed, the nation-state often remains key in articulating the transnational networks that design cultures construct and circulate in. The empirical complexity of contemporary design cultures, straddling as they do national structures and transnational networks, requires the development of new theoretical frameworks that allow for examining design as it crosses over different conceptual and contextual frames (for recent attempts in this direction, see e.g. Fallan and Lees-Maffei 2016; Gimeno Martínez and Ozorio de

Almeida Meroz 2016). This chapter contributes to the question of how to locate design cultures as these web through national agendas, transnational relations and international frameworks.

As Adrian Forty (1986: 6–8) alerted us long ago, a key difficulty with interpreting design is the use of 'society' as a stable frame according to which the meanings of design cultures can be derived. Frequently, the shape of this 'society' is imagined as congruent with that of the nation-state, an assumption that in the social sciences is known as 'methodological nationalism'. In this model, as sociologist Zsuzsa Gille (2012: 91) notes, the nation is conceptualized as a self-evident, perennial reality while the international is conceptualized merely as a relation between those bounded nations, and as such takes second place. The problem with this framework, she continues, is that it is 'a built-in obstacle to the discovery that the international may in fact precede and even affect the social space of the nation' and consequently also the dynamics of design cultures (ibid). Indeed, studies on design cultures often tend to limit their interpretations to the borders of the nation-state.

Transnationalism emerged in cross-border studies as a critique on methodological nationalism and is by now widely accepted in design studies, design history, material culture and neighbouring fields. Transnationalism neither neglects nor competes with the national paradigm. Instead, it accepts that 'the boundaries of societies, cultures or civilizations are permeable and mutually constitutive' (Amelina et al. 2012: 6). This means one can continue studying 'national' design cultures while remaining attentive to the role of transnational processes. Another valuable aspect of this approach is that it allows us to 'think of social entities as territorialized and de-territorialized as well as nationalized and cosmopolitan at the same time' (ibid: 5, 6). Since transnationalism is concerned with movement, flows and circulations it is a useful concept to better understand the transnational nature of design cultures.

To locate design cultures as these straddle national structures and transnational networks, we elaborate theoretical-methodological frameworks that borrow from the fields of new materialism, governmentality studies, cross-border studies, and historiography to capture the elusive movements of design cultures as these cross over national and transnational logics. Below we consider how these approaches can be useful to examining how transnational design cultures are construed as national phenomena. In conclusion, we propose an understanding of design cultures as bridges between narratives of national design on the one hand, and complex and utterly globalized networks on the other.

Approach 1: Transnational governance

The first section looks at the methodological possibilities that examining transnational governance provides in unravelling the national and transnational imbroglios of design cultures. The notion of 'governmentality' comes in handy when aiming to unhinge the nation from the state.[1] Coined by Michel Foucault, the notion was further developed in the humanities and social sciences. In short, governance considers all processes of governing human behaviour ranging from self-government and government of others to government of more abstract entities like populations and territory (Burchell, Gordon and Miller 1991: 1–52; Foucault 1991; Dean 2010; Hague and Harrop 2007). Institutions, communities, families and individuals at once internal and external to the state also are included in these mundane processes of governance (Mitchell 2006: 179). In political science studies, the term 'transnational governance' is used to describe organizations such as Oxfam as transnational regimes that govern populations that are not linked to a specific territory (Sharma and Gupta 2006: 24). For design cultures, this concept can be applied to approach transnational networks and organizations such as The Bureau of European Design Associations, the International Federation of Interior Architects/Designers (IFI), or the International Council of Societies of Industrial Design (ICSID) that govern transnational design communities and that, besides official state institutions, have to be taken into consideration when observing the creation of 'national' design.

To illustrate how transnational governance can be applied to design culture, this section discusses the case of the post-war phenomenon of the 'Design Centre' as a format for national design promotion that was actively shaped by transnational governance.[2] Prompted by economic challenges such as the globalization of markets, this format was mobilized by national governments and industries to increase national prestige and consequently create trade opportunities and boost the economy (Maguire and Woodham 1997; Yagou 2005; Fallan 2007; Thompson 2011). Hence, design centres are traditionally seen as excellent entry points to the study 'national' design. However, looking at institutional networks that transcend the boundaries of the nation-state, one can actually account for the importance of transnational networks in the creation of these national design centres and their policies. As such, these design bodies serve as useful starting points for examining the 'junctures' between the national and transnational spheres.

Design historian Arthur Pulos (1988: 209–21) states that design centres proliferated in almost every country that claimed to have some kind of industrial production. Many of these were actually inspired by the prominent Design Centre of the British Council of Industrial Design (CoID) that opened its doors in 1956 in London. The formula consisted of a permanent exhibition of jury-selected products, supplemented by temporary themed exhibitions, a design and designer index, and a library. The emergence of these national centres was closely connected to the global developments in the discipline of design. In 1951, the first International Design Conference was organized by the CoID and in 1957 the ICSID was established (Messel 2016). In 1967, design centres gained access to the ICSID community when member societies decided to grant official recognition to permanent exhibitions called 'Design Centres' (ICSID Vth General Assembly 1967). From then on, this kind of design bodies, wherever located in the world, could become full members. However, to obtain this official recognition, they had to conform to ICSID's definition of 'Design Centres' that was rather coloured by its modernist understanding of design as a tool of industrial growth and progress (Messel 2016). In later meetings, even more substantive guidelines were laid down, such as their attitude towards the display of objects and social questions (International meeting on Design Centre 1974). Thus, design centres not only existed within national logics, but were also part of transnational networks and answered to international design frameworks. Take, for example, the Brussels Design Centre. Established in 1962 under the protection of the Belgian Office for Foreign Trade, it 'had to exude a distinct Belgian character' (Een Design Centre te Brussel 1963: 9). The Belgian organization, as many others, adopted very consciously the British name 'Design Centre' because of its international reputation, aiming to inscribe itself into the international design community (see also Serulus 2014). This was not very surprising since the Belgian connection with the transnational community was in fact already closely-knit. The Design Centre's director Josine des Cressonnières (1926–85) was from 1961 to 1977 also the general secretary of the ICSID. Policymakers as her played a key role as an intermediary point between national and transnational structures. And this became especially apparent in the exchange of design shows with counterparts in the Netherlands, Sweden, Japan, Vienna, Spain and others.

This outward attitude was of course not only connected to the global success of the design profession and des Cressonnières' impressive network, but also to the national agenda of the Brussels organization, namely to provide Belgium with a positive image in the arena of international trade and politics. A remarkable case is the exchange with the Soviet design organization VNIITE in the early 1970s. This event took place in anticipation of the Helsinki Agreements, one of the few successes to emerge from Cold War détente where the two blocs agreed to cooperate on economic, scientific and technological levels (Dockrill and Hopkins 2006: 120). The Belgian exhibition in Moscow in 1974 was part of a large commercial mission in the Soviet Union. The Belgian Prince Albert and the minister of Foreign Trade travelled with industrialists from forty Belgian companies to explore commercial opportunities over there. The Belgian exhibition featured rational and functional design, including a Jomy collapsible fire ladder, a Meurop plastic child's chair and a Nova deep-fryer, to catch the attention of potential traders in the East.

This case shows that organizations and policymakers injected ideas that circulated in an international level into national structures, but at the same time also transformed the ideas circulating in global design networks with experiences at the national level. Looking at transnational processes of governance, one can consider the role of communities inside or outside the

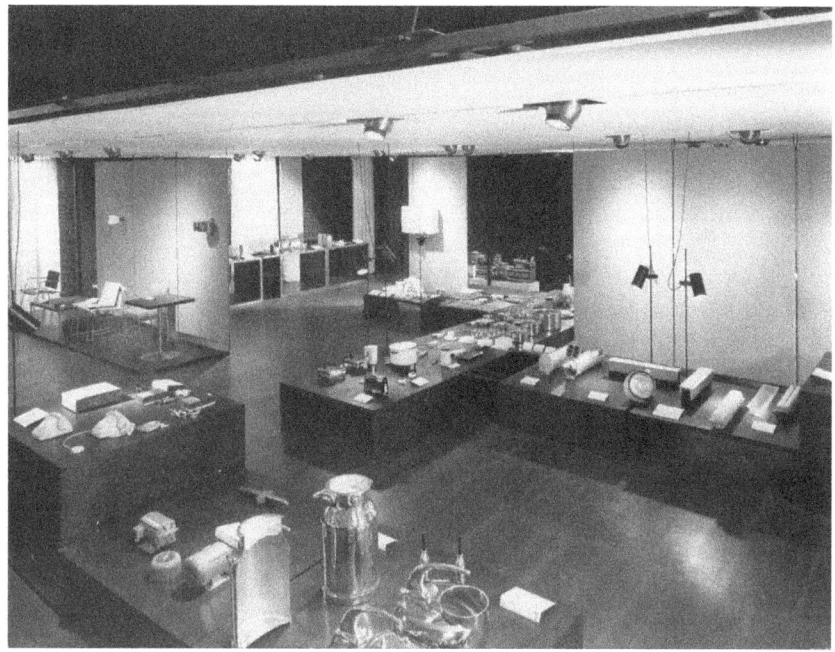

FIGURE 14.1 *The Brussels Design Centre, 1964. Source: Private Archive Des Cressonnières, Belgium.*

state, territorized or de-territorized, when studying the shaping of national design cultures.

Approach 2: Materiality – temporality

This section examines the role of materiality and temporality in the development of national design histories that bypass methodological nationalism without nevertheless dispensing with the nation by examining how the transnational bears upon the national.[3] Gille (2012: 91) points out that many models for transcending methodological nationalism 'evacuate … the nonhuman content from social institutions, social relations and change processes'. In contrast, she holds, scholars associated with the 'practice' or 'material turn' see the social 'as hybrid – that is, co-produced by humans and nonhumans' (ibid). To her, this understanding of the social as hybrid offers a privileged vantage point from which to transcend methodological nationalism since tracing the spatial movement of materiality takes us beyond the geography of the nation-state and hence offers a good opportunity to examine how the national and the transnational interact – a perspective she calls 'transnational materiality' (Gille 2014. See also Gille 2016). Anthropologist and visual culture scholar

Christopher Pinney (2005) argues that attending to the temporality of materiality also works as a means to unhinge artefacts from the 'conventional culture-object space' of the nation. A common means to interpret artefacts is to place them within their socio-political contexts, which implies that materiality is coterminous with these. Instead, Pinney contends that material artefacts have their own time, and hence that their temporality does not necessarily match that of the nation-state. Rather than placing objects in a certain time and explaining them in terms of the political, social and cultural contexts around them, Pinney instead examines what he calls objects' 'cataracts of time'. In practice, this entails tracing an artefact's string of visual, technical and material references, which results in histories that often do not coincide with the linear time of national histories.

To illustrate how attending to the materiality and temporality of artefacts can be of use to national design histories that transcend methodological nationalism, here we shortly summarize a recent study on a specific design artefact – namely, *Autarchy*, by Italian-born Andrea Trimarchi and Simone Farresin of design Studio Formafantasma – which reveals how in the process of *Autarchy* being construed as Dutch design, it in turn reconfigured 'Dutchness' and the time-space of the nation.[4]

Autarchy (2009) is a multimedia design installation that, according to its designers, 'proposes an autonomous way of producing goods ... where nature is personally cultivated, harvested and processed to feed and make tools to serve human needs ... Autarchy suggests an alternative way of producing goods in which inherited knowledge is used to find sustainable and uncomplicated solutions' (Formafantasma 2014). At the heart of the installation is a collection of vessels produced of self-made biomaterial and dyed with self-made pigments, themselves obtained from drying, boiling and filtering vegetables, spices and roots. In order to communicate the narrative that the vessels are products of a 'perfect production process without waste', where the cereal sorghum 'is harvested and used to create tools, vessels and food', the function of each element in the installation – the cereal ears, flourmill, drying ovens, loaves of bread, straw brooms – is to illustrate the different steps in the process of manufacturing the vessels.

This self-referential focus that can be perceived in *Autarchy*, in which an artefact's manufacturing process can be semiotically deduced from the object's material qualities, can be interpreted as one of the distinguishing characteristics of Dutch design. This argument can be traced back to Aaron Betsky's contribution to *Reality Machines: Mirroring the Real in Contemporary Dutch Architecture, Photography and Design* (2003) and later popularized by his book *False Flat* (2004), which, since its publication, has arguably become the canonical narrative of Dutch design. In these texts, Betsky (2003: 5) explains that the 'Dutch have kept themselves occupied for centuries by creating an artificial reality: they regain land from the sea, they create economic, social and political systems based on their own needs, and they add value by investing and trading rather than manufacturing; they

FIGURE 14.2 Autarchy *(2009)* by Studio Formafantasma. *Source:* Studio Formafantasma.

understand the importance of artificiality better than most other cultures. The whole country is a reality machine.' Thus, argues Betsky (2004: 44), the point of what one does as an artist or designer' in the Netherlands since the seventeenth century, is to help viewers/users understand the artificial nature of their reality. To achieve this, design artefacts 'must reveal their own accidental, temporary, artificial and ad hoc nature' through 'the banal but revealing reflection' of their own conditions of production (Betsky 2003: 5). This understanding of the Dutch design artefact as more than a simple object and as in essence being a 'reality machine' (a self-reflexive device, fabricating narratives that reflect on its own artificiality and conditions of production) has become a permanent fixture in the Dutch design discourse. It is better known as conceptual design.

Even though Trimarchi and Farresin have studied and worked in the Netherlands since 2007, initially the Dutch press and institutions ignored them due to their Italian nationality. At first, when the Dutch press did feature their work, the articles clearly positioned them as Italian designers. The title of a *Design.nl* article – the government-subsidized main news portal for Dutch design – reviewing Formafantasma's first pieces (both of which were produced and exhibited in the Netherlands) is revealing in this respect: 'Moulding Tradition and Baked from Italy'.

However, the particularities of the materiality of their projects have been increasingly interpreted as typical of Dutch design (e.g. narrative, critical, experimental), which is gradually resulting in Formafantasma's inclusion in Dutch design discourse. The Dutch design discourse can be interpreted as a classic 'culturalist' discourse in that it explains Dutch design artefacts merely as illustrations of a 'typical' Dutch culture allegedly bounded by its national borders and unchanged since the sixteenth century. In other words, here, an assumedly stable national background is taken as frame of reference according to which the meanings of design are derived (i.e. methodological nationalism *par excellence*).

However, the investigation of *Autarchy*'s material construction shows that the project mobilizes foreign geographies, temporalities, techniques, traditions and concerns that cannot be reduced to the interpretative framework of Dutch cultural heritage on which the Dutch design discourse is based. Indeed, the examination into the 'cataracts of time' and biography of the construction of *Autarchy* shows that it encompasses techniques from medieval Sicily and north Italian vernacular crafts, the aesthetics of eighteenth century Shakers and traditional French boulangerie, and the cosmopolitan Milanese design scene and online community. As such, *Autarchy* exceeds the linear time and the Euclidean geographical space of the nation-state. Thus, if *Autarchy* is Dutch design, then it performs a more inclusive and dynamic Dutchness, one that has recently led the main Dutch design portal to conclude that 'the pair (who have Italian passports) can and should be called Dutch designers' (Kennedy 2011).

In sum, while grounded in the Netherlands, *Autarchy*'s material construction cannot be grasped in terms of the time-space of the nation. Hence, if *Autarchy* is Dutch design, then it literally reconfigures Dutchness and reassembles the context of the nation according to its own design. Finally, *Autarchy* also requires an adjustment in the interpretative framework we use to analyse Dutch design. As briefly demonstrated above, describing the construction of *Autarchy* has entailed engaging both with the history of Dutch design and following the project as it moves beyond it and in so doing, reconfigures the boundaries of that history. An approach that entangles the material with the social and traces how artefacts create their own temporal–spatial contexts rather than contextualizes artefacts in already existing frames of reference may be of use to national design historiography as it grapples with national design in times of globalization.

Conclusion: 'National design cultures 2.0'

To conclude, in this chapter we sought to locate design cultures by considering approaches that, on the one hand, do not dismiss the empirical relevance of the nation-state, but on the other hand, do not assume it to be the only valid frame of reference in explaining the emergence and development of design cultures. In other words, from the perspective of the transnational, the existence of national design cultures does not necessarily testify to the ontological primacy of nation-states since, as we hope the examples above illustrate, the national can be and is also created as a function of transnational networks. In our research, we have found these approaches useful in that they offer a conceptualization of design cultures as a link between the local and the cosmopolitan, the vernacular and the international – a link that often remains elusive from perspectives that focus only on national frameworks. Such a design cultural framing may yet provide a fresh breath of life to the study of national design cultures, resulting perhaps, to appropriate Gille's turn of phrase, a 'National Design Cultures 2.0'.

Notes

1 This concept of governmentality in the context of design cultures is already explored in the unpublished paper 'Design and the State. A Theoretical Account of the Role of the State in the Creation of Design Cultures' which was written by Javier Gimeno Martínez and Katarina Serulus for the occasion of the international symposium *Raison D'Etre 2: Crafting a Global History of Interior Decoration and Design* on 9 and 10 March in New Orleans (Louisiana, US).

2 This case draws upon Serulus' (2016) unpublished PhD research on post-war design promotion in Belgium and research previously published in the special issue of Design and Culture on Design and Diplomacy edited by Harriet Atkinson and Verity Clarkson (Serulus 2017).

3 This concept of materiality and temporality as it relates to national design history is further elaborated in Ozorio de Almeida Meroz's (2018) unpublished PhD thesis Transnational Material Politics: Constructions of Dutch Design, 1970–2012.

4 This case draws upon Ozorio de Almeida Meroz's (2014) paper 'Autarchy. The Making of Dutch Design in Practice'.

References

Adamson, G., Riello, G. and Teasley, S. (eds) (2011), *Global Design History*, London/New York: Routledge.
Amelina, A. et al. (2012), 'Methodological Predicaments of Cross-Border Studies', in A. Amelina et al. (eds), *Beyond Methodological Nationalism: Research Methodologies for Cross-Border Studies*, New York/London: Routledge, 1–19.
Betsky, A. (2003), 'Reality Machines: De kunstmatige afspiegeling van de werkelijkheid', in L. Vlassenrood (ed.), *Reality Machines: Het alledaagse weerspiegeld in hedendaagse Nederlandse architectuur, fotografie en vormgeving*, Rotterdam: NAi.
Betsky, A. (2004), *False Flat: Why Dutch Design Is So Good*, London: Phaidon.
Burchell, G. and Miller, P. (eds) (1991), *The Foucault Effect. Studies in Governmentality*, Chicago: The University of Chicago Press.
Dean, M. (eds) (2010), *Governmentality. Power and Rule in Modern Society*, 2nd edn, London: Sage.
Dockrill, M. and Hopkins, M. (2006), *The Cold War: 1945–1991*, 2nd edn, Basingstoke/New York: Palgrave Macmillan.
'Een Design Centre te Brussel' (1963), *Informatieblad van het Instituut voor Industriële Vormgeving*, 6/2.
Fallan, K. (2007), 'How an Excavator Got Aesthetic Pretentions – Negotiating Design in 1960s' Norway', *Journal of Design History*, 20(1).
Fallan, K. and Lees-Maffei, G. (eds) (2016), *Designing Worlds: National Design Histories in an Age of Globalization*, New York/Oxford: Berghahn Books.
Formafantasma (2014), 'Autarchy'. [Online]. Available from: http://www.formafantasma.com/autarchy [Accessed: 18th May 2014].
Forty, A. 1995 (1986), *Objects of Desire: Design and Society since 1750*, London: Thames and Hudson.
Foucault, M. (1991), 'Governmentality', in G. Burchell and P. Miller (eds), *The Foucault Effect. Studies in Governmentality*, Chicago: The University of Chicago Press.
Gille, Z. (2012), 'Global Ethnography 2.0: From Methodological Nationalism to Methodological Materialism', in A. Amelina et al. (eds), *Beyond Methodological Nationalism: Research Methodologies for Cross-Border Studies*, New York/London: Routledge.
Gille, Z. (2014), 'Transnational Materiality', in H. E. Kahn and S. Sassen (eds), *Framing the Global: Entry Points for Research*, Bloomington/Indianapolis: Indiana University Press.
Gille, Z. (2016), *Paprika, Foie Gras, and Red Mud: The Politics of Materiality in the European Union*, Bloomington/Indianapolis: Indiana University Press.
Gimeno Martínez, J. and Ozorio de Almeida Meroz, J. (eds) (2016), 'Special Issue Beyond Dutch Design: Material Culture in the Netherlands in an Age of Globalization, Migration and Multiculturalism', *The Journal of Design History*, 29(3).
Hague, R. and Harrop, M. (2007), *Comparative Government and Politics*, 7th edn, Hampshire and New York: Palgrave Macmillan.
'ICSID Vth General Assembly. Ottawa - Canada - 11 & 12 September 1967' [Internal report] (1967), in ICSID Archives, 3-3-1, Brighton: University of Brighton Design Archives.

'International meeting on Design Centre' [Internal report] (1974), in ICSID Archives, 3-3-1, Brighton: University of Brighton Design Archives.

Kennedy, G. (2011), 'Why Italians Can (Sometimes) Be Dutch'. [Online]. Available from: http://www.design.nl/item/why_italians_can_sometimes_be_dutch?searchField=formafantasma [Accessed: 18th May 2014].

Maguire, P. and Woodham, J. (eds) (1997), *Design and Cultural Politics. The Britain Can Make It Exhibition of 1946*, London: Leicester University Press.

Messel, T. (2016), 'International Norms and Local Design Research:ICSID and the Promotion of Industrial Design in Latin America,1970-1979', paper read at DRS2016: Design + Research + Society-Future-Focused Thinking, Brighton.

Mitchell, T. (2006), 'Society, Economy, and the State Effect', in A. Sharma and A. Gupta (eds), *The Anthropology of the State. A Reader*, Oxford: Blackwell.

Ozorio de Almeida Meroz, J. (2014), 'Autarchy: The Making of Dutch Design in Practice', in C. Coleta et al. (eds), *A Matter of Design: Making Society through Science and Technology. Proceedings of the 5th STS Italia Conference*, Milan: STS Italia Publishing.

Ozorio de Almeida Meroz, J. (2018), Transnational Material Politics: Constructions of Dutch Design, 1970-2012, unpublished PhD thesis, Amsterdam: Vrije Universiteit Amsterdam.

Pinney, C. (2005), 'Things Happen: Or, from Which Moment Does That Object Come?', in D. Miller (ed.), *Materiality*, Durham and London: Duke University Press.

Pulos, A. (1998), *The American Design Adventure, 1940-1975*, Cambridge, MA: MIT Press.

Serulus, K. (2014), 'Caught between National Interests and European Ambitions. Design Promotion in Belgium in the 1960s', in L. Farias and P. Atkinson (eds), *Design Frontiers. Territories, Concepts, Technologies*, Mexico City: Editorial Designio.

Serulus, K. (2017), '"Well-Designed Relations": Cold War Design Exchanges between Brussels and Moscow in the Early 1970s', *Design and Culture*, 9(2).

Sharma, A. and Gupta, A. (eds) (2006), *The Anthropology of the State. A Reader*, Oxford: Blackwell.

Thompson, C. (2011), 'Modernizing for Trade: Institutionalizing Design Promotion in New Zealand', *Journal of Design History*, 24(3).

Yagou, A. (2005), 'Unwanted Innovation. The Athens Design Centre (1961–1963)', *Journal of Design History* 18(3).

CHAPTER FIFTEEN

The challenges and opportunities of introducing Design Culture in Jordan

Danah Abdulla

Introduction

Design Culture may be an area of study that is establishing itself in institutions across Europe, but the Arab region has yet to introduce this field in design education. As designers have become concerned with notions of community and social practice – under names such as social design, "good" design, design activism, humanitarian design and others (referred to as social design moving forward) – the need for integrating Design Culture in design education becomes more important, particularly as discourse continues to be Eurocentric in scope. The Global South remains non-existent and invisible within this discourse, and designers lack any professional representation for their field.

This chapter attempts to propose what the introduction of Design Culture would entail and its possibilities. It argues that introducing this field into Jordanian design education has the potential to shift from an outward-facing focus and the wholesale imports of outside models, to generating location-specific and tailored knowledge and practice. Furthermore, the placement of design programmes in universities (as the independent art and design college does not exist in the country) presents an invitation for inter/multi/transdisciplinary engagement and dialogue with other disciplines.

In this chapter, I begin to sketch out the possible content of this programme by first providing a brief overview on Jordan and Amman, the education system and the evolution of design in the country. While creating new knowledge on design culture in the country, Design Culture could provide room for Jordan, and the Arab region, to contribute to local, regional and international design discourse. The findings I draw on are from my PhD research on design education in Jordan, where I conducted twenty-five interviews, three focus groups and two workshops with designers, students and educators from Jordan. In this chapter, I refer to both Design Culture (upper case) as the academic field defined as the 'stud[y] of the interrelationships between design artefacts, in all their manifestations, the work of designers, design production (including marketing, advertising and distribution), mediation and their consumption'; and to design culture (lower case) in a descriptive way: 'the circumstances in which design is developed, circulated and used' (Julier 2015, no pagination). Therefore, design culture is something that is all around and what designers do: a process and practice informed by context and milieu, an attitude, as agency and as a pervasive but differentiated value (Julier 2014). Design Culture/ design culture provides an understanding into the interconnections between humans and things, and recognizes design as being everywhere and affecting everyone (Charman 2013).

Amman, design and design education

Relative to its neighbours, Jordan's capital city Amman is a new city and possesses one of the region's most heterogeneous societies. The city's growth is linked to the region's geo-political and political circumstances (Nortcliff et al. 2009), and historically it is known as a 'refuge city' as it 'has experienced...a succession of migrations' which has 'shaped the structure of [the country's] social and political landscape' (Hinchcliffe and Beverley 2009: 22). Jordan's most unique quality lies in the fact that over half of the population is composed of people 'from outside its own borders and a people who are still struggling for self-determination and independence' (Hinchcliffe and Beverley 2009: 99). However, this complexity contributes to how Amman has difficulty defining its identity.

Amman is described as a city in a permanent state of 'temporariness, a metropolis on the cusp of emerging' (Innab 2016: 119), exasperated by the communities that settled in Amman where the city was meant as a transit stop, but for most it ended up being their final destination. The subsequent generations of the communities that have settled 'continue to look in two directions at once: toward home/homeland and toward a preferred temporary destination of a "second home"' (Shami 2007: 215). This could explain why most of the city's inhabitants have difficulty in identifying as *Ammani* (from Amman), and see it as a temporary 'welcome mat'.

Amman is a starkly divided city, and a person's class can be determined by the neighbourhood they live in. Citizens of the East seldom interact with those from the West – and many residents from East Amman feel as though the city no longer has space for them. The segregated space persists within the university. As Nasser Eddin explains in her experience at the University of Jordan, departments are labelled based on the lifestyles of the students: 'students of education, social sciences, Islamic law and humanities were labelled as "low class", conservative, and "backward". On the other hand, people from the Business School, the Faculty of Arts and Design and Departments of Engineering and Medicine were labelled as "high class", "open", and "immoral".' (2011: 2).

The segregation is evident between public and private universities. Public institutions remain more competitive, and private institutions are largely profit-driven where tuition fees are the main source of income and cater to students with low qualifications who were unable to secure seats in public universities (Kanaan, Al-Salamat and Hanania 2009). The model of profit-driven institutions 'threatens to exacerbate one of the major deficiencies in Arab education, that is, selective exclusion for the rich and powerful in good quality education' (Fergany 2009: 45), further fuelled by limited availability of student loans and financial aid to many low-income students (Sabry 2009; United Nations Development programme and Mohammed bin Rashid Al Maktoum Foundation 2014). However, a focus on profitability – attributed to mounting demand – has led public institutions to offer spaces to students who were not admitted to their desired programmes due to an insufficient GPA through parallel programmes where students are charged higher fees (Chapman 2011, Kanaan, Al-Salamat and Hanania 2009).

Universities in Jordan are maintained by the Ministry of Higher Education and Scientific Research (MoHESR). The beginnings of design education in Jordan date back to 1980 when Yarmouk University launched a minor within fine arts. In 2001, design was granted a department within the Faculty of Fine Arts. The 1990s and early 2000s saw the establishment of more design programmes in public and private universities. Across Jordan, there are fourteen universities that teach design at the undergraduate level only, offering programmes in graphic, interior, industrial, and fashion design, design and visual communication, and design for cinema, TV and theatre. The quality of these fluctuates, as establishing design programmes have been a way to capitalize on demand and increase the profits of the university. Alongside these universities, twenty-two community colleges offer two-year diplomas mostly in graphic design (Abu Awad 2012). Unlike global trends where traditional demarcations of disciplines have started to recede (Julier 2014), separations of graphic, interior, product and fashion remain fully in place in education, and diminish slightly within practice – mostly in independent and grassroots initiatives over studios and agencies. Design education in Jordan is focused on teaching technical skills rather than formalized knowledge and critical enquiry.

However, design continues to struggle to be recognized as a professionalized practice and to differentiate itself from trades like printing, despite the number of universities and community colleges teaching design and the establishment of dedicated design studios and agencies. This could be attributed to the absence of a professional association representing designers in Jordan and regionally who are 'dedicated to the promotion of various aspects of design and the systematizing or safeguarding of its practice' (Julier 2014: 51). Representation is an issue within the entire Arab region where only two design associations claim to represent designers region-wide: the Lebanese Graphic Design Syndicate (est. 1976) and AIGA Middle East (est. 2013). These are both based in Beirut but have contributed very little to design in Lebanon or regionally. Moreover, the international affiliation to the American AIGA, and the use of English in all its communication materials is problematic. It piggy backs on a *brand* and excludes designers working in Arabic. Furthermore, the use of the term *Middle East* encompasses countries like Turkey and Iran, countries with different histories, which speak different languages, and which have more established design histories and cultures with representation.

Within education, design's struggle can be attributed to the admission requirements imposed by the MoHESR. Admission to universities in Jordan are based on the results of the matriculation exam (*tawjihi*). This controversial exam, based on memorization, dictates the choices and future of thousands of students looking to apply to university every year. Design sits at the bottom of the academic hierarchy alongside fine arts and Islamic studies. Therefore, students with low GPA scores (55%–60% for private institutions, 65%–70% for public institutions) look to design. Based on findings from my PhD research, other reasons for choosing design are:

1 Design is considered an *easy* thing to study
2 Guarantees a job
3 Luxury of having a degree in art or design increases social standing

Students enter design without knowing what it is, further hindered by a lack of information on career options prior to applying for university. Therefore, admission requirements allow anyone to be accepted into design, branding design and design students as the *rejects*, and educators are faced with obstacles teaching these students. While some universities require applicants to sit through a drawing exam, often this is for appearances, and they are left with little choice but to accept anyone who applies. At most institutions, a portfolio of work is not a requirement for applicants.

Privatization of education has increased the number of universities teaching design as it is seen to be lucrative. However, these programmes generally focus on technical software skills. The MoHESR treats design as any other discipline, imposing the same admission requirements as any other discipline, and have similar research expectations from faculty. The departments remain peripheral, generating little to no knowledge for local, regional or international output.

In the sections that follow, I outline a few challenges to design education in Jordan, and what this entails for the establishment of Design Culture programme, and attempt to lay out possible strategies for this programme.

Centre/Periphery and the Westernized university

According to Altbach (2006: 124–5), globalization has increased the dominant system of centre and periphery when it comes to the university. Powerful universities and academic systems – the centres – 'dominat[e] the production and distribution of knowledge' and 'the peripheries have tended to be dependent on them'. Peripheries also have their own regional centres, but no institution plays the 'centre' role in design regionally. Therefore, institutions and design students look to art and design colleges located in Western countries as models. Pushing Altbach's idea further, universities in Jordan are best described as Westernized universities – an institution that can be found anywhere globally, and features the same curriculum, the same authors and disciplinary divisions as any university in the West (Grosfoguel 2013).

The Westernized university – which most if not all design programmes fall under – promote or diffuse Eurocentric knowledge to produce Westernized elites in the so-called non-West that act as intermediaries between the West and the so-called non-West. Within Westernized universities, the canon of thought in all disciplines is composed of works of males from five Western countries (USA, Italy, Germany, England and France), and these structures have become 'commonsensical' (Grosfoguel 2013: 87). Knowledge is abstract from lived realities and histories. Furthermore, design programmes tend to focus on preparing students only within their specialized areas. Programmes, then, are resistant to change, where theory classes are limited, remaining within the art and design context, and students engage in no research or writing. Design education, as it currently stands, does not encourage alternative ways of thinking about design and designing. Design has no influence on other departments, rarely working with architecture or fine arts, even though they are often housed within the same department, contributing to its peripheral status within institutions themselves. The structure of the Westernized university is largely the reason for this. While we see more emphasis on design moving away from being discipline specific in Western institutions, as Anne-Marie Willis argues, higher education is highly instrumentalized, and 'theory is taught so it can be "applied" to design tasks', where 'discipline-specific design educators promp[t] defensive postures on the need to avoid of over-thinking, analysis-paralysis, and the like' (2015: 71). Theory and deeper investigation get relegated to the background in favour of outputs such as objects, websites, awareness campaigns or apps.

She argues that this enables design educators to 'feel secure because they are still turning out Graphic or Product or Interaction Designers, their disciplines remain intact and their jobs secure' (Willis 2015: 71).

The issue can also be attributed to the absence of serious research budgets, which forces universities and public research organizations to rely on foreign funding from foundations and UN institutions (Hanafi and Arvanitis 2016). The largest donors are the EU, followed by the USA, Japan and countries from the Arab Gulf – all of which are likely to have political conditions. Moreover, authoritarianism and an absence of academic freedom has contributed to the huge percentage of brain drain the region is faced with (Hanafi and Arvanitis 2016). Foreign funding often contributes to design projects centred around identity and heritage, which we now turn to.

Cultural identity and marginalization

The automatic assumption of the term design culture is that it relates to cultural identity. While the definition encompasses this, it is only one aspect of the study of Design Culture. Despite the progress that the field of design claims to have made in the integration of other discourses, this is merely decorative. Design from the Global South is constantly evaluated against Western design, stripped down to stereotypes, misunderstood and taken out of context, and the Global South often look to these design centres for models, without necessarily understanding the consequence of blindly borrowing its methods.

The design world, as Tony Fry claims, 'puts all peoples in [the] position [of marginality] – other than those who populate the few nations at the center of the rise of metropolitan capitalism' (1989: 17). Universal design attempts to universalize the experience of Western countries and its people – as if these are representative of the world – but these 'singular universal dreams of design worlds (modern "lifestyle") contradict, and certainly do not unify, great unevenness, difference, and ideological division' (Fry 1989: 24). These ideas, disguised as *universal* then travel to Westernized universities, who are reliant on knowledge produced elsewhere. It is clearly demonstrated in the divisions of classes where Westernized universities located in Arab countries have classes such as Islamic Art and History of Art, History of Modern and Contemporary Art, Typography (Latin) and Arabic typography. As Sami Zubaida reminds us, 'when it comes to "Muslim culture" the unit becomes even more indeterminate, not only because of the multiplicity of nationalities and ethnicities, but also the varieties of identification of the region itself, and its adaptations to ideologies, generations, and styles of life.' (2011: 9–10).

Is Arabic or Islamic so alien that it requires its own special study even among the people who are Arabs and Muslims themselves? These divisions emphasize difference and assume that Arab or Islamic culture is lower on the hierarchical scale than Western culture, considered modern and contemporary. The Islamic and Arabic descriptor demonstrates the power of design's universal language. Universal is Latin, rendering everything else as non-Latin because it is not part of the canon, and implies a hierarchy (Pater 2016).

A more recent example that ignores realities is the rise of the social design movement. Social design practices are finding their way in the Arab region, where largely middle-class design students are looking to *serve* the needs of poor communities composed of people with very different backgrounds from their own, or designing for refugees. Moreover, some regional initiatives are referring to such refugee movement as if they are unique to this era and to the region, disregarding the region's history where mass migration has always played a role. Designers aim to provide a *voice* for the disenfranchised, using aid discourse, offering mere technological fixes than addressing the imperial histories and neo-liberal restructuring that underpin them (Johnson 2011), and maintaining dominance over the production of knowledge by using these communities for their school projects. These ideas travel to the Westernized university and are copy-pasted into the curriculum rather than through an awareness of the context and historicity of these ideas.

Design Culture provides a possible space to question this universality of design and the blind borrowing of ideas, practices and philosophies from elsewhere, or from a distant Arab/Islamic past. It can encourage designers to engage in a deeper, more immersive process of research, fieldwork and building trust with the community they work in rather than using hasty methods from human-centred design toolkits.

Production, consumption and the designer

Production, consumption and the designer inform each other, rather than working in isolation. In Jordan, the issue of bypassing the designer – that is, not understanding the concept of the designer or the value of design – leads to these being viewed as isolated. The study of design culture can help establish design's value to society and attribute a value to design. For example, the process of production, consumption and the designer, and how these inform each other discussed by Julier (2014), serves an important purpose in a country where designers are constantly bypassed, and the differences between the production person and the designer are not understood. It would establish what it means to be a designer, as opposed to the common perceptions designers are continuously faced with such as:

- Design as software
- Design as aesthetic exercise
- Design as crafts

The first is the difficulty design has faced in its professionalization, whereas the second is partly attributed to studios and agencies dismissing design's critical thinking and ideation aspect in favour of aesthetics. The third is an interesting point of study in Jordan. Whereas some countries in the Arab region have a strong history of crafts, Jordan does not. However, this is changing due to recent political circumstances, but crafts remain captive to heritage (*turath*) and tradition, catered to tourists rather than collaborating with designers on developing new methods and generating new knowledge.

Design Culture can present a new way of looking at craft traditions locally and regionally, and how these can feed knowledge into design, as well as empower both designers and craftspeople to engage with each other. There are particularities associated with a lack of machinery in the production, where designers can begin to understand the local tools and knowledge and how this feeds design, and begin to work with craftspeople on improving the work from a functional perspective by utilizing advances in material technology.[1]

Furthermore, Design Culture – where local and regional design history has a presence – focusing not simply on pioneers and objects but 'on the shifting roles of design today including the impact of new technologies, production methods, and lifestyle, i.e. design beyond products' (Julier 2014: 59) – can prevent design from falling into the authenticity trap. Unfortunately, local design dialect with designers outside and inside the region, aside from Arabic typography and calligraphy, is dripping with stereotypes. *Arab* design is only *Arab* if it contains veils, camels, Arabesque typefaces, calligraphy, geometrical patterns, and rich sheikhs. This Orientalist *Islamic* identity associated with the region presents itself as *authentic* although it exists 'more in the imagination ... than in lived experience' (Shami 2007: 210). An example is a new-found interest in crafts and cultural heritage, heavily emphasized at Amman Design Week 2016. Example of this include the workshop *Designing Contemporary Heritage* with Studio Mieke Meijer (sponsored by the Dutch embassy), and the Raghadan tourist terminal, which was transformed into a crafts district to highlight the craftspeople as pioneers of design and making in Jordan, a largely invented tradition.

Furthermore, nostalgia has become an *it* trend in the work of Arab designers, where the work of Lebanese designer Rana Salam, which uses imagery from Arab film posters and pop culture icons from the 1940s to the 1960s, has been copied to the point of predictability. The establishment of archiving foundations, and heritage tourism projects, has fuelled the nostalgia effect. This longing of nostalgia, as Zubaida reminds us, 'conveniently forgets its imperial context', where natives were often subjected to 'a rigorous system of exclusions [...] were inferiorized and despised' as in the case of Alexandria, Egypt (2011: 148). A social and cultural knowledge of one's own history helps form 'a self-reflective awareness' (Kassab 2010: 244).

Understanding how these domains of design work can help develop inter/multi/transdisciplinary projects within the academy – emphasizing the placement of design programmes within the universities and capitalizing on the other departments and their offerings (and vice versa). Furthermore, establishing a value to design enables design graduates to be hired to generate ideas and concepts, rather than as software 'monkeys'.

Design culture as a way of understanding place

A different discussion on identity is one related to the city, and Design Culture provides a good method for investigating this. Amman finds itself in competition with regional centres, which consist of some of 'the oldest still-inhabited urban centers … aged capitals of powerful past empires, major religious sites, and centers of learning as well as notable colonial creations' (Shami 2007). Tourism and heritage initiatives display this clearly, where efforts were made to re-Orientalise the city by renovating downtown, remodelling shopfronts to add an Arabesque motif and erecting oriental fountains. However, the focus of Jordan's tourism campaign is Petra and biblical site, not Amman; and it remains a small stop on the way to these other destinations (see Jacobs 2010 for further discussion).

Amman has a lot to live up to, and the city is not the prototype for urbanism as it defies generalizations of how cities form historically and morphologically (Shami 2007). This is due to the 'fast and often arbitrary solutions that caused confusion in the city structure … exacerbated by later efforts at remediation of such confusion' (Innab 2016: 119) caused by the influx of refugees. Shami concludes that 'the historical contingency that is Amman, therefore, has to be understood in a particular context of economy, state building, and cultural production' (2007: 230). For design, this statement is crucial: by understanding these contexts, can design help construct an identity for the city? Understand its formation and future? Due to design culture's unfixed nature, where 'it embraces a complex matrix of human activities, perceptions and articulations … [a] [c]areful analysis of its visual, material, spatial and textual manifestations provides routes into this complexity' (Julier 2014: 5). The introduction of Design Culture grounded in the local and regional context can help tackle these questions and provide answers to them.

The possibility found in design culture is in providing agency to designers to take a role in establishing what happens to their city, rather than being allocated to the state. Residents are often marginalized from the city making process (al-Asad 2016), and design culture provides one way of changing this. Therefore, a programme focused on design culture must have as a primary aim the production of research, creating 'linkages between socially different worlds: different social classes, different locations, different places, different interests and different objects' (Hanafi and Arvanitis 2016: 14).

Publishing

Both Jordan and the Arab region lack publications devoted to solely to design. Currently, there are two publications dedicated to design: the monthly *TrendDesign* (based in Amman) is focused more on providing an international perspective and sound-bite type articles, and *Journal Safar*, an annual publication revolving around graphic design that is produced by Studio Safar in Beirut. Despite hundreds of publishing houses located in Jordan, publishers have contributed little to nothing to design titles. Books related to design in the region are published abroad, either by established publishers such as Gestalten, or by independent publishers based in Europe such as Khatt. What is particularly interesting is that not one Arab country 'enjoys a free press, and yet the Arab world probably has a more thriving print media than any other region in the world' (Hammond 2007: 237). Furthermore, and despite this fact, academic publishing is limited, as culture is considered sacred, since the many cultural productions that evolved 'in the colonial and postcolonial eras ... were developing under state patronage' (Ayish 2012: 83). This led to the majority of Arab intellectuals to 'evolv[e] their critical cultural perspectives outside state-patronised institutions, often in the bookshop and in independent intellectual centres' (ibid).

Whereas designers outside of educational institutions have contributed more to the discipline than those within – one initiative is the launch of Amman Design Week (ADW) in 2016 as an annual event described as 'a forum for learning, exchange and collaboration' seeking to empower designers and establish Amman as a hub regionally (Amman Design Week 2017) – there remains a large void in design writing and publishing. While ADW is a new venture, we cannot yet measure the impact it has on design culture. However, it provides one space for students, educators and designers to seek content from Jordan, as the lack of local material forces them to look for content written elsewhere, as these become the only publications available (Blankenship 2005), and while information through websites and videos has increased access to content, these are focused on software training videos or looking at portfolios and visual material. Publications provide a deeper alternative to these.

What can Design Culture do?

Introducing Design Culture within Jordanian design education presents great opportunities for the growth of design culture both locally and regionally. It could provide a platform for debate, a space for original and innovative thinking in design, critical historicization and grounding thought with lived and real experiences. Breaking the barriers between departments in universities to develop inter/multi/transdisciplinary engagement between

FIGURE 15.1 *Studio Turbo in downtown Amman. Photography by Turbo (Mothanna Hussein and Saeed Abu Jaber). Image courtesy of Turbo.*

disciplines could allow designers to engage in crucial theoretical grounding as design moves into more social practices and where designers prioritize knowledge creation by emphasizing research, criticism and writing. Looking at design from a local and regional context makes both education and practice more relevant to place and milieu as design begins to think of an epistemic pluriversality rather than a universal set of design solutions. By 'tak[ing] seriously the critical thinking of the epistemic traditions of the Global South', and shifting the direction of 'institutions appropriated by Eurocentred modernity' (Grosfoguel 2013: 88), it can help designers understand their history critically, and contribute to local, regional and international design discourse rather than attempting to play a game of catch up.

Design Culture can provide designers with the tools to become knowledgeable leaders that can help combat the ambivalent attitude designers have towards authority by granting them agency and establishing platforms that work towards promoting and establishing a value to design. Beginning to tackle these issues can promote a stronger professional identity for designers in the country, and to produce new knowledges in the field.

Note

1. French designer Christophe Pillet provides insight on this in 'Acclaimed: International Designers on Egyptian Design' by Karim Sultan in *Kalimat*

Magazine, Issue 04, pp. 118–121, http://www.kalimatmagazine.com/issue-04-winter-2012.

References

Abu Awad, E. (2012), *Identification of Competencies for Sign Designers in Jordan*, PhD. Coventry University.
Altbach, P. G. (2006), 'Globalization and the University: Realities in an Unequal World', in J. J. F. Forest and P. Altbach (eds) *International Handbook of Higher education: Part One: Global Themes and Contemporary challenges*, Dordrecht: Springer, 121–39.
Amman Design Week (2017), *About Amman Design Week, Amman Design Week*, Available at: https://www.facebook.com/pg/ammandesignweek/about/?ref=page_inter (Accessed 4 March 2017).
al-Asad, M. (2016), 'Teaching a Course on the Contemporary Arab City…for 5,700 People', in *The Arab City: Architecture and Representation*. New York: Columbia University Press, 51–4.
Ayish, M. (2012), 'Cultural Studies in Arab World Academic Communication Programmes: the Battle for Survival', in T. Sabry (ed.) *Arab Cultural Studies: Mapping the fields*, New York, NY: I.B. Tauris, 79–100.
Blankenship, S. (2005), 'Outside the Center: Defining Who We Are', *Design Issues*, 21(1): 24–41.
Chapman, R. (2011), 'Jordan Fiscal Reform Project II: Education Public Expenditures Working Paper', *Jordan Fiscal Reform Project II: Education Public Expenditures Working Paper*. Available at: http://www.frp2.org/english/Portals/0/PDFs/Mezzo-Fiscal.
Charman, H. (2013), 'Critical about Design', in N. Addison and L. Burgess (eds), *Debates in Art and design education*, Abingdon, Oxon: Routledge, 121–37.
Fergany, N. (2009), 'Education Reform Can Empower Youth in Arab Countries and Help Build Human Development', *Youth and Mediterranean Challenges: Quaderns de la Mediterrània* 11(11): 43–50.
Fry, T. (1989), 'A Geography of Power: Design History and Marginality', *Design Issues*, 6(1): 15–30.
Grosfoguel, R. (2013), 'The Structure of Knowledge in Westernized Universities: Epistemic Racism/Sexism and the Four Genocides/Epistemicides of the Long 16th Century', *Human Architecture: Journal of the Sociology of Self-Knowledge*, 11(1): 73–90.
Hammond, A. (2007), *Popular Culture in the Arab World: Arts, Politics, and the Media*, Cairo: American University in Cairo Press.
Hanafi, S. and Arvanitis, R. (2016), *Knowledge Production in the Arab World: The impossible promise*, Abingdon, Oxon: Routledge.
Hinchcliffe, P. and Beverley, M.-E. (2009), *Jordan: A Hashemite Legacy Contemporary Middle East*. Second. Abingdon, Oxon: Routledge.
Innab, S. (2016), 'Reading the Modern Narrative of Amman', in *The Arab City: Architecture and Representation*, New York: Columbia University Press, 118–35.

Jacobs, J. (2010), 'Re-branding the Levant: Contested Heritage and Colonial Modernities in Amman and Damascus', *Journal of Tourism and Cultural Change*, 8(4): 316–26.

Johnson, C. G. (2011), 'The Urban Precariat, Neoliberalization, and the Soft Power of Humanitarian Design', 27(3–4): 445–75.

Julier, G. (2014), *The Culture of Design*. 3rd edn. London: Sage.

Julier, G. (2015), *What is Design Culture?*, *DesignCulture.info*. Available at: http://www.designculture.info/main/descultintro.htm (Accessed: 10 May 2015).

Kanaan, T., Al-Salamat, M. and Hanania, M. (2009), 'Financing Higher Education in Jordan', Amman.

Kassab, E. (2010), *Contemporary Arab Thought: Cultural Critique in Comparative Perspective*, New York: Columbia University Press.

Nasser Eddin, N. (2011), *The Intersectionality of Class and Gender: Women's Economic Activities in East and West Amman*. PhD. University of Warwick. Available at: http://go.warwick.ac.uk/wrap/54468.

Nortcliff, S. et al. (2009), '"Ever-growing Amman", Jordan: Urban Expansion, Social Polarisation and Contemporary Urban Planning Issues', *Habitat International*, 33(1): 81–92.

Pater, R. (2016), *The Politics of Design*, Amsterdam: BIS Publishers.

Sabry, M. (2009), 'Funding Policy and Higher Education in Arab Countries', *Comparative & International Higher Education*, (1): 11–12.

Shami, S. (2007), 'Amman is not a City': Middle Eastern Cities in Question', in A. Cinar and T. Bender (eds), *Urban Imaginaries: Locating the Modern City*, Minneapolis: University of Minnesota Press, 208–35.

United Nations Development programme and Mohammed bin Rashid Al Maktoum Foundation (2014), *Arab Knowledge Report 2014 Youth and Localisation of Knowledge*. Dubai: United Nations Development Programme and Mohammed bin Rashid Al Maktoum Foundation. Available at: http://www.arabstates.undp.org/content/rbas/en/home/library/huma_development/arab-knowledge-report-20140/.

Willis, A.-M. (2015), 'Transition Design: The Need to Refuse Discipline and Transcend Instrumentalism', *Design Philosophy Papers*, 13(1): 69–74.

Zubaida, S. (2011), *Beyond Islam: A New Understanding of the Middle East*, London: I.B. Tauris.

Epilogue:
Towards design culture as practice

Guy Julier and Anders V. Munch

The contributions of this book demonstrate the complex configurations of design culture by approaching very different layers and topics through various disciplinary and multi and interdisciplinary approaches. This underlines the consideration in our introduction on Design Culture[1] as a multi and interdisciplinary field of enquiry. The investigations follow the changing nature and constant development of its objects, these being contemporary design cultures. They necessarily stray across disciplinary demarcations, therefore.

The sections have explored how Design Culture has developed as an emergent discipline to understand current cultural changes and challenges; how design is being positioned between market and society; how designers have to position themselves ideologically and professionally as many other actors now promote their services as design; and how design culture unfolds in and across various places, spaces and geographies. It therefore stands that these themes invite a range of disciplinary pathways that were followed both in discreet and amalgamated ways.

All these fuzzy borders, tensions, logics and ideals mean that the many actors in and observers of design culture have to keep manoeuvring in this contested field. They also have to develop overall understandings of its cultural interrelations and compositions.

Beyond its academic investigations and interpretations, the deployment of the term 'design culture' also becomes a tool of professional practice or civic aspiration. This describes a shared set of understandings of and enthusiasms for design at the centre of an organization, firm, place or other assemblage of interests. Building a design culture may involve a set of consciously enacted actions in establishing shared understandings and values. These might include the identification and establishment of specific infrastructural support, common linguistic tropes, key personalities and support systems.

Here, the task is often that of translating and mediating between different understandings of and interests in the notion of design. Design is now promoted as a tool to organize innovative processes within management and introduced to employees of many professions as strategic design or design thinking. It then becomes an increasingly wicked challenge to explicate diverging notions of design and establish an operational, common understanding across multidisciplinary teams, not to speak of larger organizations or publics. Finding ways of establishing a design culture within a government department, a city or a tech company is a process of articulation and communication as much as producing design things (Julier and Leerberg 2014; Lawson 2015). The process perhaps refers to a somewhat linear, results-driven and problem-solving approach that recognizes a particular need in a defined context and a set of steps to address this through a design sensibility.

However, more complex parameters for design culture are also apparent. Manzini (2016) identifies an expanded societal field of design culture that aligns with a transition of design itself. This transition to, what Manzini calls, 'emerging design' means that it undertakes a more consciously active role in the general contexts of everyday life, well-being and 'the socio-technical ecosystems in which we exist'. This would be in contradistinction to responding to more specific demands that are focused on 'the brief' and 'the project' within commercial parameters. In Manzini's conception, designerly attention shifts from objects for industrial production to 'ways of thinking and doing'. He describes these as meaning 'methods, tools, approaches, and … design cultures' (Manzini 2016: 53). In this, design culture becomes not just the thing that exists but as an intention towards cultural and societal change that is framed within a designerly sensibility. The outcomes here are 'hybrid, dynamic entities' (56) that incorporate multiple interests and intentions. A new design culture is expected to unfold here that may be more holistic, participatory and complex. A number of questions would subsequently arise from these. What kind of everyday assemblages do we want to live in? What material systems can be engaged to give voice to citizens in this? How do we align socio-technical devices and varying discourses?

In such an account, a concept of design culture is shifted from something that is aspirational for a brand, company, location to a process of thinking and conceptualizing within broader societal narratives. This might be compared with earlier design visionaries as László Moholy-Nagy or Victor Papanek, who saw, how design seeped into all aspects of modern society, and how it ought to enable us to organize everything appropriately. A totalizing notion of design is revealed through these words from Moholy-Nagy stated in 1947: 'There is design in the organization of emotional experiences, in family life, in labour relations, in city planning, in working together as civilized human beings. Ultimately all problems of design merge into one great problem: "design for life". This implies that it is desirable that everyone should solve his special task with the wide scope of a true "designer", with the new urge to integrated relationships' (Moholy-Nagy 1969: 42). Such visions have been repeated frequently through the twentieth century, but instead of asking all of us to perform as designers, or just the 'creative class', we ought to question, how this 'empowerment by design' might be encultured among us as users and consumers, entrepreneurs and citizens.

What seems to be missing so far in this argument is a sense of an empirical grounding with which these aspirations entangle. What, specifically, are the power structures, the economic interests, the social norms, the cultural practices and the artefactual fields that define an assemblage that makes a design culture? And how do we mobilize a fine grain understanding of these to build meaningful practices that extend them towards defined goals (e.g. reduced carbon footprints, better social inclusion and well-being and healthier populations)? Perhaps this is where a more rigorous form of design culture as a practice, born of out of academic disciplinary development and enquiry, may emerge.

This is a distinct consideration as compared with 'design thinking' in that the latter is largely assumed to exist within a project-based context of problem-solving (e.g. Lawson 1997). However, they might be linked. Kimbell (2011, 2012) opens the possibilities out for thinking about design thinking by re-aligning it with the materiality of its own processes. Visualization and prototyping within design thinking involves the production of stuff that mirrors a wider sense of the entanglements of human and non-human actors in the world.

The emergence, or reinvigoration, of design thinking from 2005 is not without coincidence with a re-emergence of concerns with regards resource scarcity, economic recession and climate change and how traditional management teaching was not equipped to deal with these complex contemporary challenges. These all demand rigorous and focused enquiry into the interlinkages of humans and things, people and systems, populations and structures. Kimbell asks for much more specific investigations of the situated, embodied practice of design thinking to critically qualify the notion within an interdisciplinary form of understanding. In short, this involves attendance to the socio-material practices – and potential ones – within specific contexts. This situatedness might be extracted from the conditions of an overarching notion of design culture. Meanwhile, embodiment might be studied close-up against the background of the specific design culture of a locality, a governmental organization, a firm, an institution and so on (Deserti and Rizzo 2014).

Beyond design thinking, we therefore offer Design Culture as a more reflexive form of practice that investigates not only the machinations of context but challenges the assumptions – including its own – of the world.

Thus, we see it as an object and discipline, but also as a way of acting in and intervening on the world. As the processes, aims and outcomes of design culture become more apparent and more *known*, so we suggest that a different kind of designing and design happens as a result. In this, we anticipate that the outcomes of a 'Design Culture practice' might reveal and communicate the structures of its own making. As part of this, we envisage a cross-disciplinary sensibility where new ontological and epistemological states surface. These may be disruptive of previous understandings, embodiments or cognitive processes and, indeed, their disciplinary counterparts in ways that we can only begin to imagine.

The chief aim of this book has been, through the contributions of its various authors, to provide a series of focal points that suggest tools and concepts for Design Culture. They are multifarious and unlikely to present a coherent whole. Indeed, we see this heterogeneity as part of the work of Design Culture: to broaden, deepen and even re-conceptualize our understandings of design and society. But we hope that this heterogeneity holds the power to open out new forms and formats for acting in and through design and society.

Note

1   In this Epilogue we revert to the distinction between 'Design Culture' (upper case) as a discipline and 'design culture' (lower case) as a phenomenon.

References

Deserti, A. and F. Rizzo (2014), 'Design and the Cultures of Enterprises', *Design Issues*, 30(1): 36–56.

Julier, G. and Leerberg, M. (2014), 'Kolding – We Design For Life: embedding a new design culture into urban regeneration', *Finnish Journal of Urban Studies*, 52(2): 39–56.

Kimbell, L. (2011), 'Rethinking Design Thinking: Part 1', *Design and Culture*, 3(3): 285–306.

Kimbell, L. (2012), 'Rethinking Design Thinking: Part 2', *Design and Culture*, 4(2): 129–48.

Lawson, B. (1997), *How Designers Think: The Design Process Demystified*, 3rd edn, London: Architectural Press.

Lawson, S. (2015), '3 Simple Ways To Create A Culture Of Design At Any Tech Company' https://www.fastcompany.com/3052979/3-simple-ways-to-create-a-culture-of-design-at-any-tech-company. Accessed 1/6/17.

Manzini, E. (2016), 'Design Culture and Dialogic Design', *Design Issues*, 32(1): 52–9.

Moholy-Nagy, L. (1969), *Vision in motion*. New York: Theobald.

INDEX

24/7 culture   131

advertising   30, 33, 79–80, 99–100, 102–4, 134
  outdoor   102
aestheticization   100–5
aesthetics   74, 79, 85, 96–7, 106–7, 221
  categories   105–6
  of existence   133
  minimalist   183
Aléx, Peder   72
altruism   111
amateur design   149
Amman Design Week   221, 223
Appadurai, Arjun   200
Apple   43–8, 165, 167
Arab world   223
assemblage   3, 4, 7, 29, 36, 38, 55, 227–9

Barry, Andrew and Georgina Born   6
bedding   31–5
Belgium   8, 88, 171, 206
Benedict, Ruth   30
Béret, Chantal   179
Betony Vernon   121–2
blankets   32–3, 35
Blåvitt   80
boundary work   132, 138
brand   2, 4, 44–8, 80, 83–5, 97, 99–100, 120–6, 172, 185, 192, 217, 228
  heritage   175–6
  identity   176, 200
  names   190
  non-   71, 78–80
  retro   92
  space   102, 104, 178–82, 185, 187
  values   119
branding   177

Brussels Design Centre   206

Candida Royalle   121
capitalism   67, 75, 219
  late   105, 133
Carrefour   79
central heating   30, 32–3
ceramics   122, 176
children, design for   83–94, 149
city making   222
class   34, 36–7, 77, 85, 215–16, 220, 222
  creative   141
clothing   71, 75–7, 83–94
coffee, Turkish   191, 193–5, 198
Comella Lyn   118–19
Comic Sans   149–50
Conran, Terence   33
consultant designer   131–42
consumer culture   68, 81
consumption   12, 17, 22, 24, 54, 57, 67, 74, 90–4, 107, 160–1, 168, 180
  as active act   100
  and production   54–5, 69, 83–4, 92–3, 104, 117, 123, 125, 132–3, 141, 180, 200–2
  rational   72
cooperative movement   72–3, 75, 77–8, 80
crafts   67, 160–1, 176, 210, 220–1
Cressonnières, J. d.   206
critical design   54, 61, 63
cultural
  authenticity   190, 196–7, 200
  heritage   176, 179, 185–7, 210, 221
  identity   133, 219–20
  production   134, 147, 222–3
cultural studies   1–2, 6–7, 55, 106–7
culture-oriented product design   42

Danida   19
degrowth   158, 161
Denmark   6, 8, 17, 93, 134, 171, 176
design aid   18–19
design authorship   193, 196, 199
design briefs   194, 198–9
design competences   40, 48
design cultural circuit   92, 94
design culture   1–7, 12, 15–16, 40, 54, 84, 97, 107, 116, 124, 132–3, 215
  as configuration   83–4, 227
  in Jordan   214–24
  national   173, 204, 207, 211
design culture as a term   1, 227–30
design education   24, 153
  in the Arab world   214–18, 223
design history   1–2, 6–7, 12, 15–25, 54–5, 107, 186, 204, 221
designification   16–19
design knowledge   48, 146, 154
design organizations   134, 138, 189, 206
design practices   41
design profession   2, 5, 7, 21, 24, 111–13, 116, 125, 131–42, 145, 147, 155, 206
  graphic   148–9
  sociology of   111
design studies   1, 6, 12, 23–4, 204
design thinking   16, 39–41, 44, 63, 116, 121, 145, 228–9
desktop publishing   145, 149
digital humanities   22–3
digitization/digitalization   21–3, 57, 172
  digital design   21–3
  digital revolution   104
disciplinarity (multi-, inter, trans- or cross-)   6–7
discourse
  analysis   84
  statements   147–8, 151, 153
distinction   36, 148, 151, 155
Doc Johnson   119–20
Dutch design   190, 208, 210
duvet   31–5

émigré   137
Erotic Economy   121
everyday design   145–55
everyday life   1, 3, 4, 7, 57, 61, 89, 106, 107, 159, 228
exhibitions   36, 112, 134, 146, 161–2, 190–2, 195–7, 200, 206
experience economy   177, 180, 186
expert   148, 157
  designers   74, 153–4
  knowledge   60, 196
expertise   113, 137, 140

fashion   76, 83–94, 120, 131–4, 146, 216
feminism, second wave   34, 119–20
financial crisis (2007/2008)   90, 158, 161
fixperts   160
flagship store   172, 176, 178–9, 186
folkhem   73
Formafantasma   208–10
Foucault, Michel   147–9, 151, 153, 205
France   172, 218
fritz-kola   96–108
Funfactory   123

gender   33–4, 36–7, 75, 87, 115–16, 125–6, 139
Germany   99, 104, 134, 162, 172, 218
glassware   191, 194, 197–9
globalization   21, 43, 172, 187, 191–3, 198, 200, 203, 205, 211
Global South   214, 224
  design from   219
Goldfrau   121–3
good design   112, 113, 148, 149, 214
Gorz, André   161
graphic design   103, 135, 145–55, 216–17, 223
green transition   87, 90

H&M   68, 81
Habitat   33–4, 37

Hammershøi, Svend 182–6
Harman, Graham 159
Haug, Wolfgang Fritz 17, 79, 107
Heidegger, Martin 159
Henrion, FHK 135–7
heritage 68, 78, 80, 176, 177, 179, 186, 187, 210, 219, 221
history
  use of 176
  self-historicization 176
home-office 138, 140–1

Iceland 88
iFixit 158, 160, 162, 165–7
Ikea 16, 37, 68, 81, 197
Illich, Ivan 161
informality 36, 146
Ingold, Tim 55
Instagram 104–5, 141
International Council of Societies of Industrial Designers 138, 173
Iran 194, 217
Iroha 127
Italy 88, 210, 218

Jackson, Steven J. 158–9
Japan 88, 206, 219
jewellery design 192–3
Jordan 214–24

Kähler 175–87
Katvig 83–94
Kenya 19
KF (Swedish Co-operative Union) 72–81
Kimbell, Lucy 40–1, 229
Kozinets, Robert 178

Larsen, Bjørn A. 19–20
Lash, Scott & Celia Lury 105, 190, 195, 199
Le Corbusier 73
Lelo 121
lifestyle 17, 102, 121–3, 125, 133, 165, 216
London 32, 132, 135, 137, 138, 140, 155, 159, 161, 205

Mah-Jong company 76
Maines, Rachel 116, 126
Manzini, Ezio 52, 228
market 7, 17, 44–8, 67, 73, 77, 85–6, 98, 112, 116–18, 121–3, 158, 178, 227
  second-hand 84
  world/global 126, 172, 191
marketing 7, 12, 16, 31, 67, 68, 69, 71, 79, 80, 83, 85–8, 93, 98, 102, 119, 121, 125, 134, 176, 178, 179, 183, 185, 186, 195, 215
Marres, Noortje and Javier Lezuan 3
material culture 2, 7, 29, 55, 133, 161, 168, 204
materiality 22, 53, 101, 164, 182–6, 195, 207–11
media 1, 4–7, 55, 84, 182–3
  artefacts 56–7
  -driven economy 172
  environment 105, 190
  fashion and lifestyle 131, 133–4
  mediagenic 4
  social 4, 30, 57, 69, 100, 104–5, 126
mediation 19, 22, 24, 54, 56, 59, 62, 101, 172, 191, 195
methological nationalism 204, 207–8, 210
Möbelinstitutet 77
Möbius band 75
modernism 53–5, 192
  Scandinavian 68
Moholy-Nagy, László 228–9
monopoly 111, 113
Myla 121

national design 173, 190, 199–200, 204–5, 207–8, 211
national design style 189–92, 196–200
nationalism 189–90, 192, 200
nation-state 171–2, 203–5, 207–8, 210–11
neo-liberalism 200
Netherlands 8, 88, 171, 173, 206, 209, 210
New Nordic Design 2
non-designers 154

Norway 18, 88
Norwegian Agency for Development Cooperation (Norad) 19
nostalgia 83, 87, 93, 221

organizational change 39, 80
organizational culture 39, 40, 42, 44

Papanek, Victor 19, 54, 228
Paris 135
Peirce, Charles Sanders 55–6
people's home. *See* folkhem
Philips Vibrators 121
physical handling 53–5, 60
plastic 88, 119, 137, 165, 193, 197, 206
platform 21, 161–5
Pocket Rocket 120
postmodernism 54
pragmatic 55–6, 59
prefigurative politics 160, 168
presumption 100, 104
produit libres 79
professional 112
    design 117, 145–55, 216–17
    design discourse 87
    designer 2, 125, 131–42, 190
    ethics 111
    identity 112
    ideology 113
professionalization 111, 133–4, 221
Proni, Giampaolo 55–7
prototyping 229
    rapid 21, 194, 195
Pye, David 159

quilts 33, 35

raunch culture 116
religion 194–6, 198
Repair Café 162
Repair Manifesto 158, 162–3, 165
retro 83, 88
'right to repair' 167

Samsung 43–4, 46–8
Schreiber, Gaby 137–40
segmentation 69
semiotics 53, 55

sex toys 116–28
sexual politics 116, 126
situatedness 41–2
social design 52, 214, 220
Society of Industrial Artists 134, 136
soft technology 32
Soviet Union 160
Spain 206
Stockholm Exhibition 1930 73, 78
Sundahl, Eskil 73
sustainability 7, 19–21, 54, 81, 88–91, 158, 163
sustainification 19–21
Svensk form 77
Sweden 33, 72–6, 79–81, 88, 134, 206
Swedish Co-operative Union. *See* KF
Swedish model 72–5
Swedish Society of Crafts and Design 74, 77
symbolism 17, 36–7, 74, 100–1, 124, 163, 167, 186, 191, 198

tableware design 194–9
Tanzania 19
taste 35–7, 54, 74, 80, 86, 107, 131, 140–1, 185
technoaesthetic 36–8
temporality 94, 207–11
theatricalization 179–80
Thompson, Grahame F. 5
traditions 35, 191–2, 196–200, 210, 224
    craft 221
    oral 160
    repair 158
    sartorial 84
transformation 43, 48, 171
transnational design 205
transnationalism 204
Turkey 8, 171, 189, 19–193, 196, 198, 217
typeface 102, 146, 149–51, 197, 221

ugly design 150
United Kingdom (UK) (also Britain) 1, 12, 29, 31, 32, 34, 36, 72, 88, 107, 121, 131, 132, 133–9, 141, 172

United States of America (USA) (also America) 37, 113, 134, 157, 158, 160, 218, 219
universal design 219
use 52–63
utility 54, 92

Vedel, Kristian 19
Vienna 206

visual culture 207
visualization 23, 195, 229

westernization 8, 171
westernized university 218–20
WeVibe 121
Wiens, Kyle 165–7
Williams, Raymond 29–30
worlding 38